ALGEBRAIC STRUCTURE THEORY
OF SEQUENTIAL MACHINES

Prentice-Hall Series in Automatic Computation

George Forsythe, editor

ARBIB, *Theories of Abstract Automata*
BATES AND DOUGLAS, *Programming Language/One*
BAUMANN, FELICIANO, BAUER, AND SAMELSON, *Introduction to ALGOL*
BLUMENTHAL, *Management Information Systems*
BOBROW AND SCHWARTZ, editors, *Computers and the Policy-Making Community: Applications to International Relations*
BOWLES, editor, *Computers in Humanistic Research*
CESCHINO AND KUNTZMANN, *Numerical Solution of Initial Value Problems*
CRESS, DIRKSEN, AND GRAHAM, *Fortran IV with Watfor*
DESMONDE, *A Conversational Graphic Data Processing System: The IBM 1130/2250*
DESMONDE, *Computers and Their Uses*
DESMONDE, *Real-Time Data Processing Systems: Introductory Concepts*
EVANS, WALLACE, AND SUTHERLAND, *Simulation Using Digital Computers*
FIKE, *Computer Evaluation of Mathematical Functions*
FORSYTHE AND MOLER, *Computer Solution of Linear Algebraic Systems*
GOLDEN, *Fortran IV: Programming and Computing*
GOLDEN AND LEICHUS, *IBM 360: Programming and Computing*
GORDON, *System Simulation*
GREENSPAN, *Lectures on the Numerical Solution of Linear, Singular and Nonlinear Differential Equations*
GRISWOLD, POAGE, AND POLONSKY, *The SNOBOL4 Programming Language*
GRUENBERGER, editor, *Computers and Communications—Toward a Computer Utility*
GRUENBERGER, editor, *Critical Factors in Data Management*
HARTMANIS AND STEARNS, *Algebraic Structure Theory of Sequential Machines*
HULL, *Introduction to Computing*
LOUDEN, *Programming the IBM 1130 and 1800*
MARTIN, *Design of Real-Time Computer Systems*
MARTIN, *Programming Real-Time Computer Systems*
MARTIN, *Telecommunications and the Computer*
MARTIN, *Teleprocessing Network Organization*
MINSKY, *Computation: Finite and Infinite Machines*
MOORE, *Interval Analysis*
SAMMET, *Programming Languages: History and Fundamentals*
SCHULTZ, *Digital Processing: A System Orientation*
SNYDER, *Chebyshev Methods in Numerical Approximation*
STERLING AND POLLACK, *Introduction to Statistical Data Processing*
STROUD AND SECREST, *Gaussian Quadrature Formulas*
TRAUB, *Iterative Methods for the Solution of Equations*
VARGA, *Matrix Iterative Analysis*
VAZSONYI, *Problem Solving by Digital Computers with PL/1 Programming*
WILKINSON, *Rounding Errors in Algebraic Processes*
ZIEGLER, *Time-Sharing Data Processing Systems*

ALGEBRAIC STRUCTURE THEORY
OF SEQUENTIAL MACHINES

J. HARTMANIS

Research Mathematician
General Electric Research and Development Center

Professor of Computer Science
Cornell University

R. E. STEARNS

Research Mathematician
General Electric Research and Development Center

PRENTICE-HALL, INC.

ENGLEWOOD CLIFFS, N. J.

WILLIAM MADISON RANDALL LIBRARY UNC AT WILMINGTON

PRENTICE-HALL INTERNATIONAL, INC., *London*
PRENTICE-HALL OF AUSTRALIA, PTY. LTD., *Sydney*
PRENTICE-HALL OF CANADA, LTD., *Toronto*
PRENTICE-HALL OF INDIA (PRIVATE), LTD., *New Delhi*
PRENTICE-HALL OF JAPAN, INC., *Tokyo*

Current printing (last digit):

10   9   8   7   6   5   4   3

Library of Congress Catalog Card No. 66-14360.

Printed in the United States of America
02227-C

PREFACE

The explosive development of information-processing technology during the last two decades has stimulated the vigorous growth of an Information Science. This new science is primarily concerned with the study of information and the laws which govern its processing and transmission. A very active part of this science is the study of sequential machines or finite automata which are abstract models of digital computers. The aim of this research is to provide a basic theoretical background for the study of digital computers and to contribute to a deeper understanding of discrete or finite information-processing devices. This area of research was started around 1954 by D. A. Huffman and E. F. Moore and has since undergone a considerable growth in several diverse directions. In the period from 1960 to 1965, a body of results we call "structure theory" was created and developed to a considerable degree of completeness and unity. This book is an exposition on the foundations, techniques, and applications of this theory.

By a structure theory for sequential machines, we mean an organized body of techniques and results which deal with the problems of how sequential machines can be realized from sets of smaller component machines, how these component machines have to be interconnected, and how "information" flows in and between these machines when they operate. The importance of machine structure theory lies in the fact that it provides a direct link between algebraic relationships and physical realizations of machines. Many structure results describe the organization of physical devices (or component machines) from which a given machine can be synthesized. Stated differently, the structure theory describes the patterns of possible realizations of a machine from smaller units. It should be stressed, however, that although many structure theory results describe possible physical realizations of machines,

v

the theory itself is independent of the particular physical components or technology used in the realization. More specifically, this theory is concerned with logical or functional dependence in machines and studies the information flow of the machine independently of how the information is represented and how the logical functions are to be implemented.

The mathematical foundations of this structure theory rest on an algebraization of the concept of "information" in a machine and supply the algebraic formalism necessary to study problems about the flow of this information in machines as they operate. The formal techniques and results are very closely related to modern algebra. Many of its results show considerable similarity with results in universal algebra, and some can be directly derived from such considerations. Nevertheless, the engineering motivation demands that this theory go its own way and raises many problems which require new mathematical techniques to be invented that have no counterpart in the development of algebra. Thus, this theory has a characteristic flavor and mathematical identity of its own. It has, we believe, an abstract beauty combined with the challenge and excitement of physical interpretation and application. It falls squarely in the interdisciplinary area of applied algebra which is becoming a part of engineering mathematics.

This book is intended for people interested in information science who have either an engineering or mathematical background. It can be read by anyone who has either some mathematical maturity, achieved through formal study, or engineering intuition developed through work in switching theory or experience in practical computer design.

Enough concepts of machine theory and machine design are introduced in the first chapter so that a mathematician may read the book without any experience with computers or switching theory. A preliminary chapter on basic algebraic concepts supplies enough mathematics to make the book self-contained for a non-mathematician. A good number of examples are given to supply the engineer with an interpretation or application of the mathematics.

J. Hartmanis

R. E. Stearns

CONTENTS

0 INTRODUCTION TO ALGEBRA 1

0.1 Sets and Functions 1
0.2 Partially Ordered Sets and Lattices 6
0.3 Groups and Semigroups 10

1 MACHINES 15

1.1 Definitions 15
1.2 Equivalence 22
1.3 Realizations 27
1.4 State Assignment Problem 32
1.5 "Don't Care" Conditions 34

2 PARTITIONS AND THE SUBSTITUTION PROPERTY 37

2.1 The Substitution Property 37
2.2 Serial Decompositions 42
2.3 Parallel Decompositions 48
2.4 Computation of S. P. Partitions 51
2.5 State Reduction 55

3 PARTITION PAIRS AND PAIR ALGEBRA 58

3.1 Partition Pairs 58
3.2 Pair Algebra 62

vii

3.3 Partition Analyses 71
3.4 Partition Pairs and State Assignment 76
3.5 Abstract Networks 82
3.6 Don't Care Conditions, First Approach 88
3.7 Don't Care Conditions, Second Approach 91
3.8 Component Machines and Local Machines 93

4 **LOOP-FREE STRUCTURE OF MACHINES** **97**

4.1 Loop-Free Networks 97
4.2 Obtaining Loop-Free Realizations 100
4.3 Implications of the S. P. Lattice 106
4.4 Properties of a Tail Machine 109
4.5 Clocks in Sequential Machines 113

5 **STATE SPLITTING** **119**

5.1 Structure and State Reduction 119
5.2 The State Splitting Problem 130
5.3 Set Systems 132
5.4 Set System Decompositions 137
5.5 Don't Care Conditions, Third Approach 146

6 **FEEDBACK AND ERRORS** **148**

6.1 Feedback Defined by Partitions 148
6.2 Feedback 156
6.3 Feedback-Free Machines 159
6.4 Decompositions with Feedback-Free Components 161
6.5 State Errors 167
6.6 Input Errors 175

7 **SEMIGROUPS AND MACHINES** **178**

7.1 The Semigroup of a Machine 178
7.2 Realization by Semigroups 182
7.3 The Structure of Group Accumulators 186
7.4 Behavior Considerations 191
7.5 Decomposition into Simple Components 195
7.6 The Complete Construction 200

REFERENCES **206**

INDEX **209**

ALGEBRAIC STRUCTURE THEORY
OF SEQUENTIAL MACHINES

O INTRODUCTION TO ALGEBRA

In this preliminary chapter we state the standard mathematical concepts and their basic properties that are used in the book. This is intended more as a review and a statement of notation than as a true introduction. Nevertheless, this chapter is self-contained and a reader with some previous exposure to set theoretic notation should be able to pick up the remaining concepts.

0.1 SETS AND FUNCTIONS

We start with a discussion of some set theoretic notation.

The set S consisting of all the elements that have the *property W* is written as

$$S = \{s \,|\, s \text{ has property } W\}.$$

Thus the set of all even numbers can be written as

$$S = \{i \,|\, i = 2k,\ k = 0, 1, 2, \ldots\}.$$

If s is an element of S, then we write

$$s \in S \text{ or } s \text{ in } S$$

and if

$$s \in S \text{ implies that } s \in T,$$

then S is a *subset* of T and we write

$$S \subseteq T.$$

1

Two sets S and T are *equal*, $S = T$, if and only if

$$S \subseteq T \quad \text{and} \quad T \subseteq S.$$

The set containing no elements, the *empty*, or *void*, set, is denoted by $\varnothing$. The *intersection* of S and T is the set consisting of all the elements in both S and T and we write

$$S \cap T = \{s \,|\, s \in S \quad \text{and} \quad s \in T\}.$$

The *union* of S and T is the set consisting of the elements in either S or T. Symbolically,

$$S \cup T = \{s \,|\, s \in S \quad \text{or} \quad s \in T\}.$$

The set operations extend naturally to families of sets:

$$\bigcup_{\alpha \in A} S_\alpha = \{s \,|\, s \in S_\alpha \text{ for some } \alpha \text{ in } A\}$$

$$\bigcap_{\alpha \in A} S_\alpha = \{s \,|\, s \in S_\alpha \text{ for all } \alpha \text{ in } A\}.$$

Two sets S and T are *disjoint* if

$$S \cap T = \varnothing,$$

and the family of sets $\{S_\alpha \,|\, \alpha \in A\}$ is disjoint if the sets are pair-wise disjoint.

The number of elements in a set S is denoted by $|S|$.

Let S and T be nonvoid sets. Then a *function f of S into T*, written

$$f : S \longrightarrow T,$$

assigns to every element s in S an element t in T, written

$$f(s) = t.$$

The function f is sometimes called a *map* or *mapping* from S to T. If

$$T = \{t \,|\, t = f(s), \, s \text{ in } S\},$$

then f is an *onto* function.

The function f is *one-to-one* if

$$s_1 \neq s_2 \text{ implies that } f(s_1) \neq f(s_2).$$

Let

$$f : S \longrightarrow T$$

and U be a subset of S; then a function

$$g : U \longrightarrow T$$

is the *restriction* of f to U if

$$f(s) = g(s)$$

for every s in U.

Conversely, if

$$f : S \longrightarrow T,$$

$S \subseteq U$ and $T \subseteq V$, then a function

$$g : U \longrightarrow V$$

is an *extension* of f if

$$f(s) = g(s)$$

for all s in S.

The *Cartesian product* of the sequence of sets $S_1, S_2, \ldots, S_n$ is the set of all *n*-tuples $(s_1, s_2, \ldots, s_n)$ with $s_i \in S_i$, and we write

$$S_1 \times S_2 \times \ldots \times S_n = \underset{1 \leqslant i \leqslant n}{\times} S_i = \{(s_1, s_2, \ldots, s_n) \mid s_i \in S_i\}.$$

When notation becomes too cumbersome, the element $(s_1, s_2, \ldots, s_n)$ in $\times \, S_i$ is sometimes written as

$$\times \, s_i \qquad \text{or} \qquad \vec{s}.$$

Next we turn to the description of relations which can exist between elements of two sets. Because the nonmathematician may not have had previous exposure to the formulation given here, we illustrate it first with a more specific example.

If $f : S \longrightarrow T$ and $f(s) = t$, then we may define a relation "s is mapped by f onto t." We can write this $s \, R \, t$, where R now designates "is mapped by f onto." Clearly, the function f is characterized by the set of all pairs

$$\{(s, t) \mid f(s) = t\} = \{(s, t) \mid s \, R \, t\},$$

which is a subset of $S \times T$. If we imagine that the function f is plotted in a plane with an s-axis and t-axis, then this characteristic set is just the graph of f on the plane. Thus this relation defined by f can be considered to be a subset of $S \times T$. With this point of view in mind, we proceed to make our definitions.

A *relation* between a set S and a set T is a subset R of $S \times T$; and for (s, t) in R we write $s \, R \, t$. Thus

$$R = \{(s, t) \mid s \, R \, t\}.$$

A relation R on $S \times S$ (sometimes called simply a relation on S) is:

> *reflexive* if, for all s, $s \, R \, s$;
>
> *symmetric* if $s \, R \, t$ implies $t \, R \, s$;
>
> *transitive* if $s \, R \, t$ and $t \, R \, u$ implies $s \, R \, u$.

A relation R on S is an *equivalence relation* on S if R is reflexive, symmetric, and transitive.

If R is an equivalence relation on S, then for every s in S, the set

$$B_R(s) = \{t \mid s \, R \, t\}$$

is an *equivalence class* (i.e., the equivalence class *defined by* s).

A *partition* π on S is a collection of disjoint subsets of S whose set union is S, i.e.

$$\pi = \{B_\alpha\}$$

such that

$$B_\alpha \cap B_\beta = \varnothing \quad \text{for} \quad \alpha \neq \beta$$

and

$$\cup \{B_\alpha\} = S.$$

We refer to the sets of π as *blocks* of π and designate the block which contains s by

$$B_\pi(s).$$

When we write out a partition, we distinguish blocks with bars and semicolons rather than with set brackets. For example, if $S = \{1, 2, 3, 4, 5, 6, 7, 8\}$ and partition π on S has blocks $\{1, 3, 4, 5\}$, $\{2, 6\}$, and $\{7, 8\}$, then we write

$$\pi = \{\overline{1,3,4,5};\ \overline{2,6};\ \overline{7,8}\}$$

instead of

$$\pi = \{\{1, 3, 4, 5\}, \{2, 6\}, \{7, 8\}\}.$$

Nevertheless, the reader should not forget that π is a set and has elements, just like any other set.

Finally, we write

$$s \equiv t\,(\pi)$$

if and only if s and t are contained in the same block of π, i.e.

$$s \equiv t\,(\pi) \text{ if and only if } B_\pi(s) = B_\pi(t).$$

If R is an equivalence relation on S, then the set of equivalence classes defines a partition π on S, and conversely every partition π on S defines an equivalence relation R on S whose equivalence classes are the blocks of π. Thus if R defines π, then

$$s\,R\,t \text{ if and only if } s \equiv t\,(\pi).$$

We now describe how partitions on a set can be "multiplied" and "added." These operations on partitions and the subsequently defined ordering of partitions play a central role in the structure theory of sequential machines and form a basic link between machine concepts and algebra.

If π_1 and π_2 are partitions on S, then:

(i) $\pi_1 \cdot \pi_2$ is the partition on S such that

$$s \equiv t\,(\pi_1 \cdot \pi_2) \text{ if and only if } s \equiv t\,(\pi_1) \text{ and } s \equiv t\,(\pi_2).$$

(ii) $\pi_1 + \pi_2$ is the partition on S such that

$$s \equiv t\,(\pi_1 + \pi_2) \text{ if and only if there exists a sequence in } S$$

$$s = s_0, s_1, s_2, \ldots, s_n = t$$

for which either

$$s_i \equiv s_{i+1}\,(\pi_1) \quad \text{or} \quad s_i = s_{i+1}\,(\pi_2)$$

$0 \leqslant i \leqslant n - 1$.

The computation of $\pi_1 \cdot \pi_2$ is very simple since the blocks of $\pi_1 \cdot \pi_2$ are obtained by intersecting blocks of π_1 and π_2,

$$B_{\pi_1 \cdot \pi_2}(s) = B_{\pi_1}(s) \cap B_{\pi_2}(s).$$

The computation of $\pi_1 + \pi_2$ is longer but also straightforward. To compute $B_{\pi_1 + \pi_2}(s)$ we proceed inductively. Let

$$B_1(s) = B_{\pi_1}(s) \cup B_{\pi_2}(s)$$

and for $i > 1$ let

$$B_{i+1}(s) = B_i(s) \cup \{B \,|\, B \text{ is a block of } \pi_1 \text{ or } \pi_2 \text{ and } B \cap B_i(s) \neq \phi\}.$$

Then

$$B_{\pi_1 + \pi_2}(s) = B_i(s)$$

for any i such that

$$B_{i+1}(s) = B_i(s).$$

To illustrate this, let

$$S = \{1, 2, 3, 4, 5, 6, 7, 8, 9\},$$

$$\pi_1 = \{\overline{1,2}; \overline{3,4}; \overline{5,6}; \overline{7,8,9}\} \text{ and } \pi_2 = \{\overline{1,6}; \overline{2,3}; \overline{4,5}; \overline{7,8}; \overline{9}\}.$$

Then

$$\pi_1 \cdot \pi_2 = \{\overline{1}; \overline{2}; \overline{3}; \overline{4}; \overline{5}; \overline{6}; \overline{7,8}; \overline{9}\}$$

and

$$\pi_1 + \pi_2 = \{\overline{1,2,3,4,5,6}; \overline{7,8,9}\}.$$

Repeated multiplication and addition are represented by the following notation:

$$\pi_1 \cdot \pi_2 \cdots \pi_n = \prod_{i=1}^{n} \pi_i$$

and

$$\pi_1 + \pi_2 + \cdots + \pi_n = \sum_{i=1}^{n} \pi_i.$$

For π_1 and π_2 on S, we say that π_2 is *larger than or equal to* π_1, and write

$$\pi_1 \leqslant \pi_2,$$

if and only if every block of π_1 is contained in a block of π_2. Thus

$$\pi_1 \leqslant \pi_2 \text{ if and only if } \pi_1 \cdot \pi_2 = \pi_1 \text{ if and only if } \pi_1 + \pi_2 = \pi_2.$$

If π and τ are partitions on S and $\pi \geqslant \tau$, then π defines a partition $\bar{\pi}$ on the set of blocks of τ if we let

$$B_\tau(s) \equiv B_\tau(t)\,(\bar{\pi}) \text{ if and only if } s \equiv t\,(\pi).$$

Thus two blocks of τ are identified by $\bar{\pi}$ if and only if they are contained in the same block of π. We refer to $\bar{\pi}$ as the *quotient partition* of π with respect to τ.

For example, if

$$\pi = \{\overline{1,2,5,6}; \overline{3,4,7}\}$$

and

$$\tau = \{\overline{1,2}; \overline{3,4}; \overline{5,6}; \overline{7}\},$$

then $\pi \geqslant \tau$ and the quotient partition is

$$\bar{\pi} = \{\overline{B_1,B_3}; \overline{B_2,B_4}\}$$

where $B_1 = \{1, 2\}$, $B_2 = \{3, 4\}$, $B_3 = \{5, 6\}$, and $B_4 = \{7\}$.

In other words, $\bar{\pi}$ is just π reinterpretated to be over the blocks of τ. If $\pi_1 \geqslant \tau$ and $\pi_2 \geqslant \tau$, then the quotient partitions with respect to τ satisfy

(i) $\pi_1 \geqslant \pi_2$ if and only if $\bar{\pi}_2 \geqslant \bar{\pi}_2$;

(ii) $\overline{\pi_1 \cdot \pi_2} = \bar{\pi}_1 \cdot \bar{\pi}_2$;

(iii) $\overline{\pi_1 + \pi_2} = \bar{\pi}_1 + \bar{\pi}_2$.

Thus the quotient partitions behave exactly as the original.

0.2   PARTIALLY ORDERED SETS AND LATTICES

A binary relation R on S is a *partial ordering* of S if and only if R is

(i) reflexive: $s\,R\,s$ for all s in S,

(ii) antisymmetric: $s\,R\,t$ and $t\,R\,s$ implies $t = s$,

(iii) transitive: $s\,R\,t$, $t\,R\,u$ implies $s\,R\,u$.

We refer to a set S with a given partial ordering R as a *partially ordered set*. When a relation R is a partial ordering, we use the more suggestive symbol "$\leqslant$" instead of R and the partially ordered set is represented by the pair $(S, \leqslant)$.

The set of all partitions on S with the previously defined ordering is seen to be a partially ordered set. Another example is provided by the set of all subsets of S which is a partially ordered set under the ordering of set inclusion.

Let $(S, \leqslant)$ be a partially ordered set and T be a subset of S. Then s (in S) is the *least upper bound* (l.u.b.) of T if and only if

(i) $s \geqslant t$ for all t in T;

(ii) $s' \geqslant t$ for all t in T implies that $s' \geqslant s$.

Dually, s is the *greatest lower bound* (g.l.b.) of T if and only if

(i) $s \leqslant t$ for all t in T

(ii) $s' \leqslant t$ for all t in T implies that $s' \leqslant s$.

A *lattice* is a partially ordered set, $L = (S, \leqslant)$, which has a l.u.b. and a g.l.b. for every pair of elements.

It is easily seen that the partially ordered set of all partitions on S is a lattice and that

$$\text{g.l.b.} \quad (\pi_1, \pi_2) = \pi_1 \cdot \pi_2$$

$$\text{l.u.b.} \quad (\pi_1, \pi_2) = \pi_1 + \pi_2.$$

Similarly, the partially ordered set of all subsets of S is a lattice and

$$\text{g.l.b.} \quad (T_1, T_2) = T_1 \cap T_2$$

$$\text{l.u.b.} \quad (T_1, T_2) = T_1 \cup T_2.$$

We now give an equivalent definition of a lattice in terms of the l.u.b. and g.l.b. operations. Although the first definition is simpler, this second formulation emphasizes some basic lattice laws which are used extensively throughout this book.

A *lattice L* is a triplet

$$L = (S, \cdot, +)$$

where S is a nonempty set of lattice elements and "$\cdot$" and "$+$" are binary operations satisfying the four postulates (i) to (iv) below, known respectively as the idempotent, commutative, associative, and absorption laws.

(i) $x \cdot x = x$ and $x + x = x$

(ii) $x \cdot y = y \cdot x$ and $x + y = y + x$

(iii) $x \cdot (y \cdot z) = (x \cdot y) \cdot z$ and $x + (y + z) = (x + y) + z$

(iv) $x \cdot (x + y) = x$ and $x + (x \cdot y) = x.$

The last definition does not use the concept of ordering explicitly, but it is easy to introduce it and establish the equivalence between the two definitions of a lattice. We carry out the proof of this equivalence in detail to give the reader an exercise in the use, the postulates, and the manipulation of the lattice operations.

Let $L = (S, \cdot, +)$ satisfy the conditions of the above definition of a lattice and define

$$x \leqslant y \text{ if and only if } x \cdot y = x.$$

Then $(S, \leqslant)$ is a lattice and

$$\text{g.l.b.} \quad (x, y) = x \cdot y \text{ and l.u.b.} \quad (x, y) = x + y.$$

To verify this, observe that $x \cdot x = x$ implies that $x \leqslant x$ and thus the relation $\leqslant$ is reflexive. If $x \geqslant y$ and $y \geqslant x$, then

$$y = x \cdot y = y \cdot x = x$$

and thus $x = y$ which shows that $\leqslant$ is antisymmetric. Finally,

$$x \geqslant y \quad \text{and} \quad y \geqslant z$$

imply that

$$x \cdot y = y \qquad \text{and} \qquad y \cdot z = z$$

and consequently

$$x \cdot z = x \cdot (y \cdot z) = (x \cdot y) \cdot z = y \cdot z = z.$$

Therefore $x \geqslant z$ and the ordering is transitive. To show that

$$x \cdot y = \text{g.l.b.} \quad (x, y),$$

note that

$$x \cdot (x \cdot y) = (x \cdot x) \cdot y = x \cdot y$$

and thus

$$x \cdot y \leqslant x \qquad \text{and similarly} \qquad x \cdot y \leqslant y.$$

On the other hand, if for some z

$$z \leqslant x \qquad \text{and} \qquad z \leqslant y,$$

then

$$(x \cdot y) \cdot z = x \cdot (y \cdot z) = x \cdot z = z,$$

and thus

$$z \leqslant x \cdot y$$

and

$$x \cdot y = \text{g.l.b.} \quad (x, y).$$

Similarly, one can show that

$$x + y = \text{l.u.b.} \quad (x, y).$$

If L is a finite lattice, then it has a l.u.b. and g.l.b. for the set of all elements in L, denoted by I and 0 respectively. Element I is called the *identity* because

$$I \cdot x = x \qquad \text{for all } x \text{ in } L.$$

Element 0 is called the *zero* because

$$x + 0 = x \qquad \text{for all } x \text{ in } L.$$

Let $L = (S, \cdot, +)$ be a lattice and T a nonvoid subset of S. Then $L' = (T, \cdot, +)$ is a *sublattice* of L if and only if x and y in T implies that $x \cdot y$ and $x + y$ are in T.

Two lattices

$$L_1 = (S_1, \cdot, +) \qquad \text{and} \qquad L_2 = (S_2, \cdot, +)$$

are *isomorphic*, written $L_1 \cong L_2$, if and only if there exists a one-to-one onto mapping

$$h : S_1 \longrightarrow S_2$$

such that

$$h(x \cdot y) = h(x) \cdot h(y) \qquad \text{and} \qquad h(x + y) = h(x) + h(y).$$

The term "isomorphic" is used more generally to indicate that two algebraic systems are identical except for names. The one-to-one mapping(s) which pairs off the names is called an "isomorphism." In this case, h is called a "lattice isomorphism."

A lattice L_1 is *homomorphic* to L_2 (or L_2 is a *homomorphic image* of L_1) if and only if there exists an onto mapping

$$h: S_1 \longrightarrow S_2$$

such that

$$h(x \cdot y) = h(x) \cdot h(y) \qquad \text{and} \qquad h(x + y) = h(x) + h(y).$$

In general, any operation preserving function from one algebraic system onto another is called a "homomorphism." In this instance, function h is a "lattice homomorphism." The lattice L_2 intuitively represents a simplified version or a coarse imitation of L_1. In Chap. 2, we discuss how a "machine homomorphism" isolates a "subcalculation" of a machine's behavior.

A lattice L is *distributive* if and only if for all x, y, z in L,

$$x \cdot (y + z) = (x \cdot y) + (x \cdot z) \qquad\qquad (D_1)$$

and dually

$$x + (y \cdot z) = (x + y) \cdot (x + z). \qquad\qquad (D_2)$$

For example, the lattice of all partitions on a set S, $|S| \geqslant 3$, is not distributive. To show this, consider Fig. 0.1 which shows the lattice of partition on $S = \{1, 2, 3\}$. We indicate the ordering relations in Fig. 0.1 by descending lines between the lattice elements. A simple calculation shows that

$$\pi_1 = \pi_1 \cdot (\pi_2 + \pi_3) \neq \pi_1 \cdot \pi_2 + \pi_1 \cdot \pi_3 = 0$$

and so this lattice is not distributive. Any other partition lattice on a larger set contains this lattice as a sublattice and thus it also fails to be distributive. We shall see later in this book that this lack of distributivity in the partition lattice has some interesting implications for machine theory.

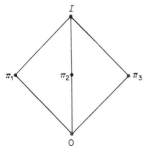

$\pi_1 = \{\overline{1, 2}; \overline{3}\}$, $\pi_2 = \{\overline{1}; \overline{2, 3}\}$, $\pi_3 = \{\overline{1, 3}; \overline{2}\}$

Fig. 0.1. Lattice of partitions on $S = \{1, 2, 3\}$.

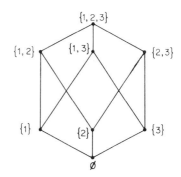

Fig. 0.2. Lattice of subsets of $\{1, 2, 3\}$.

An example for a distributive lattice is provided by the lattices of all subsets of a set S. Figure 0.2 shows the lattice of all subsets of $S = \{1, 2, 3\}$.

The reader with a little bit of skill at manipulating the lattice laws will have a distinct advantage in following the proofs and making applications. In order to further familiarize the reader with lattice concepts and give him a chance to practice the lattice properties, we offer several exercises.

EXERCISES.

1. Show that in a lattice $L = (S, \cdot, +)$,

$$x_1 \leqslant x_2 \quad \text{and} \quad y_1 \leqslant y_2$$

implies that

$$x_1 \cdot y_1 \leqslant x_2 \cdot y_2 \quad \text{and} \quad x_1 + y_1 \leqslant x_2 + y_2.$$

2. Show that the lattice of all subsets of S is a distributive lattice.

3. Show that in a lattice, the distributive law D_1 holds if and only if law D_2 holds.

4. Show that in a distributive lattice, for any x, there can exist at most one y such that

$$x \cdot y = 0 \quad \text{and} \quad x + y = I.$$

Any y that satisfies these two equations is called the *complement* of x. Thus, complements are unique in a distributive lattice.

5. Show that the partition lattice on S is complemented (i.e., every element has a complement) and that for $|S| > 2$ the complements are not unique.

6. Show that the lattice of all partitions on $S \cup a$ contains a sublattice isomorphic to the lattice of all subsets of S.

0.3 GROUPS AND SEMIGROUPS

We now define semigroups and groups and discuss some elementary properties of groups. These concepts are used only in Chap. 7 where we investigate the semigroup of a sequential machine and relate its algebraic properties to machine structure. Unless the reader has a firm grasp on the previous material, we recommend he skip this section for now and begin reading Chap. 1.

A semigroup is just a set with an associative rule of combination, such as numbers under the rule of multiplication or functions of a set into itself under the rule of composition. More precisely:

A *semigroup* G is a pair

$$G = (S, \cdot)$$

where S is a nonempty set and "$\cdot$" is a binary operation such that

(i) $x \cdot y$ is in S for all x and y in S,
(ii) $x \cdot (y \cdot z) = (x \cdot y) \cdot z$ for all $x, y,$ and z in S.

Condition (i) is called the *closure* property and (ii) the *associative* property. When the interpretation is clear, we often leave out the "·" and write

$$xy \text{ instead of } x \cdot y.$$

A *group* G is a pair

$$G = (S, \cdot)$$

such that

(i) $(S, \cdot)$ is a semigroup
(ii) there is an *identity* element e in S for which $e \cdot x = x \cdot e = x$ for all x in S
(iii) for each x in S, there is an *inverse* x^{-1} in S such that $x \cdot x^{-1} = x^{-1} \cdot x = e$.

An example of a group is provided in Fig. 0.3 where the table entry in row x and column y defines the group product xy. It is seen that 0 is the identity element, 1 and 2 are inverses of each other, and the other elements are their own inverses. This group is commonly called S_3, the symmetric or permutation group on three objects.

	0	1	2	3	4	5
0	0	1	2	3	4	5
1	1	2	0	5	3	4
2	2	0	1	4	5	3
3	3	4	5	0	1	2
4	4	5	3	2	0	1
5	5	3	4	1	2	0

Fig. 0.3. Group S_3.

A *subgroup* (*subsemigroup*) of a group G is any nonvoid subset H of G which is a group (semigroup) under the same operation.

The subgroups of S_3 are $\{0\}$, $\{0, 1, 2\}$, $\{0, 3\}$, $\{0, 4\}$, $\{0, 5\}$ and S_3. If H is a subgroup of G, then the sets

$$Ha = \{x \mid x = ya \text{ for } y \text{ in } H\}$$

for a in G are called *right cosets* of H. Similarly, we define *left cosets* aH for a in G.

We illustrate with $H = \{0, 3\}$:

$$\text{Right cosets:} \quad H = H0 = H3 = \{0, 3\}$$
$$H1 = H4 = \{1, 4\}$$
$$H2 = H5 = \{2, 5\}$$
$$\text{Left cosets:} \quad H = 0H = 3H = \{0, 3\}$$
$$1H = 5H = \{1, 5\}$$
$$2H = 4H = \{2, 4\}.$$

In a group G, two right (left) cosets, Ha and Hb are either identical or disjoint and $|Ha| = |H|$ for all a in G. To see this, observe that if

$$Ha \cap Hb \neq \phi$$

then for some x, y in H

$$xa = yb.$$

But then for any z in H, $zx^{-1}y$ is in H, and therefore

$$za = zx^{-1}xa = zx^{-1}yb \text{ is in } Hb.$$

Thus $Ha \subseteq Hb$. Similarly, we show that $Ha \supseteq Hb$. Since $x \neq y$ if and only if $xa \neq ya$, we conclude that $|H| = |Ha|$.

A subgroup H of G is a *normal* subgroup if the left and right cosets are equal,

$$aH = Ha.$$

In this case we refer simply to *cosets*.

The subgroup $\{0, 1, 2\}$ is a normal subgroup of S_3 and $\{0, 1, 2\}$ and $\{3, 4, 5\}$ are its cosets.

A *homomorphism* h of $G_1 = (S_1, \cdot)$ onto $G_2 = (S_2, \cdot)$ is a mapping

$$h : S_1 \longrightarrow S_2$$

such that

$$h(x \cdot y) = h(x) \cdot h(y).$$

If h is a one-to-one mapping, then it is an *isomorphism* between G_1 and G_2, and we write

$$G_1 \cong G_2.$$

A *congruence relation* R on a group G is an equivalence relation such that

$$x_1 \, R \, y_1 \text{ and } x_2 \, R \, y_2 \text{ implies } x_1 x_2 \, R \, y_1 y_2.$$

The equivalence classes of the congruence relation R on G define a partition π on the elements of G. In terms of this partition π, the congruence condition may be written

$$x_1 \equiv y_1 \, (\pi) \text{ and } x_2 \equiv y_2 \, (\pi) \text{ implies } x_1 x_2 \equiv y_1 y_2 \, (\pi)$$

or equivalently

$$B_\pi(x_1) = B_\pi(y_1) \text{ and } B_\pi(x_2) = B_\pi(y_2) \text{ implies } B_\pi(x_1 x_2) = B_\pi(y_1 y_2).$$

This last implication makes it possible to think of the blocks of π as forming a group with operation "$\cdot$" defined by the following equation

$$B_\pi(x) \cdot B_\pi(y) = B_\pi(xy);$$

as the block $B_\pi(xy)$ is seen to be determined by the blocks $B_\pi(x)$ and $B_\pi(y)$ independently of the particular elements x and y chosen from these blocks. We denote this group by G/π and refer to it as the *quotient* group of G with respect to the congruence relation given by π.

The three group concepts of a homomorphism, a normal subgroup, and a congruence relation can be made to correspond to each other in a natural one-to-one way. They are in effect three points of view on the same phenomenon. We now investigate this correspondence in more detail.

If R is a congruence relation on the group G, then

$$H = \{x \text{ in } G \mid x \, R \, e\}$$

is a normal subgroup and the equivalence classes of R are the cosets of H. Conversely, the cosets of a normal subgroup H of G define a congruence relation R on G.

To prove that $H = \{x \in G \mid x \, R \, e\}$ is a subgroup, let x and y be in H. By definition,

$$x \, R \, e \quad \text{and} \quad y \, R \, e$$

and therefore

$$xy \, R \, ee \quad \text{or} \quad xy \, R \, e$$

and thus H is closed under the group operation. It is easy to verify that H contains the identity element e and inverses for all its elements. Therefore H is a group.

To show that H is normal, we have to show that for all a in G, $aH = Ha$. If x is in H, then there exists a y in G such that

$$ax = ya \text{ or } axa^{-1} = y.$$

Since $x \, R \, e$, we know that

$$axa^{-1} \, R \, e$$

and therefore $y \, R \, e$. Thus y is in H and therefore

$$aH \subseteq Ha.$$

Similarly, we can show that

$$aH \supseteq Ha$$

and therefore H is normal.

To show that the cosets of a normal subgroup H define equivalence classes of a congruence relation, let

$$x_1 \text{ and } x_2 \text{ be in } aH \text{ and } y_1 \text{ and } y_2 \text{ be in } bH.$$

Then for some x_1', x_2', y_1', and y_2' in H, we must have the equations

$$x_1 = ax_1', \ y_1 = by_1', \ x_2 = ax_2', \ y_2 = by_2'$$

which combine to obtain

$$x_1 y_1 = ax_1' by_1' \text{ and } x_2 y_2 = ax_2' by_2'.$$

Since H is normal, there are elements x_1'' and x_2'' in H such that

$$x_1' b = bx_1'' \text{ and } x_2' b = bx_2''$$

and substituting these two equations into the previous equations, we obtain

$$x_1 y_1 = abx_1'' y_1' \quad \text{and} \quad x_2 y_2 = abx_2'' y_2'.$$

Thus $x_1 y_1$ and $x_2 y_2$ are both in coset abH which means that

$$x_1 y_1 \ R \ x_2 y_2$$

and the proof is completed.

This result shows that every quotient group G/π is (isomorphic to) a quotient group with respect to a normal subgroup H which is written:

$$G/H.$$

Finally, a homomorphism, h of G_1 onto G_2, defines a congruence relation,

$$x \ R \ y \qquad \text{if and only if } h(x) = h(y),$$

and this congruence relation defines a normal subgroup $H = \{x \in G \mid h(x) = e\}$ of G such that

$$G_1/H = G_2.$$

EXERCISE. Let $\{\pi_i\}$ be the set of partitions defined by the right cosets of the subgroups of G. Show that $\{\pi_i\}$ is the sublattice of the lattice of all partitions on G. Thus, if H_1 and H_2 are subgroups and π_1 and π_2 are the corresponding sets of cosets, then the (right) cosets of the largest subgroup of G contained in H_1 and H_2 is given by

$$\pi_1 \cdot \pi_2.$$

Similarly, the (right) cosets of the smallest subgroup in G containing H_1 and H_2 are given by

$$\pi_1 + \pi_2.$$

EXERCISE. Let $\{\pi_i\}$ be the set of partitions defined by the congruence relations on a group G. Show that $\{\pi_i\}$ is a sublattice of the lattice of partitions on G.

NOTES

A good basic reference on algebra is G. Birkhoff and S. MacLane [4] and a comprehensive treatment of lattice theory is given by G. Birkhoff [3].

1 MACHINES

1.1 DEFINITIONS

We begin by an abstract definition of a sequential machine which provides a mathematical model for discrete, deterministic computing devices with finite memory. Among the many physical devices modeled by sequential machines are digital computers, digital control units, or electronic circuits with synchronized delay elements. All these devices have the following common properties which are abstracted in the definition of a sequential machine.

1. A finite set of inputs which can be applied to the device in a sequential order.

2. A finite set of internal configurations or states the device can be in. These configurations correspond in the physical devices to various combinations of bits in memory, pulses in delay lines, or flip-flop settings and are usually reached at the end of some basic clock period.

3. The present internal configuration and the input uniquely determine the next configuration the device achieves. Thus, the state of the device is a function of the state the device was started in and the sequence of inputs which has been applied to it.

4. A finite set of outputs which are determined either by the configuration of the device or by the transition from one configuration to the next. Thus, these devices map inputs into outputs, and the present output depends not only on the present input but also on the past history of inputs.

With this interpretation in mind, we present the two classic machine models and derive some of their elementary properties.

15

DEFINITION 1.1A. A *Moore type sequential machine* is a quintuple

$$M = (S, I, O, \delta, \lambda)$$

where (i) S is a finite nonempty set of states;
(ii) I is a finite nonempty set of inputs;
(iii) O is a finite nonempty set of outputs;
(iv) $\delta: S \times I \longrightarrow S$ is called the transition (or next state) function;
(v) $\lambda: S \longrightarrow O$ is called the output function.

DEFINITION 1.1B. A *Mealy type sequential machine* is a quintuple

$$M = (S, I, O, \delta, \lambda)$$

where (i) S is a finite nonempty set of states;
(ii) I is a finite nonempty set of inputs;
(iii) O is a finite nonempty set of outputs;
(iv) $\delta: S \times I \longrightarrow S$ is called the transition function;
(v) $\lambda: S \times I \longrightarrow O$ is called the output function.

In those few cases when we want to emphasize the use of a Mealy machine, we designate the output function by β. Thus

$$M = (S, I, O, \delta, \lambda)$$

can be either type machine, but

$$M = (S, I, O, \delta, \beta)$$

is a Mealy machine.

Notice that these definitions are the same except for part (v). Mathematically speaking, the Moore machine is a special case of the Mealy machine because we may take

$$\beta(s, x) = \lambda(s)$$

for x in I and s in S. There is, however, a subtle difference that this formalism glosses over; the outputs of a Moore machine are thought of as occurring while the internal configuration indicates a state, whereas the outputs of a Mealy machine are thought of as occurring while the machine is going through a transition between states. This difference of interpretation is important, because a later definition does introduce a mathematical difference.

The two most common representations of a Moore machine

$$M = (S, I, O, \delta, \lambda)$$

are illustrated in Fig. 1.1 where

$$S = \{r, s, t\}, \qquad I = \{a, b\},$$

and

$$O = \{0, 1\}.$$

Inputs
a   b

		a	b			Outputs
	r	s	r		0	
States	s	t	t		0	
	t	r	s		1	

Fig. 1.1. Representation of a Moore machine by a flow
table and by a state graph.

On the left is a *flow table* with rows corresponding to each state, columns
corresponding to each input, and table entries to indicate each transition.
For example,

$$\delta(r, a) = s, \qquad \delta(r, b) = r.$$

Furthermore, there is an output column listing the value of λ for each state
of M, for example,

$$\lambda(r) = \lambda(s) = 0 \qquad \text{and} \qquad \lambda(t) = 1.$$

On the right, the same information is placed on a *state graph*. The arrow
labeled a pointing from the r node to the s node indicates that

$$\delta(r, a) = s$$

and the 0 at the r node indicates that

$$\lambda(r) = 0.$$

Similarly, there are two common representations of a Mealy machine as
illustrated in Fig. 1.2. The difference in the flow table is that an output

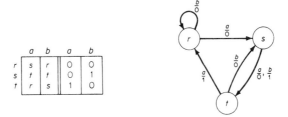

	a	b	a	b
r	s	r	0	0
s	t	t	0	1
t	r	s	1	0

Fig. 1.2. Representation of a Mealy machine by a
flow table and by a state graph.

column must be included for each input. The $a/0$ label on the arrow between
the r and s nodes in the state graph indicates that

$$\delta(r, a) = s \qquad \text{and} \qquad \beta(r, a) = 0.$$

Notice how the state graphs emphasize when the output is thought to occur. Although the state graph has proven to be a valuable research tool, the flow table is superior for most of the concepts developed here, and it is used almost exclusively throughout the remainder of this book.

In many discussions we are not directly concerned with the output of the machine, but are primarily interested in the properties of the state transitions. In order to study state transitions separately we make the following definition.

DEFINITION 1.2. A *state machine* is a triplet

$$M = (S, I, \delta)$$

where (i) S is a finite nonempty set of states;
　(ii) I is a finite nonempty set of inputs;
　(iii) $\delta: S \times I \longrightarrow S$ is called the transition function.

Given a machine description, we imagine a "device" which is built along the general format of Fig. 1.3 with "wires" to carry information in the

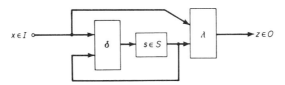

Fig. 1.3. Schematic circuit for $M = (S, I, O, \delta, \lambda)$.

direction of the arrows, "combinational logic" to compute the functions δ and λ, and a "storage element" to remember the present state of the machine. In the Moore case, the wire from the input source to the output logic is omitted. In the case of a state machine, the output logic is also omitted.

We have found that it is often useful to think in terms of a little machine chugging away from state to state rather than in terms of abstract sets and mappings. For this reason, we now incorporate this view into our formalism.

DEFINITION 1.3. Given a machine M, we say that state s *goes into* state t *under* input x if and only if

$$t = \delta(s, x).$$

For a subset B of S we define

$$\delta(B, x) = \{s \mid s = \delta(t, x), t \text{ in } B\}$$

and we say that the subset B *goes into* set B' *under* input x if and only if

$$\delta(B, x) \subseteq B'.$$

There are a few more concepts we wish to introduce at this time.

DEFINITION 1.4. A machine

$$M' = (S', I', O', \delta', \lambda')$$

is a *submachine* of the machine

$$M = (S, I, O, \delta, \lambda)$$

if and only if

$$S' \subseteq S, \qquad I' \subseteq I, \qquad O' \subseteq O,$$

$$\delta' : S' \times I' \to S' \text{ and } \delta' = \delta \text{ restricted to } S' \times I',$$

and

$$\lambda' : S' \times I' \to O' \text{ and } \lambda' = \lambda \text{ restricted to } S' \times I'$$

(and similarly for state machines).

DEFINITION 1.5. Machine M is *strongly connected* if and only if, for all submachines M' of M, $I' = I$ implies $S' = S$.

Thus, a machine is strongly connected if and only if no proper subset of S of M goes into itself under all inputs or, equivalently, if and only if each state can be sent into any other state by a properly chosen sequence of inputs.

DEFINITION 1.6. Two machines of the same type

$$M = (S, I, O, \delta, \lambda) \qquad \text{and} \qquad M' = (S', I', O', \delta', \lambda')$$

are *isomorphic* if and only if there exist three one-to-one onto mappings

$$f_1 : S \longrightarrow S'$$
$$f_2 : I \longrightarrow I'$$
$$f_3 : O \longrightarrow O'$$

such that

$$f_1[\delta(s, x)] = \delta'[f_1(s), f_2(x)]$$
$$f_3[\lambda(s, x)] = \lambda'[f_1(s), f_2(x)].$$

We refer to the triple of mappings (f_1, f_2, f_3) as an *isomorphism* between M and M'.

Thus two sequential machines are isomorphic if and only if they are identical except for a renaming of the states, inputs, and outputs.

Machine isomorphism is the most elementary case of two machines imitating each other through the use of "combinational circuits." The term *combinational circuit* refers to a device which performs the same fixed mapping of inputs into outputs, regardless of the past input history. Thus a combinational circuit may be thought of as a one-state sequential machine. If we have a machine M' that is isomorphic to M, then by just placing a combinational circuit in front of the machine M' and a combinational circuit in back of the machine, we can convert it to a machine that behaves like

M. The combinational circuit in front computes f_2, mapping I into I', and the circuit in the back computes f_3^{-1}, mapping O' into O. The schematic representation of this conversion of M' to M by use of two combinational circuits is shown in Figs. 1.4 and 1.5. The resemblance between M and M'

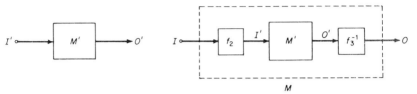

Fig. 1.4. Schematic representation of machine M'.

Fig. 1.5. Schematic representation of M' with combinational circuits to simulate the isomorphic machine M.

is so strong that we often think of them as being two names for the "same" machine.

Later in this chapter, we define the most general concept of when one machine can simulate (realize) another machine by means of two combinational circuits placed in front and back of the machine. The next and final concept of this section serves as an intermediate realization concept and is the key idea behind the elementary decompositions introduced later.

DEFINITION 1.7. A sequential machine

$$M' = (S', I', O', \delta', \lambda')$$

is a *homomorphic image* of the machine

$$M = (S, I, O, \delta, \lambda)$$

if and only if there exists three onto mappings

$$h_1 : S \longrightarrow S'$$
$$h_2 : I \longrightarrow I'$$
$$h_3 : O \longrightarrow O'$$

such that

$$h_1[\delta(s, a)] = \delta'[h_1(s), h_2(a)]$$
$$h_3[\lambda(s, a)] = \lambda'[h_1(s), h_2(a)].$$

We refer to the triple (h_1, h_2, h_3) of mappings as a *homomorphism* of M onto M'.

To illustrate these ideas, consider machines A and A' shown in Figs. 1.6 and 1.7. It is easily checked that the following three mappings define a homomorphism of A onto A'.

	a	b	c	
1	5	6	4	2
2	6	5	4	0
3	4	4	2	1
4	3	3	6	2
5	2	1	3	2
6	1	2	3	0

Fig. 1.6.   Machine A.

	0	1	
p	s	r	z_0
q	r	p	z_1
r	q	s	z_0
s	p	q	z_0

Fig. 1.7.   Machine A'.

$$h_1: \quad 1 \longrightarrow p \qquad h_2: \quad a \longrightarrow 0 \qquad h_3: \quad 0 \longrightarrow z_0$$
$$2 \longrightarrow p \qquad\qquad b \longrightarrow 0 \qquad\qquad 1 \longrightarrow z_1$$
$$3 \longrightarrow q \qquad\qquad c \longrightarrow 1 \qquad\qquad 2 \longrightarrow z_0$$
$$4 \longrightarrow r$$
$$5 \longrightarrow s$$
$$6 \longrightarrow s$$

For example,

$$h_1[\delta(1, a)] = h_1(5) = s = \delta'[h_1(1), h_2(a)] = \delta'(p, 0) = s$$

and

$$h_3[\lambda(1, a)] = h_3[\lambda(1)] = z_0 = \lambda'[h_1(1)] = \lambda'(p) = z_0.$$

DEFINITION 1.8. A state machine

$$M' = (S', I', \delta')$$

is a *homomorphic image* of the machine M if and only if there exist two onto mappings

$$h_1: S \longrightarrow S'$$
$$h_2: I \longrightarrow I'$$

such that

$$h_1[\delta(s, a)] = \delta'[h_1(s), h_2(a)].$$

In applications we are often interested in homomorphisms between machines which have the same input and output alphabet. In such cases, if h_2 and h_3 are identity mappings, we refer to this homomorphism as a *state homomorphism*. If M' is a state machine, then only h_2 has to be an identity mapping to have a state homomorphism.

If M' is a homomorphic image of M, then by using two combinational circuits, M can be used to simulate M'. The schematic representation of this simulation is shown in Fig. 1.8. If h_2 does not have a unique inverse, then $h_2^{-1}(a)$ is interpreted to be any input symbol which is mapped onto a by h_2. Intuitively speaking, the machine M does more than M' can, but it can be modified by attaching combinational circuits to imitate its homomorphic image M'. It will be seen that this simple interpretation provides the basis for motivating and understanding many later results.

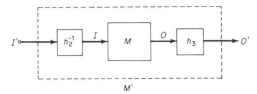

Fig. 1.8. Simulation of the homomorphic image M' of M.

EXERCISE. Show that the homomorphic image of a strongly connected machine is strongly connected.

EXERCISE. Show that if M_1 is a homomorphic image of M_2 and M_2 is a homomorphic image of M_3, then M_1 is a homomorphic image of M_3.

1.2 EQUIVALENCE

Any notion of equivalence between machines, be they both Moore, both Mealy, or one of each type, must be based on some precise concept as to when two machines can do the "same thing." Intuitively, we think of machines doing the same thing if the same inputs give the same outputs. In this section we explore equivalence from the ground up, beginning with input sequences and states.

NOTATION. If I is an input set, we let $\mathscr{I}$ represent the set of all finite non-null input sequences and let $\mathscr{I}_0$ represent the set of all finite sequences, including the null (or length zero) sequence which we represent by the symbol Λ. Symbolically,

$$\mathscr{I}_0 = \mathscr{I} \cup \{\Lambda\}.$$

We generally represent an input sequence by an input symbol with a bar over it or as a string of input symbols without punctuation. For example, we might write

$$\bar{x} = x_1 x_2 \ldots x_n$$

for x_i in I, and we would say that $\bar{x}$ has length n.

We now extend the next state function δ to input sequence in the natural manner and expand λ (or β) in a way suitable for the study of equivalence.

DEFINITION 1.9. Let $\bar{\delta}$ be the function δ of Def. 1.1 extended inductively over the set $S \times \mathscr{I}_0$ as follows:

(i) $\bar{\delta}(s, \Lambda) = s$ for all s in S;

(ii) if $\bar{\delta}$ is defined for sequences of length $k \geqslant 0$ and $\bar{x} = \bar{x}'x$ where $\bar{x}'$ is of length k and x is in I, let

$$\bar{\delta}(s, \bar{x}) = \delta(\bar{\delta}(s, \bar{x}'), x).$$

Let (Moore case)

$$\bar{\lambda}(s, \bar{x}) = \lambda(\bar{\delta}(s, \bar{x})) \qquad \text{for } \bar{x} \text{ in } \mathscr{I}_0$$

and (Mealy case)

$$\bar{\beta}(s, \bar{x}) = \beta(\bar{\delta}(s, \bar{x}'), x) \qquad \text{for } \bar{x}' \text{ in } \mathscr{I}_0 \text{ and } x \text{ in } I.$$

In plain English, $\bar{\delta}(s, \bar{x})$ is computed by starting the machine in state s, feeding in the input sequence $\bar{x}$, and looking at the final state. In the Moore case, $\bar{\lambda}(s, \bar{x})$ is the output associated with this last state. In the Mealy case, $\bar{\beta}(s, \bar{x})$ is associated with the final transition. Since there are no transitions associated with the null sequence, $\bar{\beta}$ is only defined for $\bar{x} \in \mathscr{I}$.

DEFINITION 1.10. If

$$M_1 = (S_1, I, O, \delta_1, \lambda_1) \quad \text{and} \quad M_2 = (S_2, I, O, \delta_2, \lambda_2)$$

are two Moore (Mealy) machines with the same input and output alphabets, then states s_1 in S_1 and s_2 in S_2 are said to be *equivalent* if and only if

$$\bar{\lambda}_1(s_1, \bar{x}) = \bar{\lambda}_2(s_2, \bar{x})$$

for all $\bar{x}$ in $\mathscr{I}_0$ (Moore case) or $\bar{x}$ in $\mathscr{I}$ (Mealy case).

Notice that this definition also applies to the special case where $M_1 = M_2$. It is easily verified that this is an equivalence relation among the states of all machines with the input set I and output set O.

LEMMA 1.1. Equivalent states s_1 and s_2 of machines M_1 and M_2 go into equivalent states under each input.

Proof. Let $\bar{x}$ be an arbitrary element of $\mathscr{I}_0$. Then by Defs. 1.9 and 1.10

$$\bar{\lambda}_1[\delta_1(s_1, x), \bar{x}] = \bar{\lambda}_1(s_1, x\bar{x}) = \bar{\lambda}_2(s_2, x\bar{x}) = \bar{\lambda}_2[\delta_2(s_2, x), \bar{x}]$$

and thus

$$\delta_1(s_1, x) \text{ is equivalent to } \delta_2(s_2, x). \quad \blacksquare$$

DEFINITION 1.11. Two machines M_1 and M_2 (of the same type) are *equivalent* if and only if each s_1 in S_1 has an equivalent state s_2 in S_2 and each s_2 in S_2 has an equivalent state s_1 in S_1.

One example of equivalent machines is shown in Fig. 1.9. Here states r, s, and u are equivalent and states t, v, and w are equivalent.

DEFINITION 1.12. A machine M is *reduced* if and only if state s_1 equivalent to state s_2 implies that $s_1 = s_2$.

The importance of this definition is brought home by the following:

THEOREM 1.1. Given a machine M_1, there is a reduced machine M

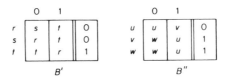

Fig. 1.9. Two equivalent machines B' and B''.

equivalent to M_1. Furthermore, if M_2 is any machine equivalent to M_1, then there exists a state homomorphism which maps M_2 onto M.

Proof. We divide S_1 into classes B_i of equivalent states and take $S = \{B_i\}$. Let $\delta(B_i, x)$ be the class B_j such that $\delta_1(s, x)$ is in B_j for some s in B_i. By Lemma 1.1, all choices of s give the same B_j. Take $\lambda(B_i) = \lambda_1(s)$ or $\beta(B_i, x) = \beta_1(s, x)$ for any s in B_i. By definition of equivalent states, any choice of s gives the same value. Thus we have defined a reduced machine $M = (S, I, O, \delta, \lambda)$ equivalent to M_1. Let M_2 be equivalent to M_1. Then by the definition of equivalent machines, each s in S_2 must be equivalent to the states in some B_i and there can only be one such B_i because states in other B_j are not equivalent to the states in B_i. We may thus set

$$h_1(s) = B_i$$

which defines the state homomorphism of M_2 onto M. ∎

One illustration of the proof is given in Fig. 1.10 which shows a reduced machine for those of Fig. 1.9. The state homomorphism map

Fig. 1.10. Reduced machine B for B' and B''.

$$h_1 : \{u, v, w\} \longrightarrow \{B_1, B_2\}$$

is given by

$$h_1(u) = B_1 \quad \text{and} \quad h_1(v) = h_1(w) = B_2.$$

COROLLARY 1.1.1. If two reduced machines are equivalent, then they are isomorphic. We are therefore justified in referring to *the* reduced machine.

Proof. The desired isomorphism (f_1, f_2, f_3) between two equivalent reduced machines is given by $f_1 = f$ (of Theorem 1.1) and f_2 and f_3 equal to identity mappings. ∎

These results show that, for any set of equivalent machines, there exists a unique equivalent reduced machine and this machine has the smallest number of states among all the machines equivalent to it, because any other equivalent machine with the same number of states must be isomorphic to this reduced machine.

We are now ready to discuss "equivalence" between Moore and Mealy machines. We prefer to use the term "similar" since there is no true equivalence relation.

DEFINITION 1.13. A Moore machine

$$M_1 = (S_1, I, O, \delta_1, \lambda_1)$$

and a Mealy machine

$$M_2 = (S_2, I, O, \delta_2, \beta_2)$$

defined on the same input and output sets are said to be *similar* if and only if for each state s_1 in S_1 (or s_2 in S_2), there is a state s_2 in S_2 (s_1 in S_1) such that

$$\bar\lambda_1(s_1, \bar x) = \bar\beta_2(s_2, \bar x)$$

for all $\bar x \in \mathscr{I}$.

Note that nothing is said about $\bar\lambda_1(s_1, \Lambda) = \lambda_1(s_1)$. Thus the output of a given state may not be compared with any Mealy output and consequently several nonequivalent Moore machines may be similar to a single Mealy machine. Figure 1.11 provides a simple example of this.

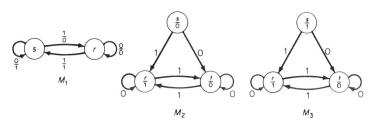

Fig. 1.11. A Mealy machine, M_1, similar to two non-equivalent Moore machines, M_2 and M_3.

THEOREM 1.2. All the Mealy machines similar to a given Moore machine

$$M = (S, I, O, \delta, \lambda)$$

are equivalent. One such machine is given by

$$M' = (S, I, O, \delta, \beta = \lambda(\delta)).$$

Proof. Let M_1 and M_2 be two Mealy machines similar to M. Let s_1 be an arbitrary element of S_1. Let s be the state in S such that

$$\bar\beta_1(s_1, \bar x) = \bar\lambda(s, \bar x)$$

for all $\bar x$ in $\mathscr{I}$, and let s_2 in S_2 be such that

$$\bar\beta_2(s_2, \bar x) = \bar\lambda(s, \bar x)$$

for all $\bar x$ in $\mathscr{I}$. But then

$$\bar{\beta}_1(s_1, \bar{x}) = \bar{\beta}_2(s_2, \bar{x})$$

for all $\bar{x}$ in $\mathscr{I}$, and s_1 and s_2 are equivalent. By a similar argument, it follows that for every state in S_2 there is an equivalent state in S_1 and thus M_1 and M_2 are equivalent machines. The second statement is immediate from Definitions 1.10 and 1.11. ∎

Once again, some subtleties of the Moore-Mealy contrast come to the surface. To consider Definition 1.1A as a special case of 1.1B, we took

$$\beta(s, x) = \lambda(s);$$

but to construct a Mealy machine similar to a Moore machine, we see that we must take

$$\beta(s, x) = \lambda(\delta(s, x)).$$

Thus Definition 1.13 introduces a second way of viewing a Moore machine as a Mealy machine and exposes the limitation of regarding the Moore machine as a special case of the Mealy machine.

Next we take the state point of view and consider the advantages of converting from a Moore to a Mealy machine.

THEOREM 1.3. Let

$$M = (S, I, O, \delta, \lambda)$$

be a reduced Moore machine and M' be a similar reduced Mealy machine. Let $\{B_i\}$ be equivalence classes on S such that s_1 and s_2 are in the same B_i if and only if

$$\delta(s_1, x) = \delta(s_2, x)$$

for all x in I. Then M' has one state corresponding to each B_i.

Proof. We construct M' using $\{B_i\}$ for states. By Theorem 1.2,

$$M^* = (S, I, O, \delta, \beta = \lambda(\delta))$$

is a Mealy machine similar to M and if we show that the B_i are the classes of equivalent states on M^*, then the construction in the proof of Theorem 1.1 will give the desired representation of M' and map of S into $\{B_i\}$. Suppose that

$$\delta(s_1, x) = \delta(s_2, x)$$

for all x in I. Then obviously

$$\bar{\delta}(s_1, \bar{x}) = \bar{\delta}(s_2, \bar{x})$$

for all $\bar{x}$ in $\mathscr{I}$ and by definition of M^*,

$$\bar{\beta}(s_1, \bar{x}) = \lambda(\bar{\delta}(s_1, \bar{x})) = \lambda(\bar{\delta}(s_2, \bar{x})) = \bar{\beta}(s_2, \bar{x})$$

for all $\bar{x}$ in $\mathscr{I}$, and hence s_1 and s_2 are equivalent states in M^*. On the other hand, if

$$\delta(s_1, x) = s_1', \qquad \delta(s_2, x) = s_2', \qquad \text{and} \qquad s_1' \neq s_2',$$

then there exists an $\bar{x}$ in $\mathscr{I}_0$ such that

$$\bar{\lambda}(s_1', \bar{x}) \neq \bar{\lambda}(s_2', \bar{x}).$$

But then

$$\bar{\beta}(s_1, x\bar{x}) = \bar{\lambda}(s_1, x\bar{x}) = \bar{\lambda}(s_1', \bar{x}) \neq \bar{\lambda}(s_2', \bar{x}) = \bar{\lambda}(s_2, x\bar{x}) = \bar{\beta}(s_2, x\bar{x})$$

and $x\bar{x}$ is in $\mathscr{I}$; hence s_1 and s_2 are not equivalent. Thus the B_i are the classes of equivalent states of M^*, as was to be shown. ∎

COROLLARY 1.3.1. A reduced Moore machine has the same number of states as the corresponding reduced Mealy machine if and only if all the next-state rows in its state table are distinct.

Thus, we have an easy test for deciding if the Mealy machine gives fewer states.

To illustrate this result, consider the reduced Moore machine C of Fig. 1.12. For this machine states 1 and 3 have identical next state rows, and thus it can be replaced by a similar five-state Mealy machine, which is shown in Fig. 1.13. Note that for this machine, states 4 and 5 have identical next state rows, but these states are not equivalent and it is easily seen that this is a reduced machine.

	0	1	
1	2	1	1
2	6	5	0
3	2	1	0
4	1	3	0
5	3	1	0
6	5	4	0

Fig. 1.12.   Machine C.

	0	1	0	1
1	2	1	0	1
2	6	5	0	0
4	1	1	1	0
5	1	1	0	1
6	5	4	0	0

Fig. 1.13.   Mealy machine similar to C.

1.3 REALIZATIONS

So far, we have treated machines on an abstract level and have discussed the case in which two flow tables specify the same machine from the input-output point of view. The purpose of this section is to define and elucidate the relation between these ideas and physical circuits, which so far have only been mentioned informally. It is through such physical interpretation that the theoretical results become interesting and useful to people interested in physical applications.

The next two definitions describe how a machine M', which is not necessarily equivalent to M, can be used to imitate M after a renaming of the inputs and outputs. Again it is helpful to think of the mappings performed by ι and ζ of this definition as combinational circuits placed in front and back of the machine M' to make it behave like M.

DEFINITION 1.14. If M and M' are two machines, then the triple (α, ι, ζ) is said to be an *assignment* of M into M' if and only if

α is a mapping of S into nonvoid subsets of S',

ι is a mapping of I into I',

ζ is a mapping from O' into O,

and these mappings satisfy the following relations:

(i) $\delta'[\alpha(s), \iota(x)] \subseteq \alpha[\delta(s, x)]$ for all s in S and x in I,

(ii) $\zeta(\lambda'(s')) = \lambda(s)$ for all s' in $\alpha(s)$ (Moore case), or

(ii') $\zeta(\lambda'(s', \iota(x))) = \lambda(s, x)$ for all s' in $\alpha(s)$ and x in I (Mealy case).

DEFINITION 1.15. A machine M' is said to be a *realization* of machine M if and only if there is an assignment (α, ι, ζ) of M into M'. If M and M' are state machines, then we require an α and ι satisfying condition i and such that α maps S into disjoint subsets of S'.

The next result states that if M' is a realization of M, then M' started in a state $\alpha(s)$ behaves like M under the interpretation of ι and ζ when started in s.

THEOREM 1.4. If M' is a realization of M through the assignment (α, ι, ζ), then for s' in $\alpha(s)$ and $\bar{x}$ in $\mathscr{I}$

$$\bar{\lambda}(s, \bar{x}) = \zeta[\bar{\lambda}'(s', \iota(\bar{x}))].$$

Proof. Left as an exercise.

THEOREM 1.5. If M and M' are equivalent machines, then M is realized by M' and M' is realized by M.

Proof. To prove this we show that there exists an assignment of M into M' and vice versa. Let ι and ζ be identity mappings and let

$$\alpha(s) = \{s' | s' \text{ is equivalent to } s\}.$$

Then

$$\delta'[\alpha(s), x] \subseteq \alpha[\delta(s, x)]$$

since, by Lemma 1.1, equivalent states go into equivalent states. Since s' and s are equivalent,

$$\lambda'(s', x) = \lambda(s, x).$$

Thus M' realizes M. A similar argument shows that M realizes M'. ∎

EXERCISE. Show that if M_1 realizes M_2 and M_2 realizes M_3, then M_1 realizes M_3.

EXERCISE. Show that if M' realizes M and

$$s' \text{ is in } \alpha(s_1) \text{ and } s' \text{ is in } \alpha(s_2),$$

then s_1 and s_2 are equivalent states of M. Thus, if M' realizes a reduced machine, then for any s' there exists at most one s of M such that s' is in $\alpha(s)$.

It should be noted that if M' realizes M, then these two machines do not necessarily have to be isomorphic or related by homomorphisms. There is though, as shown in the next theorem, a homomorphism which relates M' to the reduced machine equivalent to M in the case when ι is a one-to-one mapping.

THEOREM 1.6. Machine M' is a realization of machine M such that ι is one-to-one mapping if and only if the reduced form M_R of M is a homomorphic image of a submachine M'' of M'.

Proof. We can assume that M is a reduced machine. Since a machine realizes its reduced form (by Theorem 1.5) and since the relation "realized by" is a transitive, M' realizes the reduced form of M. Furthermore, if the mapping ι is one-to-one in the realization of M by M', then it is one-to-one in the realization of the reduced form of M by M'. Thus we have to show that there exists a submachine M'' of M' which can be mapped homomorphically onto M. Let

$$S'' = \cup \{\alpha(s) | s \in S \text{ of } M\}$$
$$I'' = \cup \{\iota(x) | x \in I \text{ of } M\}$$
$$O'' = O'$$
$$\delta'' = \delta' \text{ restricted to } S'' \times I''$$
$$\lambda'' = \lambda' \text{ restricted to } S'' \times I''.$$

Then

$$M'' = (S,'' I'', O'', \delta'', \lambda'')$$

is a submachine of M'. By definition of (α, ι, ζ), s' in S'' implies that

$$\delta''[\alpha(s), \iota(x)] \subseteq \alpha[\delta(s, x)]$$

and therefore

$$\delta''[\alpha(s), \iota(x)] \subseteq S''.$$

To see that M'' can be mapped homomorphically onto M define:

$$h_1(s') = s \qquad \text{if and only if } s' \text{ in } \alpha(s),$$
$$h_2 = \iota^{-1}$$
$$h_3 = \zeta.$$

Since, for all s' in $\alpha(s)$,

$$\delta''[s', \iota(x)] \text{ is in } \alpha[\delta(s, x)]$$

and

$$\zeta[\lambda''(s', \iota(x))] = \lambda(s, x),$$

we obtain

$$h_1[\delta''(s', \iota(x))] = \delta(s, x) = \delta(h_1(s'), h_2[\iota(x)])$$

and

$$h_3[\lambda''(s', \iota(x))] = \lambda(s, x) = \lambda(h_1(s'), h_2[\iota(x)]).$$

Thus (h_1, h_2, h_3) is a homomorphism.

Conversely, if M is a homomorphic image of M'', then the homomorphism $h = (h_1, h_2, h_3)$ defines an assignment of M into M' if we let

$$\alpha(s) = \{s' \mid h_1(s') = s\},$$

$$\iota(x) = \text{some } x' \text{ such that } h_2(x') = x,$$

$$\zeta = h_3.$$

If s' is in $\alpha(s)$ then by definition of α,

$$h_1(s') = s.$$

Therefore,

$$h_1[\delta''(s', \iota(x))] = \delta(h_1(s'), h_2[\iota(x)]) = \delta(s, x)$$

and thus

$$\delta''[s', \iota(x)] \text{ is in } \alpha[\delta(s, x)].$$

Therefore

$$\delta''[\alpha(s), \iota(x)] \subseteq \alpha[\delta(s, x)].$$

Finally,

$$\zeta[\lambda''(s', \iota(x))] = \lambda(s, x)$$

and (α, ι, ζ) is an assignment of M into M''; but then M' realizes M. ∎

EXERCISE. Show that Theorem 1.6 does not hold when ι is not one-to-one.

We now wish to name a special case of Definition 1.15.

DEFINITION 1.16. Machine M' is said to *realize the state behavior* of machine M if and only if M' realizes M with an assignment (α, ι, ζ) such that α maps each state of M onto a single state of M' and α is one-to-one.

In this case, the relations of Definition 1.14 reduce to the following equations:

(i) $\delta'[\alpha(s), \iota(x)] = \alpha[\delta(s, x)]$ for all s in S and x in I.

(ii) $\zeta[\lambda'(\alpha(s))] = \lambda(s)$ for s in S

(ii') $\zeta[\lambda'(\iota(x), \alpha(s))] = \lambda(s, x)$ for s in S and x in I.

We shall see that for some applications a complete analysis can be made for realizations of this type, whereas the analysis for other realizations can be done only by more cumbersome techniques or by good guesswork. Further, most of the realizations of the general type have too many states and require extra memory to build. Considerable attention will be focused on such matters in later sections.

We show two realizations for machine D of Fig. 1.14. The more general type is illustrated in Fig. 1.15 and a state behavior realization is given in Fig. 1.16.

	a	b	
1	3	2	0
2	1	2	1
3	3	1	1

$\alpha(1) = \{00, 10\}$

$\alpha(2) = \{11\}$

$\alpha(3) = \{01\}$

$\iota(a) = 0$
$\iota(b) = 1$
$\zeta(0) = 0$
$\zeta(1) = 1$

$(y_1\ y_2)$	x = 0	x = 1	
0 0	01	11	0
1 0	01	11	0
1 1	00	11	1
0 1	01	10	1

D'

Fig. 1.14. Machine D.   **Fig. 1.15.** Machine D', a realization of machine D.

$\alpha(1) = 00$

$\alpha(2) = 01$

$\alpha(3) = 10$

$\iota(a) = 0$
$\iota(b) = 1$
$\zeta(0) = 0$
$\zeta(1) = 1$

$(y_1\ y_2)$	x = 0	x = 1	
0 0	10	01	0
0 1	00	01	1
1 0	10	00	1
1 1	00	00	1

D''

Fig. 1.16. Machine D'', a state realization of machine D.

The states, inputs, and outputs of machines D' and D'' are expressed in terms of binary variables, and the functions α, ι, and ζ explain how these are interpreted. After the next definition, we show how these can be expressed in function form and synthesized by a physical device.

DEFINITION 1.17. Input binary variables

$$x_i \text{ for } 1 \leqslant i \leqslant m,$$

state binary variables

$$y_j \text{ for } 1 \leqslant j \leqslant n,$$

transition functions

$$Y_j : \{(y_1, \ldots, y_n, x_1, \ldots, x_m)\} \longrightarrow \{0, 1\},$$

and output functions

$$z_k : \{(y_1, \ldots, y_n)\} \longrightarrow \{0, 1\} \qquad i \leqslant k \leqslant r \qquad \text{(Moore case)}$$

or

$$z_k : \{(y_1, \ldots, y_n, x_1, \ldots, x_m)\} \longrightarrow \{0, 1\} \qquad \text{(Mealy case)}$$

are said to *define* the following machine
   (i) $S = \{(y_1, \ldots, y_n)\}$, the set of all n-tuples on $\{0, 1\}$;
   (ii) $I = \{(x_1, \ldots, x_m)\}$;
   (iii) $O = \{(z_1, \ldots, z_r)\}$;
   (iv) $\delta(\vec{y}, \vec{x}) = \vec{Y}(\vec{y}, \vec{x})$;
   (v) $\lambda(\vec{y}) = \vec{z}(\vec{y})$ or $\beta(\vec{y}, \vec{x}) = \vec{z}(\vec{y}, \vec{z})$.

Thus, machine D' is defined by the Boolean equations:

$$Y_1 = x$$
$$Y_2 = \bar{y}_2 + \bar{x}\bar{y}_1 + xy_1$$
$$z = y_2$$

and D'' is defined by the equations:

$$Y_1 = \bar{y}_2\bar{x}$$
$$Y_2 = \bar{y}_1 x$$
$$z = y_1 + y_2.$$

We say that the equations realize a machine M if they define a machine M' that realizes M. Thus the previous sets of equations both realize machine D. The term "realize" is used because the logical equations determine a schematic circuit diagram from which an engineer can build a physical device to behave like the machine. The equations for D' lead to the diagram of Fig. 1.17. The interpretation of Fig. 1.17 is that, at each time pulse (or end

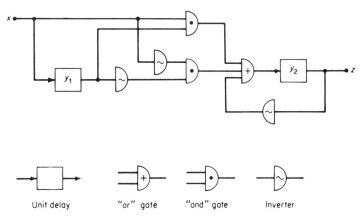

Fig. 1.17.   Circuit diagram for machine D'.

of fixed time intervals), the contents of delays y_1 and y_2 are released, combined with the input to compute the next values, and the new values are stored in the delays.

1.4   STATE ASSIGNMENT PROBLEM

One of the central problems in the physical realization of sequential machines is the selection of "desirable" (binary) codes to represent the internal states of the machine. Most often "desirable" means fewest number of components in the resulting realization though other criteria can be imposed and will become more prevalent with changing technical demands. A traditional measure of complexity is the number of diodes used in the realizations, where one diode is required for each wire entering an "and" or "or" gate. Thus the circuit of Fig. 1.17 is said to require seven diodes.

To illustrate the large variation in complexity that different state assignments can have on machine realization, consider machine E of Fig. 1.18.

	0	1	
1	4	3	0
2	6	3	0
3	5	2	0
4	2	5	1
5	1	4	0
6	3	4	0

	y_1 y_2 y_3		y_1 y_2 y_3
1 →	0 0 0	1 →	1 1 0
2 →	0 0 1	2 →	1 0 1
3 →	0 1 0	3 →	1 0 0
4 →	0 1 1	4 →	0 0 0
5 →	1 0 0	5 →	0 0 1
6 →	1 0 1	6 →	0 1 0

Fig. 1.18. Machine E. **Fig. 1.19.** Two state assignments for machine E.

In Fig. 1.19 are shown two state assignments for E. The logical equations which define the machine obtained by means of the first assignment are

$$Y_1 = \bar{y}_1\bar{y}_2y_3\bar{x} + y_2\bar{y}_3\bar{x} + y_2y_3x$$
$$Y_2 = \bar{y}_2x + \bar{y}_1\bar{y}_2\bar{y}_3 + y_1y_3$$
$$Y_3 = y_1x + y_2\bar{y}_3x + y_2y_3\bar{x} + \bar{y}_1\bar{y}_2\bar{x}$$
$$z = y_2y_3.$$

The second assignment leads to

$$Y_1 = y_1x + \bar{y}_1\bar{x}$$
$$Y_2 = y_3\bar{x}$$
$$Y_3 = \bar{y}_2\bar{y}_3$$
$$z = \bar{y}_1\bar{y}_2\bar{y}_3.$$

(In both cases, there was some latitude in assigning values of Y_i over those values of the y_i which do not represent a state of the machine. Using standard Venn diagram techniques, we assigned these values so as to simplify the equations. In the terminology of the next section, we filled the "don't care conditions" judiciously.) The contrast between these equations is obvious, and in a physical realization, the first assignment requires about three times as many diodes as the realization using the second assignment.

In this example, the second state assignment leads to simpler logical equations because the functional dependence between the state variables has been reduced. It is seen that Y_1 does not depend on y_2 and y_3, and Y_2 and Y_3 do not depend on y_1. The corresponding schematic realization in Fig. 1.20 shows that this realization actually consists of two independent machines operating in parallel (these concepts are made precise in the next chapter). This example, which is not an isolated one, shows that machine

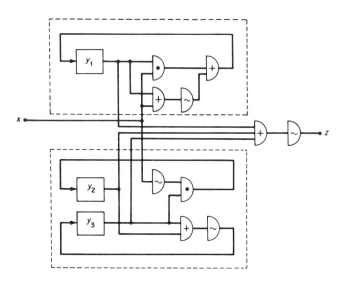

Fig. 1.20. Realization of machine E using the second assignment.

decomposition can lead to economical state assignments. Furthermore, one feels intuitively that the reduction of the number of state variables and inputs on which the state variables depend should simplify the logical circuits in the corresponding realization. Because the structure theory for sequential machines is concerned with realizations of machines from smaller component machines and the general understanding of the logical dependence or information flow, structure theory can be viewed as an approach to the state assignment problem. Thus, this problem supplies additional motivation for the development of a structure theory. Explicit applications of structure theory to the state assignment problem are discussed later.

1.5 "DON'T CARE" CONDITIONS

In applying machine theory to engineering problems, it sometimes happens that the problem requirements do not completely specify a machine

	0	1	
1	4	2	0
2	–	1	–
3	1	–	1
4	2	3	1

Fig. 1.21. Machine with d. c. conditions.

table. The machine designer may thereby be left with several complex alternatives for completing the machine table. The most common option is the so-called *"don't care"* (or d.c.) condition. These are generally represented by dashes in the flow table such as in Fig. 1.21. The dashes are interpreted to mean that the engineer doesn't care what transition or output occurs when the corresponding input and state combination occur. Such conditions arise when the machine, in its normal operation as applied to the particular problem, is not expected to be confronted with that particular input-state combination, or when certain outputs are to be ignored anyway. Certain later sections of this book discuss methods of extending the structure theorems to machines with d.c. conditions.

There is one aspect of completely specified machines which leads to d.c. conditions of a special type. Consider machine F and realization of Fig. 1.22. Notice that even though the machine is completely specified, the

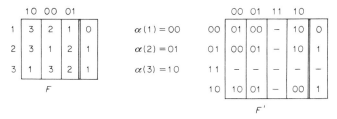

Fig. 1.22.   Machine F and realization F'.

realization in binary variables is not. The realization has a fictitious input which is never used and a state which is never entered. The result is a column and row of d.c. conditions. We refer to such conditions as *incidental* d.c. conditions.

In Fig. 1.23 the incidental d.c. conditions of Fig. 1.22 have been filled with zeros to obtain realization F', and the corresponding equations are

$$Y_1 = \bar{x}_1\bar{x}_2 y_1 \bar{y}_2 + x_1\bar{x}_2\bar{y}_1$$
$$Y_2 = \bar{x}_1\bar{x}_2\bar{y}_1\bar{y}_2 + \bar{x}_1 x_2 \bar{y}_1 y_2 + \bar{x}_1 x_2 y_1 \bar{y}_2$$
$$z = y_1\bar{y}_2 + \bar{y}_1 y_2.$$

These equations require thirty diodes. Contrast this to the realization F'' of Fig. 1.24 which was obtained by filling the d.c.'s judiciously. Now the equations are

$$Y_1 = \bar{x}_1\bar{x}_2 y_1 + x_1\bar{y}_1$$
$$Y_2 = x_2 y_2 + x_2 y_1 + \bar{x}_1\bar{x}_2\bar{y}_1\bar{y}_2$$
$$z = y_1 + y_2.$$

Here only twenty diodes are required and y_1 has been made independent of y_2. Techniques for filling d.c. conditions to simplify equations are well known and are not elaborated here. There are, however, two things we wish to point out. First, we always fill the d.c. conditions carefully and to our advantage, often without saying so (as in Fig. 1.24). Secondly, to obtain the reduced dependence realizations promised by our later theorems, the reader has to fill d.c. conditions properly.

	00	01	11	10	
00	01	00	00	10	0
01	00	01	00	10	1
11	00	00	00	00	0
10	10	01	00	00	1

	00	01	11	10	
00	01	00	10	10	0
01	00	01	11	10	1
11	10	01	01	00	1
10	10	01	01	00	1

Fig. 1.23. Machine F' with d. c. conditions filled with zeros.

Fig. 1.24. Machine F' with d. c. conditions judiciously filled.

NOTES

The study of sequential machines was started by D. A. Huffman [19] and E. F. Moore [25]. Huffman published the first systematic study of sequential circuits whereas Moore gave a more abstract formulation and started the formal study of sequential machines. In Moore's formulation, the output of a machine is dependent only on the state of the machine. This was generalized by G. H. Mealy [24] which led to the differentiation between Moore and Mealy machines. A number of the original papers on sequential machines have been reprinted in a book edited by E. F. Moore [26]. Further results on sequential machines can be found in the books by S. Ginsburg [9] and A. Gill [8].

The structure theory developed in this book gives one approach to the state assignment problem. This was first discussed by the authors in [12, 28] and further developed by C. H. Curtis [5, 6], R. M. Karp [20], and Z. Kohavi [21]. Other approaches to the state assignment problem are discussed by D. B. Armstrong [1, 2], T. A. Dolotta and E. J. McCluskey [7], and D. R. Haring [10].

2 PARTITIONS AND THE SUBSTITUTION PROPERTY

2.1 THE SUBSTITUTION PROPERTY

In this chapter we begin to develop some mathematical tools and theorems which are fundamental to the structure theory of sequential machines. These tools yield results which show how and when complex sequential machines can be realized from interconnected sets of simpler machines, how these simpler machines are related to the machine under consideration, and what the laws are which govern their interconnections. We are interested in those results which characterize possible circuit layouts, but which do not depend on which actual components will be used to realize the computing device. Thus we are primarily concerned with the nature of the *computing process*, and seek to determine the simpler operations from which this process is composed.

The study of machine structure is begun in this section with a formal study of the intuitive concept of a "subcomputation." Imagine a man who is adding a series of integers and a second man who is keeping track of whether the sum is even or odd. Since the result of the second man's computation is evident from the result of the first man's computation, we say that the second man is doing a subcomputation of the first man's computation. In a similar way, we want to think of a small machine as doing a subcomputation of a large machine if the state or output of the large machine determines the state or output of the small machine. The small machine then gives partial information about the large machine. One can see that we are actually close to the concept of a homomorphism. Since a machine M can be used to realize its homomorphic image M', one can say informally

37

that M' does a part or a subcomputation of the computation performed by M. The results of this chapter give some elementary structure of decomposition results obtainable from the homomorphism concept.

The previously given definition of a homomorphism is not ideally suited for computational purposes and tests, for it involves two machines and the operation-preserving mappings between these machines. The next definition leads to a different characterization of state homomorphisms that involves only one machine and leads to direct computational methods.

DEFINITION 2.1. A partition π on the set of states of the machine

$$M = (S, I, O, \delta, \lambda)$$

is said to have the *substitution property* if and only if

$$s \equiv t\,(\pi)$$

implies that

$$\delta(s, a) \equiv \delta(t, a)\,(\pi)$$

for all a in I.

We refer sometimes to partitions with the substitution property as S.P. partitions.

It follows from this definition that the partition π on S of M has the substitution property if and only if each input maps blocks of π into blocks of π. That is, for a in I and B_π in π, there exists a (unique) B'_π in π such that

$$\delta(B_\pi, a) \subseteq B'_\pi.$$

Since the operation of M determines unique block to block transformations on S.P. partition π, we can think of these blocks as the states of a new state machine defined by π and M. This justifies our next definition.

DEFINITION 2.2. Let π be a S.P. partition on the set of states of the machine

$$M = (S, I, O, \delta, \lambda).$$

Then the π-*image of* M is the state machine

$$M_\pi = (\{B_\pi\}, I, \delta_\pi)$$

with

$$\delta_\pi(B_\pi, x) = B'_\pi \qquad \text{if and only if} \qquad \delta(B_\pi, x) \subseteq B'_\pi.$$

We can think of M_π as a machine which does only part of the computation performed by M, since it only keeps track of which block of π contains the state of M.

This can also be thought about in terms of the uncertainty or ignorance which can exist about the state of M. If π has S.P. on M and we know the block of π which contains the state of M, then we can compute the block of π to which this state of M is transformed by any input sequence. As a matter of fact, M_π performs this computation. On the other hand, if a partition π does not have S.P., then this computation is not possible for some input sequence and initial block. Thus we can say informally that the S.P. partitions define a sort of uncertainty about the state of M which does not spread as the machine operates.

To illustrate these ideas, consider machine A of Fig. 2.1. It is easily seen that the partitions

$$\pi_1 = \{\overline{1,2,3}; \overline{4,5,6}\} \qquad \text{and} \qquad \pi_2 = \{\overline{1,6}; \overline{2,5}; \overline{3,4}\}$$

have the substitution property on A. The corresponding image machines A_{π_1} and A_{π_2} are shown in Fig. 2.2.

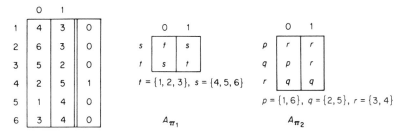

Fig. 2.1.   Machine A.   Fig. 2.2.   The image machines A_{π_1} and A_{π_2}.

To get a preview of how these concepts are used later for machine decomposition, consider what happens when machines A_{π_1} and A_{π_2} are operated side by side. Each machine separately does only part of the computation performed by A, since it only determines the block of π_i which contains the state of A. Operating jointly, these two machines determine the exact state of A. This is because every block of π_1 has exactly one state of A in common with every block of π_2. Thus, the states of A_{π_1} and A_{π_2} uniquely determine a state of A and so, operating in parallel, these two machines compute the state transitions of A. These ideas are made precise and investigated in the two sections which follow.

The next result shows that there exists a one-to-one correspondence between state homomorphisms and S.P. partitions.

THEOREM 2.1. Let $h = (h_1, e)$ be a state homomorphism of

$$M = (S, I, O, \delta, \lambda) \text{ onto } M' = (S', I, \delta')$$

such that e is the identity map. Then the partition π defined by

$$s \equiv t\,(\pi) \qquad \text{if and only if} \qquad h_1(s) = h_1(t),$$

has S.P. on M and

$$M' \cong M_\pi.$$

Conversely, if π has S.P. on M, then M_π is a homomorphic image of M and the homomorphism $h = (h_1, e)$ is given by

$$h_1(s) = B_\pi \qquad \text{if and only if} \qquad s \text{ is in } B_\pi.$$

Proof. Since h is a homomorphism, $h_1(s) = h_1(t)$ implies

$$\delta'[h_1(s), a] = \delta'[h_1(t), a] = h_1[\delta(s, a)] = h_1[\delta(t, a)].$$

Therefore

$$\delta(s, a) \equiv \delta(t, a)\ (\pi)$$

and π is a S.P. partition. The isomorphism (f, e) of M_π onto M' is given by

$$f(B_\pi) = s' \qquad \text{if } h(s) = s' \text{ for } s \text{ in } B_\pi.$$

To prove the second part, let

$$s \text{ be in } B_\pi \qquad \text{and} \qquad \delta(s, a) \text{ in } B'_\pi.$$

Then

$$h_1(s) = B_\pi \qquad \text{and} \qquad h_1[\delta(s, a)] = B'_\pi$$

and thus

$$h_1[\delta(s, a)] = \delta_\pi[h_1(s), a].$$

But then h is a homomorphism of M onto M_π. ∎

The next result shows how one can combine S.P. partitions on M to obtain new S.P. partitions.

THEOREM 2.2. *If π_1 and π_2 are S.P. partitions on the set of states of a sequential machine M, then so are the partitions*

$$\pi_1 \cdot \pi_2 \text{ and } \pi_1 + \pi_2.$$

Proof. Assume that

$$s \equiv t\ (\pi_1) \qquad \text{and} \qquad s \equiv t\ (\pi_2).$$

Then by definition,

$$s \equiv t\ (\pi_1 \cdot \pi_2).$$

For any input a in I

$$\delta(s, a) \equiv \delta(t, a)\ (\pi_1)$$

and

$$\delta(s, a) \equiv \delta(t, a)\ (\pi_2)$$

by the hypotheses of the theorem, but then clearly

$$\delta(s, a) \equiv \delta(t, a)\ (\pi_1 \cdot \pi_2)$$

by the definition of $\pi_1 \cdot \pi_2$.

To show that $\pi_1 + \pi_2$ has S.P. we recall that

$$s \equiv t\ (\pi_1 + \pi_2)$$

implies that there exists a chain

$$s = s_0, s_1, s_2, \ldots, s_m = t$$

such that

$$s_j \equiv s_{j+1}(\pi_1) \qquad \text{or} \qquad s_j \equiv s_{j+1}(\pi_2), \qquad j = 0, 1, 2, \ldots, m - 1.$$

We now use this to show that for every input a in I,

$$\delta(s, a) \equiv \delta(t, a)(\pi_1 + \pi_2).$$

Since π_1 and π_2 have S.P.,

$$\delta(s, a) \equiv \delta(s_1, a)(\pi_1) \qquad \text{or} \qquad \delta(s_1, a) \equiv \delta(s, a)(\pi_2)$$

and since π_1 and π_2 are both finer than $\pi_1 + \pi_2$, we conclude that

$$\delta(s, a) \equiv \delta(s_1, a)(\pi_1 + \pi_2).$$

Similarly,

$$\delta(s_1, a) \equiv \delta(s_2, a)(\pi_1 + \pi_2)$$
$$\delta(s_2, a) \equiv \delta(s_3, a)(\pi_1 + \pi_2)$$
$$\cdots$$
$$\delta(s_{m-1}, a) \equiv \delta(t, a)(\pi_1 + \pi_2).$$

Thus, since the equivalence relation is transitive, we have

$$\delta(s, a) \equiv \delta(t, a)(\pi_1 + \pi_2),$$

as was to be shown. ∎

THEOREM 2.3. The set of all S.P. partitions on the set of states of a sequential machine M forms a lattice L_M, under the natural partition ordering. Furthermore, L_M contains the trivial partitions 0 and I.

Proof. From the previous theorem, we know that the set of S.P. partitions on S of M is closed under the "·" and "+" operations. Thus, the set of all S.P. partitions forms a sublattice of the lattice of all partitions on S, and therefore a lattice in the natural ordering of partitions. The last statement of the theorem is obvious. ∎

Two applications of the lattice L_M are brought out in later chapters. First, it will be seen that the plot of L_M permits a simple visualization of all the important multiple series-parallel state behavior realizations. Thus, the lattice is, in a sense, a picture of some machine structure. Secondly, algebraic properties (modularity, distributivity, complementation, etc.) of the lattice L_M are reflected in machine properties and vica versa, which supply means of the classification of sequential machines according to their L_M lattices.

To practice some of the ideas of this section, consider machine B shown in Fig. 2.3. This machine has eight S.P. partitions:

$$0 = \{\overline{1}; \overline{2}; \overline{3}; \overline{4}; \overline{5}; \overline{6}; \overline{7}; \overline{8}\},$$
$$\pi_1 = \{\overline{1,2}; \overline{3,4}; \overline{5,6}; \overline{7,8}\},$$

$$\pi_2 = \{\overline{1,2,3,4}; \overline{5,6,7,8}\},$$
$$\pi_3 = \{\overline{1}; \overline{2}; \overline{3}; \overline{4,5}; \overline{6}; \overline{7}; \overline{8}\},$$
$$\pi_4 = \{\overline{1,2}; \overline{3,4,5,6}; \overline{7,8}\},$$
$$\pi_5 = \{\overline{1}; \overline{2}; \overline{3,6}; \overline{4}; \overline{5}; \overline{7}; \overline{8}\},$$
$$\pi_6 = \{\overline{1}; \overline{2}; \overline{3,6}; \overline{4,5}; \overline{7}; \overline{8}\},$$
$$I = \{\overline{1,2,3,4,5,6,7,8}\}.$$

These partitions may be found by a constructive method discussed later in Section 2.5. The lattice L_B is shown in Fig. 2.4.

EXERCISE. Construct the image machines B_{π_1}, B_{π_2}, B_{π_4} and exhibit the homomorphisms which map B onto these machines.

EXERCISE. Show that L_B is not distributive.

EXERCISE. Find all S. P. partitions for machine C of Fig. 2.5, plot L_C, and determine the corresponding image machines.

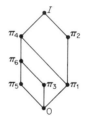

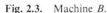

	0	1	
1	3	7	0
2	4	8	0
3	1	6	0
4	2	5	0
5	2	4	0
6	1	3	1
7	4	4	1
8	3	3	0

Fig. 2.3. Machine B.

Fig. 2.4. Lattice L_B.

	0	1	
1	5	2	0
2	6	1	0
3	1	6	0
4	2	5	0
5	3	4	0
6	4	3	1

Fig. 2.5. Machine C.

2.2 SERIAL DECOMPOSITIONS

We now make precise what we mean by a serial connection of two machines.

DEFINITION 2.3. The serial connection of two machines
$$M_1 = (S_1, I_1, O_1, \delta_1, \lambda_1) \qquad \text{and} \qquad M_2 = (S_2, I_2, O_2, \delta_2, \lambda_2)$$
for which
$$O_1 = I_2$$
is the machine
$$M = M_1 \ominus M_2 = (S_1 \times S_2, I_1, O_2, \delta, \lambda)$$
where
$$\delta[(s, t), x] = (\delta_1(s, x), \delta_2[t, \lambda_1(s, x)])$$

and

$$\lambda[(s, t), x] = \lambda_2[t, \lambda_1(s, x)].$$

A schematic representation of a serial connection is shown in Fig. 2.6. The next definition describes how state machines can be interconnected.

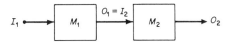

Fig. 2.6.   Serial connection of M_1 and M_2.

DEFINITION 2.4. Given the state machines

$$M_1 = (S_1, I_1, \delta_1) \qquad \text{and} \qquad M_2 = (S_2, I_2, \delta_2)$$

with

$$I_2 = S_1 \times I_1,$$

a set of output symbols O and an output function

$$\lambda: S_1 \times S_2 \times I_1 \longrightarrow O,$$

then the serial connection of M_1 and M_2 with the output function λ is the machine

$$M = (S_1 \times S_2, I_1, O, \delta, \lambda)$$

where

$$\delta[(s, t), x] = (\delta_1(s, x), \delta_2[t, (s, x)])$$

and

$$\lambda: S_1 \times S_2 \times I_1 \longrightarrow O.$$

A schematic representation of this realization is shown in Fig. 2.7.

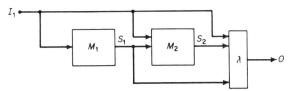

Fig. 2.7. Serial connection of the state machines M_1 and M_2 with output function λ.

It should be noted that there are two different ways in which serially connected machines can operate. If two Mealy machines are serially connected as prescribed by Definition 2.3, then the first machine has to compute its output before the second machine can compute its next state and output. Thus, if we assume that each machine computation requires a certain time interval, the output of the serial connection appears after two time intervals. This time delay grows with the number of the serially connected machines and may be undesirable in some practical applications. Further, such connections of Mealy machines can lead to difficult or impossible timing problems in more general series-parallel connections.

The situation is quite different when we consider the serial connection of state machines (Definition 2.4). (This may also be regarded as the Moore case.) When an input x is applied to the connection specified by Definition 2.4, then both machines can operate simultaneously to compute their next states. This is possible since the input to M_2 is the present state of M_1 and the external input (x in I_1). When this type of connection is generalized to more than two machines, the time delay for the output does not grow with the number of serially connected machines as in the previous case. Note that the machine obtained by such a connec-

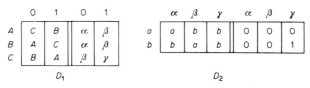

Fig. 2.8.   Machines D_1 and D_2.

<table>
<tr><td></td><td></td><td>0</td><td>1</td><td>0</td><td>1</td></tr>
<tr><td>(A, a)</td><td>1</td><td>5</td><td>4</td><td>0</td><td>0</td></tr>
<tr><td>(A, b)</td><td>2</td><td>6</td><td>3</td><td>0</td><td>0</td></tr>
<tr><td>(B, a)</td><td>3</td><td>1</td><td>6</td><td>0</td><td>0</td></tr>
<tr><td>(B, b)</td><td>4</td><td>2</td><td>5</td><td>0</td><td>0</td></tr>
<tr><td>(C, a)</td><td>5</td><td>4</td><td>2</td><td>0</td><td>0</td></tr>
<tr><td>(C, b)</td><td>6</td><td>3</td><td>2</td><td>0</td><td>1</td></tr>
</table>

Fig. 2.9.   Machine D.

tion of concurrently operating machines can be either a Moore or a Mealy machine, depending only on whether λ is a function of the inputs.

To illustrate these points with actual machines, note that the serial connection of machines D_1 and D_2 of Fig. 2.8 results in the machine D shown in Fig. 2.9. For example,

$$\delta(1, 1) = \delta[(A, a), 1] = [\delta_1(A, 1), \delta_2(a, \lambda_1(A, 1))]$$
$$= [B, \delta_2(a, \beta)] = (B, b) = 4.$$

$$\lambda[(A, a), 1] = \lambda_2[a, \lambda_1(A, 1)] = \lambda_2(a, \beta) = 0.$$

Similarly, the serial connection of the state machines E_1 and E_2 and the

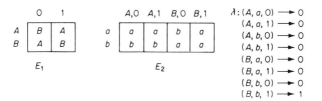

Fig. 2.10.   Machines E_1, E_2 and output function.

output function λ shown in Fig. 2.10 result in the machine E shown in Fig. 2.11. For example,

$$\delta(1, 0) = \delta[(A, a), 0]$$
$$= [\delta_1(A, 0), \delta_2(a, (A, 0))]$$
$$= (B, a) = 3$$
$$\lambda[(A, a), 0] = 0.$$

		0	1	0	1
(A, a)	1	3	1	0	0
(A, b)	2	4	2	0	0
(B, a)	3	2	3	0	0
(B, b)	4	1	3	0	1

Fig. 2.11. Machine E.

We now turn our attention to the realization of a machine M by a serial connection of two other machines.

DEFINITION 2.5. The machine $M_1 \ominus M_2$ is a *serial decomposition* of M if and only if $M_1 \ominus M_2$ realizes M.

If $M_1 \ominus M_2$ is a state behavior realization of M, then we say that $M_1 \ominus M_2$ is a *serial decomposition of the state behavior* of M.

For the present, we restrict ourselves to the study of state behavior decompositions. In Chapter 5, after the full structural value of the S.P. concept is explored in Chapter 4, we consider relaxing the state behavior condition.

NOTATION. We say that the state behavior decomposition of M into $M_1 \ominus M_2$ is *nontrivial* if and only if M_1 and M_2 have fewer states than M.

THEOREM 2.4. The sequential machine M has a nontrivial serial decomposition of its state behavior if and only if there exists a nontrivial S.P. partition π on the set of states S of M.

Proof. Assume the state behavior of M is realized by $M_1 \ominus M_2$ and let (α, ι, ζ) be the assignment map where α is a one-to-one map

$$\alpha: S \longrightarrow S_1 \times S_2.$$

The mapping α induces an equivalence relation or partition π on S if we consider all those states equivalent whose first components under α are identical; that is

$$s \equiv t\ (\pi) \qquad \text{if and only if } s_1 = t_1$$

where

$$\alpha(s) = (s_1, s_2) \quad \text{and} \quad \alpha(t) = (t_1, t_2).$$

To show that π is a S.P. partition, note that by definition

$$\alpha[\delta(s, a)] = (\delta_1(s_1, \iota(a)), \delta_2[s_2, \lambda_1(s_1, \iota(a))])$$
$$\alpha[\delta(t, a)] = (\delta_1(t_1, \iota(a)), \delta_2[t_2, \lambda_1(t_1, \iota(a))])$$

and so if $s \equiv t(\pi)$, then $s_1 = t_1$ and thus

$$\delta_1(s_1, \iota(a)) = \delta_1(t_1, \iota(a)).$$

This means that

$$\delta(s, a) \equiv \delta(t, a)\,(\pi)$$

and so π has S.P.

Finally, we cannot have $\pi = 0$ because M_1 has fewer states than M and we cannot have $\pi = I$ because M_2 has fewer states than M; thus, π has to be a nontrivial partition on S. This completes the proof going one way.

Now we show that if there exists a nontrivial S.P. partition π on S of M, then M has a nontrivial serial realization of its state behavior. We assume that π has l blocks and that the largest block has k states. Since π is nontrivial, $n > k$ and $n > l$. Let τ be a k block partition on S such that

$$\pi \cdot \tau = 0$$

(Such a τ can be constructed by labeling the states of each block B_i of π by $1, 2, \ldots, n_i$, $n_i \leqslant k$, and then placing all the states with the same label in one block of τ). The basic idea of the proof is to design two machines M_1 and M_2 which, when connected in series operate so that M_1 computes the block of π which contains the state of M and M_2 computes the corresponding block of τ. Since

$$\pi \cdot \tau = 0,$$

the serial connection of M_1 and M_2 computes the state of M and we can obtain a realization of M by defining the proper output function. To construct M_1, let

$$M_1 = M_\pi$$

and let its output be the present state and input. Thus

$$M_1 = (\{B_\pi\},\, I,\, \{B_\pi\} \times I,\, \delta_1 = \delta_\pi,\, e).$$

Let

$$M_2 = (\{B_\tau\},\, \{B_\pi\} \times I,\, O,\, \delta_2,\, \lambda_2 = \lambda)$$

where

$$\delta_2[B_\tau,\, (B_\pi,\, x)] = B'_\tau,$$

B'_τ such that

$$\delta(B_\tau \cap B_\pi,\, x) \in B'_\tau.$$

The output

$$\lambda_2[B_\tau,\, (B_\pi,\, x)] = \lambda(B_\tau \cap B_\pi,\, x).$$

(Note that if $B_\tau \cap B_\pi = \varnothing$, then we have a don't care condition, but this pair of states is never entered by $M_1 \ominus M_2$ in the simulation of M.) Thus $M_1 \ominus M_2$ is a realization of M which proves that M has a nontrivial serial decomposition of its state behavior.

Stated less formally: M_1 computes the block of π that contains the present state of M. Since the states of M_2 are blocks of τ and the input to M_2 is a block of π and an element of I, the present state of M and its input is known in M_2 ($\pi \cdot \tau = 0$) and thus M_2 can compute the block of τ which contains the next state of M. To store this, we need only a k state machine and thus the desired machines M_1 and M_2 exist. ∎

EXAMPLE. Consider machine F of Fig. 2.12. It is easily seen that

$$\pi = \{\overline{1,2}; \overline{3,4,5}\}$$

has S.P. on F. Thus we know from the proof of Theorem 2.4 that F can be realized by a serial connection of a two-state and a three-state machine, F_1

	0	1	0	1
1	5	3	1	0
2	3	4	0	0
3	1	5	0	1
4	2	3	0	0
5	1	4	0	0

Fig. 2.12.   Machine F.

	0	1	0	1
A	B	B	A,0	A,1
B	A	B	B,0	B,1

$\pi = \{\overline{1,2}; \overline{3,4,5}\} = \{A, B\}$

Fig. 2.13.   Machine F_1.

and F_2, respectively. The machine F_1 can be constructed directly from the flow table of F and is given in Fig. 2.13. To construct machine F_2, we have to choose a three-block partition τ on S such that

$$\pi \cdot \tau = 0.$$

Let

$$\tau = \{\overline{1,3}; \overline{2,4}; \overline{5}\} = \{a, b, c\}.$$

To construct F_2 in easy steps, we rewrite the flow table of F by replacing its states by the corresponding blocks of τ, and rearrange the information to obtain F_2, as shown in Fig. 2.14. It can easily be seen that by proper

		0	1	0	1
A	a	c	a	1	0
	b	a	b	0	0
B	a	a	c	0	1
	b	b	a	0	0
	c	a	b	0	0

	A0	A1	B0	B1	A0	A1	B0	B1
a	c	a	a	c	1	0	0	1
b	a	b	b	a	0	0	0	0
c	$-$	$-$	a	b	$-$	$-$	0	0

$\tau = \{\overline{1,3}; \overline{2,4}; \overline{5}\} = \{a, b, c\}$

Fig. 2.14.   Construction of machine F_2.

filling of the don't care conditions, we can obtain two pairs of identical next state columns in F_2 and thus we actually need only a two input machine as F_2 and we can simplify the output of F_1. The two simplified machines which realize F are shown in Fig. 2.15.

EXERCISE. Construct the two machines F_1' and F_2' which realize F of Fig. 2.12 if $\tau = \{\overline{1,5}; \overline{2,3}; \overline{4}\}$.

	0	1	0	1
A	B	B	α	β
B	A	B	β	α

	α	β	α	β
a	c	a	1	0
b	a	b	0	0
c	b	a	0	0

Fig. 2.15. Machines F_1 and F_2 whose serial connection realizes F.

EXERCISE. Construct the two machines D_1' and D_2' which realize D of Fig. 2.9 if $\tau = \overline{\{1,4,5; \; 2,3,6\}}$.

In Chapter 4 we investigate the properties of the second, or "tail," machine in serial decompositions and relate them to the choice of τ and the properties of M. In the next section, we study decompositions of a machine into two parallel machines.

2.3   PARALLEL DECOMPOSITIONS

In this section we study the decomposition of a machine into two machines which operate in parallel.

DEFINITION 2.6. The *parallel connection* of the two machines

$$M_1 = (S_1, I_1, O_1, \delta_1, \lambda_1) \qquad \text{and} \qquad M_2 = (S_2, I_2, O_2, \delta_2, \lambda_2)$$

is the machine

$$M = M_1 \,||\, M_2 = (S_1 \times S_2, I_1 \times I_2, O_1 \times O_2, \delta, \lambda)$$

with

$$\delta[(s_1, s_2), (x_1, x_2)] = (\delta_1(s_1, x_1), \delta_2(s_2, x_2))$$

and

$$\lambda[(s_1, s_2), (x_1, x_2)] = (\lambda_1(s_1, x_1), \lambda_2(s_2, x_2)).$$

DEFINITION 2.7. The machine $M_1 \,||\, M_2$ is a *parallel decomposition* of M if and only if $M_1 \,||\, M_2$ realizes M.

If $M_1 \,||\, M_2$ is a state behavior realization of M, then we refer to $M_1 \,||\, M_2$ as a *parallel decomposition of the state behavior* of M. We say that the state behavior decomposition of M into $M_1 \,||\, M_2$ is *nontrivial* if and only if M_1 and M_2 each have fewer states than M.

For the present, we restrict ourselves to the study of parallel state behavior decompositions.

THEOREM 2.5. A sequential machine M has a nontrivial parallel decomposition of its state behavior if and only if there exist two nontrivial S.P. partitions π_1 and π_2 on M such that

$$\pi_1 \cdot \pi_2 = 0.$$

Proof. Let the state behavior of M be realized by $M_1 \,\|\, M_2$. Let (α, ι, ζ) be the assignment map such that $\alpha: S \longrightarrow S_1 \times S_2$ is one-to-one. The mapping α defines two equivalence relations π_1 and π_2 on S as follows:

$s \equiv t\,(\pi_1)$ if and only if $s_1 = t_1$ where $\alpha(s) = (s_1, s_2)$ and $\alpha(t) = (t_1, t_2)$,

$s \equiv t\,(\pi_2)$ if and only if $s_2 = t_2$ where $\alpha(s) = (s_1, s_2)$ and $\alpha(t) = (t_1, t_2)$.

Since the mapping α is one-to-one onto, we know that

$$s \equiv t\,(\pi_1 \cdot \pi_2) \text{ implies } s = t$$

and thus

$$\pi_1 \cdot \pi_2 = 0.$$

To see that π_1 and π_2 have S.P., note that if

$$s \equiv t\,(\pi_1)$$

then

$$\alpha(s) = (s_1, s_2) \qquad \text{and} \qquad \alpha(t) = (s_1, t_2).$$

But then

$$\alpha[\delta(s, x)] = [\delta_1(s_1, \iota(x)), \delta_2(s_2, \iota(x))]$$
$$\alpha[\delta(t, x)] = [\delta_1(s_1, \iota(x)), \delta_2(t_2, \iota(x))]$$

and therefore, the first components of the next states are again identical under α and we have

$$\delta(s, x) \equiv \delta(t, x)\,(\pi_1).$$

The same argument shows that π_2 also has S.P. Finally, if $M_1 \,\|\, M_2$ is a nontrivial realization, then

$$|S| > |S_1|, |S| > |S_2|, |S_1| \cdot |S_2| \geqslant |S|.$$

Thus π_1 and π_2 have less than $|S|$ blocks and more than one block and are therefore nontrivial partitions.

To show the converse, assume that π_1 and π_2 are nontrivial S.P. partitions on M such that

$$\pi_1 \cdot \pi_2 = 0.$$

To construct M_1 and M_2, we take their image machines M_{π_1} and M_{π_2} and add outputs:

$$M_1 = (\{B_{\pi_1}\}, I, \{B_{\pi_1}\} \times I, \delta_1 = \delta_{\pi_1}, e)$$
$$M_2 = (\{B_{\pi_2}\}, I, \{B_{\pi_2}\} \times I, \delta_2 = \delta_{\pi_2}, e).$$

Obviously since $\pi_1 \cdot \pi_2 = 0$, the output of $M_1 \,\|\, M_2$ determines a unique pair in $S \times I$ and thus there is a mapping ζ which maps $O_1 \times O_2$ onto O so that $M_1 \,\|\, M_2$ realizes M. More precisely, the realization is given by the mappings

$$\alpha(s) = (B_{\pi_1}(s), B_{\pi_2}(s))$$
$$\iota(x) = (x, x)$$

$$\zeta[(B_{\pi_1}, x), (B_{\pi_2}, x)] = \lambda(B_{\pi_1} \cap B_{\pi_2}, x).$$

Since π_1 and π_2 are nontrivial partitions, the decomposition is also nontrivial. ∎

Consider machine G of Fig. 2.16. For this machine the partitions

$$\pi_1 = \{\overline{0,1,2}; \overline{3,4,5}\} \qquad \text{and} \qquad \pi_2 = \{\overline{0,5}; \overline{1,4}; \overline{2,3}\}$$

have S.P. and since

$$\pi_1 \cdot \pi_2 = 0,$$

they define a parallel decomposition of G. The two image machines (with outputs added) are shown in Figs. 2.17 and 2.18. Since G is a Moore machine,

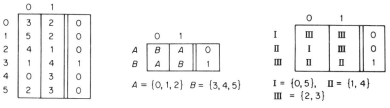

Fig. 2.16.   Machine G.   Fig. 2.17.   Machine G_1.   Fig. 2.18.   Machine G_2.

the component machines can be Moore machines. We have chosen outputs so that

$$\lambda(s) = \lambda_1(s_1) \cdot \lambda_2(s_2).$$

This parallel decomposition is shown schematically in Fig. 2.19.

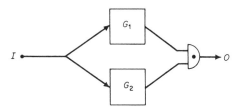

Fig. 2.19.   The parallel decomposition of G.

For another illustration, consider machine H of Fig. 2.20. The partitions

$$\pi_1 = \{\overline{1,3,5}; \overline{2,4,6}\} \qquad \text{and} \qquad \pi_2 = \{\overline{1,2}; \overline{3,4}; \overline{5,6}\}$$

both have S.P. and since

$$\pi_1 \cdot \pi_2 = 0,$$

they define a parallel decomposition of H. The two component machines, namely H_1 and H_2 with suitable outputs, are shown in Figs. 2.21 and 2.22. Note that H_1 is actually an input independent machine and thus our reali-

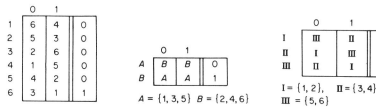

	0	1	
1	6	4	0
2	5	3	0
3	2	6	0
4	1	5	0
5	4	2	0
6	3	1	1

Fig. 2.20. Machine H.

	0	1	
A	B	B	0
B	A	A	1

$A = \{1, 3, 5\}$ $B = \{2, 4, 6\}$

Fig. 2.21. Machine H_1.

	0	1	
I	III	II	0
II	I	III	0
III	II	I	1

$I = \{1, 2\}$, $II = \{3, 4\}$
$III = \{5, 6\}$

Fig. 2.22. Machine H_2.

zation has the form shown in Fig. 2.23. A study of input independent machines (or clocks) and their detection is included in Chapter 4.

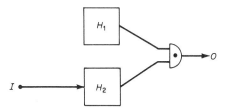

Fig. 2.23.   The parallel decomposition of H.

2.4 COMPUTATION OF S.P. PARTITIONS

The results of the two previous sections indicate the important role which S.P. partitions play in the study of sequential machines. In this section we show how S.P. partitions can be efficiently and systematically computed for any sequential machine.

There are basically two ways of obtaining S.P. partitions. The first way is to work with the machine description until a partition is found which satisfies Definition 2.1. The second way is to combine previously obtained S.P. partitions using the sum and product operations. Since the second way is much easier than the first, the most efficient procedures are those which rely most heavily on the second way. Of course, some use must be made of the first way since no nontrivial partitions are known a priori to have S.P. In view of these observations, we suggest a general procedure following two steps:

(1) For every pair of states s and t, compute the smallest S.P. partition, $\pi_{s,t}^m$, which identifies the pair.

(2) Find all possible sums of the $\pi_{s,t}^m$. These sums constitute all the S.P. partitions.

To show that this procedure gives all the S.P. partitions, it must be shown that every S.P. partition is the sum of some subset of $\{\pi_{s,t}^m\}$. The reader may verify this by doing the next exercise.

EXERCISE. If π is a S.P. partition on M, show that

$$\pi = \sum \{\pi_{s,t}^m \mid s \equiv t\,(\pi)\}.$$

Before we illustrate this procedure, a couple of remarks are in order.

1. Note that we did not say exactly how the $\pi_{s,t}^m$ are to be computed. Several similar ways of doing this can be specified to the last detail, all amounting to looking ahead (in the state table) and identifying only those states which have to be identified. After a little practice, a person should find that he is not following one set procedure, but is instead following little short cuts dictated by his intuition. Thus hand calculations are easier than might appear at first glance.

2. Note that step 2 requires that one *find* all possible sums, not *take* all possible sums. Many of the sums are equal and it is not necessary to perform all possible derivations of that partition. This economy is obtained by taking pairs of $\pi_{s,t}^m$ to obtain "second-generation" partitions and then using only new "second-generation" partitions to find "third-generation" partitions, and so on.

	a	b	c
1	6	3	2
2	5	4	1
3	2	5	4
4	1	6	3
5	4	1	6
6	3	2	5

Fig. 2.24. Machine J.

EXAMPLE. To illustrate the procedure and some bookkeeping techniques, consider machine J of Fig. 2.24.

We start by computing the S.P. partitions obtained by identifying a pair of states.

If $\pi_{1,2}^m$ identifies states 1 and 2, then

$$\delta(1, a) = 6, \qquad \delta(2, a) = 5$$

and

$$\delta(1, b) = 3, \qquad \delta(2, b) = 4$$

imply that states 6, 5 and 3, 4 must also be identified by $\pi_{1,2}^m$. Therefore

$$\pi_{1,2}^m \geqslant \{\overline{1,2};\ \overline{3,4};\ \overline{5,6}\}.$$

Since

$$\delta(3, a) = 2, \qquad \delta(4, a) = 1,$$
$$\delta(3, b) = 5, \qquad \delta(4, b) = 6,$$
$$\text{etc.,}$$

we see that

$$\pi_{1,2}^m = \{\overline{1,2};\ \overline{3,4};\ \overline{5,6}\}.$$

In the actual computation, we just look at the flow table and check onto what states the state pair 1, 2 is mapped by different inputs. All that we actually write is as follows:

$$1,2 \longrightarrow \overline{5,6}\ \overline{3,4}\ \overline{1,2}.$$

Since these pairs do not overlap and are mapped back into themselves, we know that we have computed the smallest S.P. partition which identifies the states 1 and 2.

Next consider states 1 and 3. In our shorthand

$$\overline{1,3} \longrightarrow \overline{2,6}\ \overline{3,5}\ \overline{2,4}.$$

Since the pairs $\overline{1,3}$, $\overline{3,5}$ and $\overline{2,6}$, $\overline{2,4}$ overlap we use the transitive law and obtain that

$$\pi_{1,3}^m \geqslant \{\overline{1,3,5};\ \overline{2,4,6}\}.$$

Since these blocks are mapped by all inputs into themselves, we note that

$$\pi_{1,3}^m = \{\overline{1,3,5};\ \overline{2,4,6}\}.$$

In our shorthand we write all this computation:

$$\overline{1,3} \longrightarrow \overline{2,6}\ \overline{3,5}\ \overline{2,4} \longrightarrow \underline{\overline{1,3,5}\ \overline{2,4,6}}$$

and underline the last partition to show that it has S.P. Next we obtain the following

$$\overline{1,4} \longrightarrow \overline{1,6}\ \overline{3,6}\ \overline{2,3} \longrightarrow \overline{1,2,3,4,6} \longrightarrow \underline{\overline{1,2,3,4,5,6}}.$$

Thus $\pi_{1,4}^m$ is the trivial partition on S. We indicate this for easy reference by now placing an asterisk in front of this computation. As the computation proceeds it becomes much faster since we now can consult the previous results. For example,

$$\overline{1,5} \longrightarrow \overline{4,6}\ \overline{1,3}\ \overline{2,6}.$$

Since $\pi_{1,5}^m$ must identify states 1 and 3, we know that

$$\pi_{1,5}^m \geqslant \pi_{1,3}^m.$$

Since 1 and 5 are identified by $\pi_{1,3}^m$ we have that

$$\pi_{1,3}^m = \pi_{1,5}^m.$$

Proceeding this way we obtain

$$*\overline{1,6} \longrightarrow \overline{3,6}\ \overline{2,3}\ \overline{2,5} \longrightarrow \overline{1,2,3,5,6} \longrightarrow \underline{\overline{1,2,3,4,5,6}}.$$

Next

$$\overline{2,3} \longrightarrow \overline{2,5}\ \overline{4,5}\ \overline{1,4}$$

since $\overline{1,4}$ is starred in our list we know without further computation that $\pi_{2,3}^m$ is also the trivial partition. All the computations of the first step are summarized below.

$$\overline{1,2} \longrightarrow \overline{5,6}\ \overline{3,4}\ \overline{1,2}$$

$$\overline{1,3} \longrightarrow \overline{2,6}\ \overline{3,5}\ \overline{2,4} \longrightarrow \overline{1,3,5}\ \overline{2,6,4}$$

$$*\overline{1,4} \longrightarrow \overline{1,6}\ \overline{3,6}\ \overline{2,3} \longrightarrow \overline{1,2,3,4,6} \longrightarrow I$$

$$\overline{1,5} \longrightarrow \overline{4,6}\ \overline{1,3}\ \overline{2,6} \longrightarrow \overline{1,3,5}\ \overline{2,4,6}$$

$$*\overline{1,6} \longrightarrow \overline{3,6}\ \overline{2,3}\ \overline{2,5} \longrightarrow \overline{1,2,3,5,6} \longrightarrow I$$

$$*\overline{2,3} \longrightarrow \overline{2,5}\ \overline{4,5}\ \overline{1,4} \longrightarrow I$$

$$\overline{2,4} \longrightarrow \overline{1,5}\ \overline{4,6}\ \overline{1,3} \longrightarrow \pi_{1,3}^m$$

$$*\overline{2,5} \longrightarrow \overline{4,5}\ \overline{1,4}\ \overline{1,6} \longrightarrow I$$

$$\overline{2,6} \longrightarrow \overline{3,5}\ \overline{2,4}\ \overline{1,5} \longrightarrow \pi_{1,3}^m$$

$$\overline{3,4} \longrightarrow \overline{1,2}\ \overline{5,6}\ \overline{3,4} \longrightarrow \pi_{1,2}^m$$

$$\overline{3,5} \longrightarrow \overline{2,4}\ \overline{1,5}\ \overline{4,6} \longrightarrow \pi_{1,5}^m$$

$$*\overline{3,6} \longrightarrow \overline{2,3}\ \ldots \qquad \longrightarrow I$$

$$*\overline{4,5} \longrightarrow \overline{1,4}\ \ldots \qquad \longrightarrow I$$

$$\overline{4,6} \longrightarrow \overline{1,3}\ \overline{2,6}\ \overline{3,5} \longrightarrow \pi_{1,3}^m$$

$$\overline{5,6} \longrightarrow \overline{1,2}\ \overline{3,4}\ \overline{5,6} \longrightarrow \pi_{1,2}^m$$

There are only two nontrivial S.P. partitions in this list and their sum

$$\{\overline{1,2};\ \overline{3,4};\ \overline{5,6}\} + \{\overline{1,3,5};\ \overline{2,4,6}\} = \{\overline{1,2,3,4,5,6}\}.$$

Thus the second step does not yield any new partitions and we have computed all S.P. partitions on machine J.

To show how rapid the computations of the first step can become, consider machine K of Fig. 2.25. Part of these computations are summarized below:

$$\overline{1,2} \longrightarrow \overline{1,2}\ \overline{5,6}\ \overline{7,8}\ \overline{3,4}$$

$$\overline{1,3} \longrightarrow \overline{2,4}\ \overline{1,3}\ \overline{5,6}\ \overline{6,8} \longrightarrow \overline{1,3}\ \overline{2,4}\ \overline{5,6,8} \longrightarrow \overline{1,2,3,4}\ \overline{5,6,7,8}$$

$$\overline{1,4} \longrightarrow \overline{2,3}\ \overline{1,4}\ \overline{8,5} \longrightarrow \overline{7,6} \longrightarrow \overline{1,4}\ \overline{2,3}\ \overline{5,8}\ \overline{6,7}$$

$$*\overline{1,5} \longrightarrow \overline{2,5}\ \overline{1,6}\ \overline{3,5}\ \overline{7,8} \longrightarrow \overline{1,2,3,5}\ \overline{4,8} \longrightarrow I\ (\text{using } \pi_{1,3}^m)$$

$$*\overline{1,6} \longrightarrow \overline{2,6}\ \overline{1,5}\ \ldots \longrightarrow I\ (\text{using } \pi_{1,5}^m)$$

$$\overline{1,7} \longrightarrow \overline{2,7}\ \overline{1,8}\ \overline{4,5}\ \overline{2,8}\ \overline{3,5} \longrightarrow \overline{1,2,7,8}\ \overline{3,4,5} \longrightarrow \overline{1,2,7,8}\ \overline{3,4,5,6}$$

$$\overline{1,8} \longrightarrow \overline{2,8}\ \overline{1,7}\ \ldots \longrightarrow \pi_{1,7}^m$$

$$\overline{2,3} \longrightarrow \overline{1,4}\ \ldots \longrightarrow \pi_{1,4}^m$$

$$\overline{2,4} \longrightarrow \overline{1,3}\ \ldots \longrightarrow \pi_{1,3}^m$$

$$*\overline{2,5} \longrightarrow \overline{1,5}\ \ldots \longrightarrow I$$

$$*\overline{2,6} \longrightarrow \overline{1,6}\ \ldots \longrightarrow I$$

$$\overline{2,7} \longrightarrow \overline{1,7}\ \ldots \longrightarrow \pi_{1,7}^m$$

$$\overline{2,8} \longrightarrow \overline{1,8}\ \ldots \longrightarrow \pi_{1,7}^m$$

$$\overline{3,4} \longrightarrow \overline{5,6}\ \overline{1,2} \longrightarrow \pi_{1,2}^m$$

$$\overline{3,5} \longrightarrow \overline{1,7}\ \ldots \longrightarrow \pi_{1,7}^m$$

$$\overline{3,6} \longrightarrow \overline{1,8}\ \ldots \longrightarrow \pi_{1,7}^m$$

	x_1	x_2	x_3	x_4	x_5	
1	2	1	5	8	3	0
2	1	2	6	7	4	0
3	4	3	6	6	1	0
4	3	4	5	5	2	0
5	5	6	3	4	7	0
6	6	5	4	3	8	0
7	7	8	4	2	5	0
8	8	7	3	1	6	1

Fig. 2.25. Machine K.

$$* \overline{3,7} \longrightarrow \overline{1,5} \dots \longrightarrow I$$
$$* \overline{3,8} \longrightarrow \overline{1,6} \dots \longrightarrow I$$

etc.

In this way we obtain that there are four nontrivial S.P. partitions on machine K:

$$\pi_1 = \{\overline{1,2}; \overline{3,4}; \overline{5,6}; \overline{7,8}\}, \qquad \pi_2 = \{\overline{1,2,3,4}; \overline{5,6,7,8}\},$$
$$\pi_3 = \{\overline{1,4}; \overline{2,3}; \overline{5,8}; \overline{6,7}\}, \qquad \pi_4 = \{\overline{1,2,7,8}; \overline{3,4,5,6}\}.$$

Again the sums do not yield any new partitions, and thus we have computed all the S.P. partitions on K. The corresponding lattice L_K is shown in Fig. 2.26.

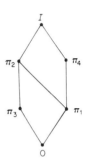

Fig. 2.26.   Lattice L_K.

EXERCISE. Compute all S.P. partitions for machines D, F, G, and H.

EXERCISE. Construct the parallel realization of machine K defined by π_3 and π_4. Construct the serial realization of K by using

$$\pi = \pi_1 \qquad \text{and} \qquad \tau = \{\overline{1,3,5,7}; \overline{2,4,6,8}\}.$$

2.5   STATE REDUCTION

We have seen how elementary (or two-machine) serial and parallel decompositions can be obtained from the S.P. partitions. Here we describe another application; the use of partitions with S.P. to find the reduced machine equivalent to a given machine M (see Theorem 1.1 and Corollary 1.1.1). Other aspects of state reduction are covered in Chapter 5. The first step is to relate state reduction to the Substitution Property. To do this, we define a special partition.

DEFINITION 2.8. If M is a machine, we define π_R to be the partition on the states of M such that

$$s \equiv t\,(\pi_R)$$

if and only if state s is equivalent to state t.

The subscript R stands for "reduction," as suggested by our next result which links S.P. partitions and state reduction.

THEOREM 2.6. If M is a sequential machine, then π_R has S.P. and M_{π_R} with the output

$$\lambda_R(B_{\pi_R}, x) = \lambda(s, x) \qquad \text{for } s \text{ in } B_{\pi_R}$$

is the reduced machine equivalent to M.

Proof. Lemma 1.1 asserts that π_R has S.P. The output is well defined because states in B_{π_R} are equivalent and all have the same output. The proof of Theorem 1.1 shows that M_{π_R} is the reduced machine. ∎

Once the S.P. lattice of a machine is determined, finding the reduced machine is just a matter of deciding which S.P. partition is π_R. Next we work up to Theorem 2.7 which gives an easy test to determine π_R from the S.P. lattice.

DEFINITION 2.9. A partition π on the state of a machine M is *output consistent* if and only if

$$s \equiv t\,(\pi) \text{ implies } \lambda(s) = \lambda(t) \qquad \text{or} \qquad \beta(s, x) = \beta(t, x)$$

for all inputs x.

LEMMA 2.1. A partition π with S.P. for a machine M is output consistent if and only if $s \equiv t\,(\pi)$ implies s and t are equivalent.

Proof. Left as an exercise. ∎

We now characterize π_R.

THEOREM 2.7. If M is a sequential machine, then π_R is the maximal output consistent partition with S.P. Furthermore, S.P. partition π is output consistent if and only if $\pi \leqslant \pi_R$.

Proof. Any $\pi \leqslant \pi_R$ is a refinement of the relation of state equivalence (i.e., π_R) and hence π is output consistent by Lemma 2.1. On the other hand, any output consistent S.P. partition π is a refinement on π_R by Lemma 2.1 and so $\pi \leqslant \pi_R$. ∎

COROLLARY 2.7.1. The output consistent S.P. partitions form a sublattice of the S.P. lattice.

Proof. The sum and product of partitions finer than π_R are also finer than π_R. ∎

It is very easy to test a partition to see if it is output consistent and the lattice properties of the output consistent S.P. partitions make it even easier to find the maximal output consistent S.P. partition. Thus, once the S.P. lattice is given, π_R is easily determined. It is also possible, by using techniques of the next chapter, to compute π_R directly from the machine.

EXAMPLE. In Fig. 2.27 we have machine L and its S.P. partitions are:

$$\pi_0 = 0$$

$$\pi_1 = \{\overline{1,2}; \bar{3}; \bar{4}; \bar{5}; \bar{6}\}$$

$$\pi_2 = \{\bar{1}; \bar{2}; \bar{3}; \bar{4}; \overline{5,6}\}$$

$$\pi_3 = \{\overline{1,2}; \bar{3}; \bar{4}; \overline{5,6}\}$$

$$\pi_4 = \{\overline{1,4}; \overline{2,3,5,6}\}$$

$$\pi_5 = I.$$

	0	1	
1	2	3	0
2	1	3	0
3	4	5	0
4	3	2	1
5	1	6	1
6	1	5	1

Fig. 2.27.   Machine L.

Partitions π_1 and π_2 are seen to be output consistent and so

$$\pi_3 = \pi_1 + \pi_2$$

must also be output consistent. The partition π_4 is not output consistent and so neither is $\pi_5 \geqslant \pi_4$. Therefore

$$\pi_3 = \pi_R.$$

The S.P. lattice is shown in Fig. 2.28 with the output consistent partitions circled. Notice how they form a sublattice. The reduced machine L_{π_R} is shown in Fig. 2.29. Note that L_{π_R} has only trivial S.P. partitions. The effect of state reduction on machine structure is investigated in Chapter 5.

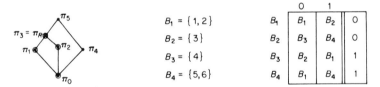

$$B_1 = \{1, 2\}$$
$$B_2 = \{3\}$$
$$B_3 = \{4\}$$
$$B_4 = \{5,6\}$$

	0	1	
B_1	B_1	B_2	0
B_2	B_3	B_4	0
B_3	B_2	B_1	1
B_4	B_1	B_4	1

Fig. 2.28.   S. P. lattice and output-consistent sublattice for machine L.

Fig. 2.29.   Reduced machine L_{π_R}.

NOTES

The use of partitions with the substitution property or congruence relations for machine decomposition was first discussed by one of the authors in [11]. The results of this chapter are contained in [14, 16], some of which were obtained independently by M. Yoeli [30, 32].

3 PARTITION PAIRS
AND PAIR ALGEBRA

3.1 PARTITION PAIRS

In the previous chapter, we derived the elementary structure theory of serial-parallel realizations. This was achieved through state partitions which represented self-dependent information. These concepts of information and information dependence are very basic and underlie all the structure results. In this chapter we wish to consider more powerful and more general mathematical tools for describing the two concepts of information and information dependence. The principles of this chapter are the hard-core ideas from which the applications of Chapters 4, 5, and 6 are obtained.

We recall that if a partition π on the set of states of a machine M has the substitution property, then as long as we know the block of π which contains a given state of M, we can compute the block of π to which that state is transformed by any given input sequence. Intuitively we say that the "ignorance" about the given state (as specified by the partition π) does not spread as the machine operates. Therefore, the S.P. partitions on a machine describe the cases in which the "ignorance" about the exact state of the machine does not increase as the machine operates. The concept of partition pairs is more general and is introduced to study how "ignorance spreads" or "information flows" through a sequential machine when it operates.

DEFINITION 3.1. A *partition pair* (π, π') on the machine

$$M = (S, I, O, \delta, \lambda)$$

is an ordered pair of partitions on S such that

$$s \equiv t\,(\pi) \text{ implies } \delta(s, x) \equiv \delta(t, x)\,(\pi')$$

for all x in I.

Thus (π, π') is a partition pair (p. p.) on M if and only if the blocks of π are mapped into the blocks of π' by M. That is, for every x in I and B_π in π, there exists a $B_{\pi'}$ in π' such that

$$\delta(B_\pi, x) \subseteq B_{\pi'}.$$

In other words, if we only know the block of π which contains the state of M, then we can compute for every input the block of π' to which this state is transferred by M.

Clearly, a partition π has S.P. if and only if (π, π) is a p.p. on M.

EXAMPLE. Consider machine A of Fig. 3.1. For this machine

$$(\pi_1, \pi_2) = (\{\overline{1,2}; \overline{3,4}\}, \{\overline{1,3}; \overline{2,4}\})$$

$$(\pi_2, \pi_1) = (\{\overline{1,3}; \overline{2,4}\}, \{\overline{1,2}; \overline{3,4}\})$$

$$(\pi_3, \pi_3) = (\{\overline{1,4}; \overline{2,3}\}, \{\overline{1,4}; \overline{2,3}\})$$

are partition pairs. It is also seen that π_3 is an S.P. partition on this machine.

To show a use of partition pairs, which is developed in more detail later in this chapter, let us assign the binary variables to the states and inputs of A as shown in Fig. 3.2. The variable y_1 is assigned according to the partition

	a	b	c	d	
1	1	2	3	4	1
2	3	4	1	2	1
3	2	1	4	3	0
4	4	3	2	1	0

Fig. 3.1.   Machine A.

	x_1 y_2
1	$\longrightarrow$ 0 0
2	$\longrightarrow$ 0 1
3	$\longrightarrow$ 1 0
4	$\longrightarrow$ 1 1

	x_1 x_2
a	$\longrightarrow$ 0 0
b	$\longrightarrow$ 0 1
c	$\longrightarrow$ 1 0
d	$\longrightarrow$ 1 1

Fig. 3.2.   Assignment of state and input variables for A.

π_1 (that is $y_1 = 0$ for states in the first block of π_1 and $y_1 = 1$ for the states in the second block) and y_2 is assigned according to π_2. Since

$$\pi_1 \cdot \pi_2 = 0,$$

we have assigned a different code to each state of A. Because (π_1, π_2) and (π_2, π_1) are partition pairs on A, Y_1 is not a function of y_1 and Y_2 is not a function of y_2. The actual equations are

$$Y_1 = \bar{x}_1 y_2 + x_1 \bar{y}_2$$

$$Y_2 = \bar{x}_2 y_1 + x_2 \bar{y}_1$$

$$z = \bar{y}_1.$$

The reduced logical dependence in the equations leads to a very economical assignment (few diodes). Observe how the schematic realization of

A shown in Fig. 3.3. mimics the logical independence described by the partition pairs (π_1, π_2) and (π_2, π_1). We can also think of this as a decompo-

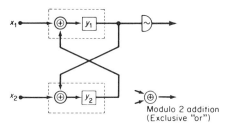

Fig. 3.3.   Realization of machine A.

sition of A into component machines (enclosed by the dotted lines). Such "cross decompositions" cannot be detected by S.P. partitions. These decompositions are investigated later in this chapter after some further algebraic tools are developed.

> **EXERCISE.** Determine the logical equations for a realization of A by the serial connection defined by π_3 and $\tau = \{\overline{1,2}; \overline{3,4}\}$. Compare the number of diodes of this realization to the above one.

As in the case of S.P. partitions, the partitions pairs on M can be combined by means of partition operations.

> **LEMMA 3.1.** If (π, π') and (τ, τ') are partition pairs on M, then
> (i) $(\pi \cdot \tau, \pi' \cdot \tau')$ is a p.p. on M and
> (ii) $(\pi + \tau, \pi' + \tau')$ is a p.p. on M.

Proof. (i) If

$$s \equiv t \, (\pi \cdot \tau)$$

then

$$s \equiv t \, (\pi) \qquad \text{and} \qquad s \equiv t \, (\tau).$$

Therefore for any input x,

$$\delta(s, x) \equiv \delta(t, x) \, (\pi') \qquad \text{and} \qquad \delta(s, x) \equiv \delta(t, x) \, (\tau')$$

and hence,

$$\delta(s, x) \equiv \delta(t, x) \, (\pi' \cdot \tau'),$$

which shows that

$$(\pi \cdot \tau, \pi' \cdot \tau')$$

is a partition pair.

(ii) If

$$s \equiv t \, (\pi + \tau),$$

then there exists a sequence of states

$$s \equiv s_0, s_1, s_2, \ldots, s_n = t$$

such that

$$s_i \equiv s_{i+1}\,(\pi) \qquad \text{for } i \text{ even} \qquad \text{and} \qquad s_i \equiv s_{i+1}\,(\tau) \qquad \text{for } i \text{ odd.}$$

Therefore, for any input x,

$$\delta(s_i, x) \equiv \delta(s_{i+1}, x)\,(\pi') \qquad \text{for } i \text{ even}$$

and

$$\delta(s_i, x) \equiv \delta(s_{i+1}, x)\,(\tau') \qquad \text{for } i \text{ odd,}$$

hence

$$\delta(s, x) \equiv \delta(t, x)\,(\pi' + \tau')$$

by transitivity and we conclude that

$$(\pi + \tau, \pi' + \tau')$$

is a p.p. ∎

Next we consider the problem of determining, for a given partition π, which partitions π' can be used to make a partition pair (π, π') on M. At the same time, we consider the dual problem of finding partitions π to match a given π'. Eventually, we show that the possible choices for π' are characterized by a smallest π' such that (π, π') is a p.p. on M; and the possible π are characterized by a largest π such that (π, π') is a p.p.

First, note that for any π on S of M,

$$(\pi, I) \text{ and } (0, \pi)$$

are trivially partition pairs. But then, using Lemma 3.1, we know that for a given partition π, there exists a minimal partition π' such that (π, π') is a p.p. on M. The partition π' is given by

$$\pi' = \prod \{\pi_i \,|\, (\pi, \pi_i) \text{ is a p.p. on } M\}.$$

Similarly, for a given π' there exists a maximal partition π such that (π, π') is a p.p. on M. This justifies one next definition.

DEFINITION 3.2. If π is a partition on S of M, let

$$m(\pi) = \prod \{\pi_i \,|\, (\pi, \pi_i) \text{ is a p.p. on } M\}$$

and

$$M(\pi) = \sum \{\pi_i \,|\, (\pi_i, \pi) \text{ is a p.p. on } M\}.$$

We think of the $m(\ )$ as an operator which gives the minimal second partition ("m" for minimum) and $M(\ )$ as the operator which gives the maximum front partition ("M" for maximum).

Informally speaking, for a given partition π, the partition $m(\pi)$ describes the largest amount of information which we can compute about the next state of M knowing only π (i.e., the block of π which contains the present state of M). Similarly, for a given π', the partition $M(\pi')$ describes the least amount of information we must have about the present state of M to compute π' for the next state. Thus these partitions give precise meaning to our intuitive concepts "*how much can we find out about the next state if we know only . . .*" and "*how much do we have to know about the present state to compute . . . about the next state.*"

The description of $m(\pi)$ and $M(\pi)$ in Definition 3.2 is not well suited for their computation. The computation of $m(\pi)$ is easily carried out by computing all sets of states onto which the blocks of π are mapped and then constructing the minimal partition which contains these sets. To illustrate this, consider machine B of Fig. 3.4.
Let

$$\pi_1 = \{\overline{1,2}; \overline{3,4}; \overline{5}\}.$$

The blocks of π_1 are mapped onto the sets

$$\{4, 5\}, \{1,4\} \text{ and } \{2,3\}.$$

Joining the first two sets because they overlap, we obtain that

$$m(\pi_1) = \{\overline{1,4,5}; \overline{2,3}\}.$$

The computation of $M(\pi')$ is also quite simple. For a given π', we have to identify all the (present) states which are mapped by all inputs into common blocks of π'. We do this for partition

$$\pi' = \{\overline{1,2}; \overline{3,4,5}\}$$

on machine B. In order to spot quickly those states to be identified, we replace each state in the flow table for B by a symbol representing the block of B containing that state. Figure 3.5 results. Now we identify states with identical modified next state rows and obtain that

$$M(\pi') = \{\overline{1}; \overline{2,3}; \overline{4,5}\}.$$

	0	1	
1	5	3	0
2	4	2	0
3	4	1	1
4	1	4	1
5	2	5	0

Fig. 3.4. Machine B.

	0	1
1	b	b
2	b	a
3	b	a
4	a	b
5	a	b

$a = \{1,2\}$
$b = \{3,4,5\}$

Fig. 3.5. Table for the computation of $M(\pi')$.

3.2 PAIR ALGEBRA

In the last section, we introduced the concepts of a partition pair, an m operator, and an M operator. In this section, we want to work out some algebraic relationships these concepts satisfy and then proceed in later sections to applications. However, later in the book, we want to study other partition pairlike systems. We want to study how input information is transformed into state information, state information to output, and input information to output. We want to investigate other concepts of "information" or "information flow." In view of these goals and in view of other possible applications yet undiscovered, we extract the common properties of all these systems, and derive the algebraic relationships in terms of these properties.

Anything satisfying the fundamental properties of a partition pairlike system will be called a "pair algebra"; the basic mathematical framework of pair algebras is to be established in this section once and for all. Later, when different interpretations of the pair algebras are given, the abstract theorems in this section translate into more practical results requiring no further proof. Thus the initial abstract approach is justified by later economies. Another advantage is that this approach brings out the unifying principles behind a variety of different results.

DEFINITION 3.3. Let L_1 and L_2 be finite lattices. Then a subset Δ of $L_1 \times L_2$ is a pair algebra on $L_1 \times L_2$ if and only if the two following postulates hold:

P_1. (x_1, y_1) and (x_2, y_2) in Δ implies that $(x_1 \cdot x_2, y_1 \cdot y_2)$ and $(x_1 + x_2, y_1 + y_2)$ are in Δ.

P_2. For any x in L_1 and y in L_2, (x, I) and $(0, y)$ are in Δ.

Thus a pair algebra is a binary relation on $L_1 \times L_2$ which is closed under component-wise operations (P_1) and contains all the elements specified by P_2.

Note that [because of Lemma 3.1 and the fact that (π, I) and $(0, \pi)$ are p.p. on M] the set of all partition pairs on M is a pair algebra on $L \times L$, where L is the lattice of partitions on S. Thus all the results which we now derive about a pair algebra hold for partition pairs on M.

For all the applications of pair algebra in this book, L_1 describes the ordering of the information which we can have about the machine and L_2 describes the ordering of the information to which this information can be transformed by M. The pairs in Δ then characterize some transformation of this information that transpires in the operation of M. In light of this, P_2 can be interpreted to mean that "any information is sufficient to compute total ignorance" (i.e., $(x, I) \in \Delta$) and "perfect information is sufficient to compute anything" (i.e., $(0, y) \in \Delta$). Property P_1 can be interpreted to mean "the combination of the information in x_1 and x_2 is sufficient to compute the combined information y_1 and y_2" (i.e., $(x_1 \cdot x_2, y_1 \cdot y_2) \in \Delta$) and "the combined ignorance in x_1 and x_2 is sufficient to calculate the combined ignorance in y_1 and y_2" (i.e., $(x_1 + x_2, y_1 + y_2) \in \Delta$). Except for the property $(x_1 + x_2, y_1 + y_2) \in \Delta$, one would expect these properties to hold for any system describing "information flow," since the interpretations are so natural. The property $(x_1 + x_2, y_1 + y_2) \in \Delta$ is more of a convenience that has been added in order to obtain stronger results. This addition is finally justified by the number of systems which do satisfy it.

LEMMA 3.2. If Δ is a pair algebra on $L_1 \times L_2$ and (x, y) is in Δ, then $x' \leqslant x$ and $y \leqslant y'$ implies that (x', y), (x, y'), and (x', y') are in Δ.

Proof. By P_2, (x', I) in Δ. By P_1, (x', I) and (x, y) in Δ implies that

$$(x' \cdot x, I \cdot y) = (x', y) \text{ in } \Delta.$$

The other two cases follow by a similar argument. ∎

Thus, if a pair is in the pair algebra Δ on $L_1 \times L_2$, we can obtain another pair by replacing the first component by a smaller element and/or the second component by a larger element. The next definition characterizes the largest possible first component of a pair in Δ and the smallest possible second component.

DEFINITION 3.4. Let Δ be a pair algebra on $L_1 \times L_2$. For x in L_1 we define

$$m(x) = \prod \{ y_i \mid (x, y_i) \text{ in } \Delta \}.$$

For y in L_2 we define

$$M(y) = \sum \{ x_i \mid (x_i, y) \text{ in } \Delta \}.$$

Definition 3.2 is actually a special case of Definition 3.4 and so we are consistent in repeating the notation. Also, if one now replaces the words "pair algebra Δ" by the words "set of partition pairs Δ", the results of this section hold for the definitions of the previous section. This is because the partition pairs on a machine satisfy P_1 and P_2 and are a pair algebra.

DEFINITION 3.5. For (x, y) and (x', y') in $L_1 \times L_2$ we define $(x, y) \leqslant (x', y')$ if and only if

$$x \leqslant x' \text{ in } L_1 \quad \text{and} \quad y \leqslant y' \text{ in } L_2.$$

Any pair algebra Δ on $L_1 \times L_2$ is obviously a lattice under this ordering, with zero element $(0, 0)$, unit element (I, I), and component-wise g.l.b. and l.u.b. operations.

We now single out a special subset Q_Δ of a pair algebra Δ. This set is discussed in some detail after the theorem.

DEFINITION 3.6. An element (x, y) in a pair algebra Δ is called an *Mm pair* if and only if

$$y = m(x) \quad \text{and} \quad x = M(y).$$

The set of all *Mm* pairs in Δ will be called Q_Δ.

THEOREM 3.1. If Δ is a pair algebra, then:
(i) $[M(y), y]$ and $[x, m(x)]$ are in Δ;

(ii) $x_1 \geqslant x_2$ implies that $m(x_1) \geqslant m(x_2)$;

(iii) $m(x_1 + x_2) = m(x_1) + m(x_2)$;

(iv) $m(x_1 \cdot x_2) \leqslant m(x_1) \cdot m(x_2)$;

(v) $y \geqslant m(x)$ if and only if (x, y) in Δ;

(vi) $y_1 \geqslant y_2$ implies that $M(y_1) \geqslant M(y_2)$;

(vii) $M(y_1 + y_2) \geqslant M(y_1) + M(y_2)$;

(viii) $M(y_1 \cdot y_2) = M(y_1) \cdot M(y_2)$;

(ix) $x \leqslant M(y)$ if and only if (x, y) in Δ;

(x) $M[m(x)] \geqslant x$;

(xi) $m[M(y)] \leqslant y$;

(xii) $M\{m[M(y)]\} = M(y)$;

(xiii) $m\{M[m(x)]\} = m(x)$;

(xiv) $\{M(y), m[M(y)]\}$ and $\{M[m(x)], m(x)\}$ are in Q_Δ;

(xv) if (x_1, y_1) and (x_2, y_2) are in Q_Δ, then

$$x_1 \leqslant x_2 \qquad \text{if and only if} \qquad y_1 \leqslant y_2;$$

(xvi) the set Q_Δ under the ordering on Δ is a lattice in which

$$\text{g.l.b. } \{(x_1, y_1), (x_2, y_2)\} = [(x_1 \cdot x_2), m(x_1 \cdot x_2)]$$
$$\text{l.u.b. } \{(x_1, y_1), (x_2, y_2)\} = [M(y_1 + y_2), (y_1 + y_2)].$$

Proof. (i) Follows directly from Definitions 3.3 and 3.4.

(ii) By (i), $[x_1, m(x_1)]$ is in Δ and hence $x_1 \geqslant x_2$ implies (Lemma 3.2) that $[x_2, m(x_1)]$ is in Δ. Therefore (Definition 3.4),

$$m(x_1) \geqslant m(x_2).$$

(iii) Since

$$x_1 + x_2 \geqslant x_1 \qquad \text{and} \qquad x_1 + x_2 \geqslant x_2,$$

part (ii) implies that

$$m(x_1 + x_2) \geqslant m(x_1) \qquad \text{and} \qquad m(x_1 + x_2) \geqslant m(x_2)$$

and thus

$$m(x_1 + x_2) \geqslant m(x_1) + m(x_2).$$

From (i) we know that

$$[x_1, m(x_1)] \text{ and } [x_2, m(x_2)] \text{ are in } \Delta.$$

Therefore (P_1),

$$[x_1 + x_2, m(x_1) + m(x_2)] \text{ is in } \Delta$$

and thus (Definition 3.4)

$$m(x_1 + x_2) \leqslant m(x_1) + m(x_2).$$

Combining the two inequalities, we obtain

$$m(x_1 + x_2) = m(x_1) + m(x_2).$$

(iv) Since

$$x_1 \cdot x_2 \leqslant x_1 \qquad \text{and} \qquad x_1 \cdot x_2 \leqslant x_2$$

we know from (ii) that

$$m(x_1 \cdot x_2) \leqslant m(x_1) \quad \text{and} \quad m(x_1 \cdot x_2) \leqslant m(x_2).$$

Therefore,

$$m(x_1 \cdot x_2) \leqslant m(x_1) \cdot m(x_2).$$

(v) Since $[x, m(x)]$ is in Δ by (i), $y \geqslant m(x)$ implies by Lemma 3.2 that (x, y) is in Δ. If (x, y) is in Δ then by Definition 3.4, $y \geqslant m(x)$.

(vi) By (i) $[M(y_2), y_2]$ is in Δ and hence $y_1 \geqslant y_2$ implies (Lemma 3.2) that $[M(y_2), y_1]$ is in Δ. Therefore (Definition 3.4),

$$M(y_1) \geqslant M(y_2).$$

(vii) Since

$$y_1 + y_2 \geqslant y_1 \quad \text{and} \quad y_1 + y_2 \geqslant y_2,$$

we know (vi) that

$$M(y_1 + y_2) \geqslant M(y_1) \quad \text{and} \quad M(y_1 + y_2) \geqslant M(y_2).$$

Therefore,

$$M(y_1 + y_2) \geqslant M(y_1) + M(y_2).$$

(viii) Since

$$y_1 \cdot y_2 \leqslant y_1 \quad \text{and} \quad y_1 \cdot y_2 \leqslant y_2$$

we have by (vi) that

$$M(y_1 \cdot y_2) \leqslant M(y_1) \cdot M(y_2).$$

By (i)

$$[M(y_1), y_1] \text{ and } [M(y_2), y_2] \text{ are in } \Delta.$$

Therefore (P_1),

$$[M(y_1) \cdot M(y_2), y_1 \cdot y_2] \text{ is in } \Delta,$$

and thus

$$M(y_1) \cdot M(y_2) \geqslant M(y_1 \cdot y_2).$$

Combining these inequalities we obtain

$$M(y_1 \cdot y_2) = M(y_1) \cdot M(y_2).$$

(ix) By (i) $[M(y), y]$ is in Δ; and if $x \leqslant M(y)$, we have, by Lemma 3.2, that (x, y) in Δ. If (x, y) is in Δ then by Definition 3.4, $x \leqslant M(y)$.

(x) Since $[x, m(x)]$ is in Δ, we know (Definition 3.4) that

$$M[m(x)] \leqslant x.$$

(xi) Follows by an argument similar to (x).

(xii) By (xi)

$$m[M(y)] \leqslant y.$$

By (vi), we have

$$M\{m[M(y)]\} \leqslant M(y).$$

On the other hand, because $\{M(y), m[M(y)]\}$ is in Δ,

$$M\{m[M(y)]\} \geqslant M(y).$$

Thus the equality holds.

(xiii) This equality follows by an argument similar to (xii).

(xiv) $\{M(y), m[M(y)]\}$ is in Δ, and since by (xi)

$$M\{m[M(y)]\} = M(y),$$

we conclude that it is an Mm pair. The second case follows by a similar argument.

(xv) The condition $x_1 \leqslant x_2$ implies $m(x_1) \leqslant m(x_2)$ by (ii) and, therefore, $y_1 \leqslant y_2$ since $y_1 = m(x_1)$ and $y_2 = m(x_2)$. Similarly, $y_1 \leqslant y_2$ implies $x_1 \leqslant x_2$.

(xvi) If (x_1, y_1) and (x_2, y_2) are in Q_Δ, then by (iii) and (xiv)

$$[M(y_1 + y_2), y_1 + y_2] = (M[m(x_1 + x_2)], m(x_1 + x_2))$$

is also in Q_Δ. This is obviously an upper bound for (x_1, y_1) and (x_2, y_2) since by (vii),

$$M(y_1 + y_2) \geqslant M(y_1) + M(y_2) = x_1 + x_2.$$

Any other upper bound (x, y) must satisfy

$$y \geqslant y_1 + y_2,$$

since by (xv),

$$(x, y) \geqslant [M(y_1 + y_2), y_1 + y_2]$$

and we have our l.u.b. By a similar argument, we conclude that

$$\text{g.l.b. } \{(x_1, y_1), (x_2, y_2)\} = [x_1 \cdot x_2, m(x_1 \cdot x_2)]. \quad \blacksquare$$

The lattice Q_Δ, sometimes referred to as an "Mm lattice," takes on a central importance in the structure theory because Q_Δ characterizes Δ as described next.

COROLLARY 3.1.1. Let Δ be a pair algebra on $L_1 \times L_2$ and let x be in L_1 and y in L_2. Then (x, y) is in Δ if and only if there is an (x', y') in Q_Δ such that

$$x' \geqslant x \quad \text{and} \quad y' \leqslant y.$$

Proof. Suppose (x, y) is in Δ. Let

$$x' = M(y) \quad \text{and} \quad y' = m(M(y)).$$

By (ix), (xi), and (xii), we have

$$x' \geqslant x, \quad y' \leqslant y, \quad \text{and} \quad (x', y') \text{ in } Q_\Delta.$$

Therefore, (x', y') satisfies all the conditions. Assume now that we are given a (x', y') in Q_Δ and an x and y satisfying $x' \geqslant x$ and $y' \leqslant y$. Because of Lemma 3.2, (x, y) is also in Δ. $\quad \blacksquare$

Thus Q_Δ, whose size is usually a fraction of the size of Δ, forms a sort of skeleton for Δ. Any pair in Δ can be obtained from a pair in Q_Δ by refining the first component and enlarging the second. From the intuitive standpoint, an Mm pair describes the possibility of obtaining some maximum amount of information for some minimum information. Other pairs (x, y) in Δ represent "inefficient" use of information; either not taking full advantage of the information given $[y > m(x)]$ or using more information than necessary $[x < M(y)]$.

In addition to being smaller than Δ, Q_Δ also has the advantage of a simplified ordering relation.

COROLLARY 3.1.2. If (x_1, y_1) and (x_2, y_2) are in Q_Δ, then the following three statements are equivalent:

(i) $(x_1, y_1) \geqslant (x_2, y_2)$;
(ii) $x_1 \geqslant x_2$;
(iii) $y_1 \geqslant y_2$.

Proof. This is a direct consequence of Definition 3.5 and condition xv of the theorem. ∎

Thus the order of Q_Δ is the same as the order on the first components of the pairs or as the order on the second components. The one unpleasant aspect is that Q_Δ is not a sublattice of Δ and the l.u.b. and g.l.b. operations must be computed by the formulas in part xvi of Theorem 3.1.

The remaining corollaries of this section are specialized to the case where $L_1 = L_2$. This case is of special interest in machine theory because one often wants to study the flow of state information into state information. We are now able to give a more general definition of the substitution property.

DEFINITION 3.7. If Δ is a pair algebra on $L \times L$, then we say x in L has the *substitution property* (S.P.) *with respect to* Δ if and only if

$$(x, x) \text{ is in } \Delta.$$

We write L_Δ for the set of x in L with S.P., that is

$$L_\Delta = \{x \in L \,|\, (x, x) \in \Delta\}.$$

COROLLARY 3.1.3. If Δ is a pair algebra on $L \times L$, then the S.P. lattice L_Δ is a sublattice of L containing 0 and I. Furthermore,

$$L_\Delta = \{x \in L \,|\, x \geqslant m(x)\} = \{x \in L \,|\, x \leqslant M(x)\}.$$

Proof. L_Δ is a sublattice by P_1 and contains 0 and I because (P_2) Δ contains $(0, 0)$ and (I, I). The last statement follows directly from parts (v) and (ix) of the theorem. ∎

Thus we have characterizations of x in L_Δ in terms of the two operators:

x has S.P. if and only if $x \geqslant m(x)$ if and only if $x \leqslant M(x)$. There is a third characterization which enables one to read off the S.P. elements from Q_Δ.

COROLLARY 3.1.4. *If Δ is a pair algebra on $L \times L$, then*

$$L_\Delta = \{z \in L \,|\, x \geqslant z \geqslant y \text{ for some } (x, y) \in Q_\Delta\}.$$

Proof. Given z in L_Δ, choose $y = m(z)$ and $x = M(m(z))$. We leave the details as an exercise. ∎

In generating the S.P. lattice for a machine M, the algorithm calls for computing

$$\pi^m_{s,t} = \min \{\tau \in L_M \,|\, \tau \geqslant \pi_{s,t}\}.$$

But this must be done before the lattice L_M is known, and so we suggested a method of "looking ahead" to see what must be identified. The next corollary tells us in effect that this method applies to any L_Δ where "looking ahead" is interpreted to mean the proper use of the m operator.

NOTATION. For a pair algebra Δ on $L \times L$ and x in L, we write

$$m^0(x) = x \qquad \text{and} \qquad m^i(x) = m(m^{i-1}(x)), \qquad \text{for } i \geqslant 1.$$

COROLLARY 3.1.5. *Given a pair algebra Δ on $L \times L$, there exists an integer K such that for all x in L and $k \geqslant K$,*

$$\min \{y \in L_\Delta \,|\, y \geqslant x\} = \sum_0^k m^i(x).$$

Proof. Let

$$y_j = \sum_0^j m^i(x).$$

Because of (iii),

$$y_{j+1} = x + m(y_j) = y_j + m(y_j).$$

Therefore,

$$y_0 \leqslant y_1 \leqslant \ldots \leqslant y_j$$

and because L is a finite lattice,

$$y_k = y_{k+1} \qquad \text{for some } k.$$

Therefore

$$y_{k+1} = y_k = y_k + m(y_k)$$

and so we must have

$$m(y_k) \leqslant y_k$$

which means y_k is in L_Δ by Corollary 3.1.3. Now we must show that y_k is the minimum. Let y' be any element of L_Δ such that

$$y' \geqslant x.$$

By repeated application of (ii) and using $y' \geqslant m(y')$,

$$y' \geqslant m^i(y') \geqslant m^i(x) \qquad \text{for } 0 \leqslant i \leqslant k$$

and therefore

$$y' \geqslant \sum_0^k m^i(x) = y_k.$$

Therefore y_k is the minimum. Finally, we have to show that k can be chosen larger or equal to some K for all x. But by induction,

$$y_k = y_{k+1} \text{ implies } y_k = y_{k+n} \qquad \text{for } n \geqslant 0.$$

Since each x determines a k and since L is finite, some K must be good for all x. ∎

In the case where L_Δ is L_M for some n-state machine M, one can choose $K = n - 1$ since a partition on n states can only be refined $n - 1$ times (from a one-block partition to an n-block partition). But for any given x, it is only necessary to sum up the series until a k is reached such that

$$m^{k+1}(x) \leqslant \sum_0^k m^i(x).$$

In most applications, we have found this "convergence" to be very fast for most x.

Next we give a "computational procedure" for the maximum operator.

COROLLARY 3.1.6. Given a pair algebra Δ on $L \times L$, there exists an integer K such that for all x in L and $k \geqslant K$,

$$\max \{y \in L_\Delta \mid y \leqslant x\} = \prod_0^k M^i(x).$$

Proof. Exercise. ∎

EXERCISE. As an application of the last corollary, show that if M is an n-state machine and τ is given by

$$s \equiv t \, (\tau) \qquad \text{if and only if} \qquad \lambda(s, x) = \lambda(t, x) \qquad \text{for } x \text{ in } I,$$

then

$$\pi_R = \prod_0^{n-1} M^i(\tau);$$

where π_R is the largest output consistent S.P. partition on M and M_{π_R} with the natural output is the reduced machine for M.

We finish this section with three corollaries which are used extensively in later chapters.

COROLLARY 3.1.7. If Δ is a pair algebra on $L \times L$, then

$$m^k(x) = 0 \qquad \text{if and only if} \qquad x \leqslant M^k(0).$$

Proof. If $m^k(x) = 0$, then

$$M^k(0) = M^k[m^k(x)] \geqslant M^{k-1}[m^{k-1}(x)] \geqslant \ldots \geqslant x,$$

using the relation

$$M[m(x)] \geqslant x.$$

Conversely,

$$x \leqslant M^k(0)$$

implies by a similar argument [using Theorem 3.1 (xi)] that

$$m^k(x) \leqslant m^k[M^k(0)] \leqslant 0,$$

which completes the proof. ∎

COROLLARY 3.1.8. If Δ is a pair algebra on $L \times L$, then

$$M^k(x) = I \qquad \text{if and only if} \qquad x \geqslant m^k(I).$$

Proof. Exercise. ∎

COROLLARY 3.1.9. If Δ is a pair algebra on $L \times L$, then

$$M^k(0) = I \qquad \text{if and only if} \qquad 0 = m^k(I).$$

Proof. This is just the combination of Corollaries 3.1.7 and 3.1.8. ∎

3.3 PARTITION ANALYSES

In this section we define several (partition) pair algebras associated with a machine and discuss their computation.

DEFINITION 3.8. For a machine $M = (S, I, O, \delta, \lambda)$, define:

a. (π, τ) is an *S-S pair* if and only if π and τ are partitions on S and for all x in I,

$$s \equiv t\ (\pi) \text{ implies } \delta(s, x) \equiv \delta(t, x)\ (\tau);$$

b. (ξ, τ) is an *I-S pair* if and only if ξ is a partition on I, τ is a partition on S, and for all s in S,

$$a \equiv b\ (\xi) \text{ implies } \delta(s, a) \equiv \delta(s, b)\ (\tau);$$

c. (π, ω) is an *S-O pair* if and only if π is a partition on S, ω is a partition on O, and for all x in I,

$$s \equiv t\ (\pi) \text{ implies } \lambda(s, x) \equiv \lambda(t, x)\ (\omega);$$

d. (ξ, ω) is an *I-O pair* if and only if ξ is a partition on I, ω is a partition on O, and for all s in S,

$$a \equiv b\ (\xi) \text{ implies } \lambda(s, a) \equiv \lambda(s, b)\ (\omega).$$

Note that Definition 3.8a is just a repeat of Definition 3.1. Note also that in the Moore case, any (ξ, ω) is an *I-O* pair because the degenerate condition $\lambda(s) \equiv \lambda(s)(\omega)$ must always hold. In other words, given the state of Moore machine M, any information about the output can be computed regardless of the input information; or more simply stated, the output is independent of the input.

THEOREM 3.2. For a machine $M = (S, I, O, \delta, \lambda)$
(a) the set of all *S-S* pairs, Ω_{S-S},
(b) the set of all *I-S* pairs, Ω_{I-S},
(c) the set of all *S-O* pairs, Ω_{S-O},
(d) the set of all *I-O* pairs, Ω_{I-O},

are all pair algebras.

Proof. (a) Because (π, I) and $(0, \pi)$ are obviously in Ω_{S-S} and because of Lemma 3.1, Ω_{S-S} is a pair algebra.

By interchanging the role of S and O or δ and λ, the same reasoning proves the other cases. ∎

EXERCISE. Work out the details in the previous proof.

We now know that all the properties of Theorem 3.1 hold for *I-S*, *S-O*, and *I-O* pairs in addition to the *S-S* pairs. The M and m operations with respect to these new pairs are distinguished by subscripts; we write, for example

$$M_{I-S}(\tau) \qquad \text{or} \qquad m_{S-O}(\omega).$$

We may sometimes write

$$M_{S-S}(\tau) \qquad \text{or} \qquad m_{S-S}(\pi),$$

although these operators are usually written without subscripts as before.

Now we concentrate on the computation of the Mm lattice for the *S-S* pairs on a given machine M. We use the symbol Q_M to represent this lattice.

Let $\pi_{s,t}$ denote the partition which identifies the states s and t but leaves the other states in one-element blocks.

THEOREM 3.3. If (π, π') is in Q_M, then

$$\pi' = \sum \{m(\pi_{s,t}) \,|\, \pi_{s,t} \leqslant \pi\}.$$

Proof. Since $\pi \geqslant \pi_{s,t}$ we know that $(\pi_{s,t}, \pi')$ is a partition pair and therefore $m(\pi_{s,t}) \leqslant \pi'$. Hence

$$\sum \{m(\pi_{s,t}) \,|\, \pi_{s,t} \leqslant \pi\} \leqslant \pi'.$$

But

$$[\sum \pi_{s,t}, \sum m(\pi_{s,t})] = [\pi, \sum m(\pi_{s,t})]$$

is a partition pair. Therefore,

$$\Sigma \, m(\pi_{s,t}) \leqslant m(\pi) = \pi'$$

and the theorem is proved. ∎

Theorem 3.3 states that every m partition is the sum of partitions of the form $m(\pi_{s,t})$ and Theorem 3.1 (iii) states that every sum of m partitions is again an m partition. Thus we have a set of generators for the m partitions. Each m partition $m(\tau)$ determines a unique element of Q_M (namely, $[M(m(\tau)),\ m(\tau)]$), and so we have generators for Q_M. In applying these principles to the generation of Q_M, we have found it useful to follow these two general steps:

STEP 1. Compute all the $m(\pi_{s,t})$ for distinct s and t. This is the only part of the procedure that requires reference to the flow table. Next, compare the $m(\pi_{s,t})$ and remove those which are redundant from the list. While this comparison is being made, it is an easy matter to compute the $M[m(\pi_{s,t})]$ by using the obvious relationship:

$$M(\pi) = \Sigma \, \{\pi_{s,t} \mid m(\pi_{s,t}) \leqslant \pi\}.$$

That is, in making the comparisons, if one notices that $m(\pi_{s,t}) \leqslant m(\pi_{s',t'})$, one makes a little note to the effect that $\pi_{s',t'} \leqslant M[m(\pi_{s,t})]$. At the end, one has enough notes to complete the corresponding M partitions. The alternative of computing the $M[m(\pi_{s,t})]$ directly from the flow table is not recommended for hand calculations.

STEP 2. The next step is to find all possible sums of the $m(\pi_{s,t})$. This does not mean taking all possible sums. The m partitions generated in step 1 are now added pair-wise to get a second generation of m partitions. Again redundancies are eliminated and the corresponding M partitions computed during this process. A third generation is computed from the second, etc., until no more are generated. Finally, it may be necessary to toss in the zero partition [which is $m(\pi_{s,s})$].

We now apply the principles developed above to an analysis of machine C given in Fig. 3.6.

First we calculate the $m(\pi_{s,t})$. To find $m(\pi_{1,2})$, we look at the flow table and see that to identify rows 1 and 2, we must set states 1 and 3, 1 and 5 equivalent; and by transitivity, we must also have 3 and 5 equivalent. Thus

	00	01	11	10
1	3	1	4	2	0
2	1	5	4	2	0
3	3	4	3	5	0
4	5	1	4	2	0
5	5	4	3	5	1

Fig. 3.6.   Machine C.

$$m(\pi_{1,2}) = \{\overline{1,3,5};\, \overline{2};\, \overline{4}\}.$$

Continuing, we arrive at the following list of $m(\pi_{s,t})$ for machine C.

$$m(\pi_{1,2}) = \{\overline{1,3,5};\, \overline{2};\, \overline{4}\} = \pi'_1,$$

$$m(\pi_{1,3}) = m(\pi_{4,5}) = \{\overline{1,3,4};\, \overline{2,5}\} = \pi'_2,$$

$$m(\pi_{1,4}) = m(\pi_{3,5}) = \{\overline{1};\, \overline{2};\, \overline{3,5};\, \overline{4}\} = \pi'_3,$$

$$m(\pi_{1,5}) = m(\pi_{2,3}) = m(\pi_{2,5}) = m(\pi_{3,4}) = I,$$
$$m(\pi_{2,4}) = \{\overline{1,5}; \overline{2}; \overline{3}; \overline{4}\} = \pi_4'.$$

Now that we have the $m(\pi_{s,t})$, we can forget about the flow table and work only with these partitions.

In this particular example, the pair-wise sums of this first generation of m partitions does not yield any new partitions. Only the zero partition needs to be added.

Now we work on the M partitions. Summing over $m(\pi_{s,t}) \leqslant \pi_1'$, we get

$$M(\pi_1') = \sum \pi_{s,t} = \pi_{1,2} + \pi_{1,4} + \pi_{3,5} + \pi_{2,4} = \{\overline{1,2,4}; \overline{3,5}\}.$$

Continuing, we get all the M partitions:

$$M(I) = I,$$
$$M(\pi_1') = \pi_1 = \{\overline{1,2,4}; \overline{3,5}\},$$
$$M(\pi_2') = \pi_2 = \{\overline{1,3}; \overline{2}; \overline{4,5}\},$$
$$M(\pi_3') = \pi_3 = \{\overline{1,4}; \overline{3,5}; \overline{2}\},$$
$$M(\pi_4') = \pi_4 = \{\overline{1}; \overline{2,4}; \overline{3}; \overline{5}\},$$
$$M(0) = 0.$$

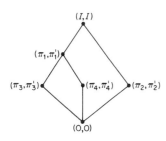

Fig. 3.7.   The Mm lattice, Q_c, for machine C.

Combining the previous calculations, we obtain a complete list of the Mm pairs. The Mm lattice Q_C is shown in Fig. 3.7 and the Mm pairs are as follows:

$(0, 0),$

$(I, I),$

$(\pi_1, \pi_1') = (\{\overline{1,2,4}; \overline{3,5}\}, \{\overline{1,3,5}; \overline{2}; \overline{4}\}),$

$(\pi_2, \pi_2') = (\{\overline{1,3}; \overline{2}; \overline{4,5}\}, \{\overline{1,3,4}; \overline{2,5}\}),$

$(\pi_3, \pi_3') = (\{\overline{1,4}; \overline{3,5}; \overline{2}\}, \{\overline{1}; \overline{2}; \overline{3,5}; \overline{4}\}),$

$(\pi_4, \pi_4') = (\{\overline{1}; \overline{2,4}; \overline{3}; \overline{5}\}, \{\overline{1,5}; \overline{2}; \overline{3}; \overline{4}\}).$

These six pairs are a compact representation of the state information flow in the machine.

As promised, the S.P. partitions are easily read off using Corollary 3.1.4. In this case, they are the partitions π which satisfy

$$\pi_3 \geqslant \pi \geqslant \pi_3', \qquad I \geqslant \pi \geqslant I, \qquad \text{or} \qquad 0 \geqslant \pi \geqslant 0.$$

Thus there are two nontrivial partitions with S.P., namely,

$$\{\overline{1}; \overline{2}; \overline{3,5}; \overline{4}\} \qquad \text{and} \qquad \{\overline{1,4}; \overline{2}; \overline{3,5}\}.$$

EXERCISE. Construct some random-looking machines with five or six states and three or four inputs. Then compute the Q_M for these machines. Machines of this size generally have a rich enough structure to acquaint one with the procedure; yet they are small enough so that the calculations are not too lengthy.

The computation of the Mm pairs in $\Omega_{I\text{-}S}$, $\Omega_{S\text{-}O}$, and $\Omega_{I\text{-}O}$ proceeds similarly. This is illustrated in machine D of Fig. 3.8. The corresponding Mm pairs and four lattices are shown in Fig. 3.9. In Fig. 3.10 is shown a Moore machine E with the same state transitions as D, and in Fig. 3.11 is shown the corresponding $Mm_{S\text{-}O}$. The $Mm_{I\text{-}O}$ lattice must necessarily be

	a	b	c	a	b	c
1	1	2	3	z_1	z_3	z_2
2	3	4	4	z_3	z_1	z_3
3	2	1	1	z_2	z_2	z_1
4	4	3	2	z_3	z_2	z_3

Fig. 3.8. Machine D.

	a	b	c	
1	1	2	3	z_1
2	3	4	4	z_1
3	2	1	1	z_2
4	4	3	2	z_3

Fig. 3.10. Machine E.

$P_1 = (\{\overline{1,2,3,4}\}, \{\overline{1,2,3,4}\})$

$P_2 = (\{\overline{1,3}; \overline{2}; \overline{4}\}, \{\overline{1,2,3,4}\})$

$P_3 = (\{\overline{1,4}; \overline{2,3}\}, \{\overline{1,4}; \overline{2,3}\})$

$P_4 = (\{\overline{1}; \overline{2,4}; \overline{3}\}, \{\overline{1,2,3,4}\})$

$P_5 = (\{\overline{1}; \overline{2}; \overline{3}; \overline{4}\}, \{\overline{1}; \overline{2}; \overline{3}; \overline{4}\})$

(a)

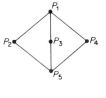

$P_1 = (\{\overline{a,b,c}\}, \{\overline{1,2,3,4}\})$

$P_2 = (\{\overline{a,b}; \overline{c}\}, \{\overline{1,2}; \overline{3,4}\})$

$P_3 = (\{\overline{a}; \overline{b,c}\}, \{\overline{1}; \overline{2,3}; \overline{4}\})$

$P_4 = (\{\overline{a}; \overline{b}; \overline{c}\}, \{\overline{1}; \overline{2}; \overline{3}; \overline{4}\})$

(b)

$P_1 = (\{\overline{1,2,3,4}\}, \{\overline{z_1, z_2, z_3}\})$

$P_2 = (\{\overline{1}; \overline{2,4}; \overline{3}\}, \{\overline{z_1, z_2}; \overline{z_3}\})$

$P_3 = (\{\overline{1}; \overline{2}; \overline{3}; \overline{4}\}, \{\overline{z_1}; \overline{z_2}; \overline{z_3}\})$

(c)

$P_1 = (\{\overline{a,b,c}\}, \{\overline{z_1, z_2, z_3}\})$

$P_2 = (\{\overline{a,c}; \overline{b}\}, \{\overline{z_1, z_2}; \overline{z_3}\})$

$P_3 = (\{\overline{a}; \overline{b}; \overline{c}\} \{\overline{z_1}; \overline{z_2}; \overline{z_3}\})$

(d)

Fig. 3.9. The Mm lattices for machine D. (a) $Mm_{S\text{-}S}$ lattice, Q_D. (b) $Mm_{I\text{-}S}$ lattice. (c) $Mm_{S\text{-}O}$ lattice. (d) $Mm_{I\text{-}O}$ lattice.

a single element lattice $(I, 0)$, since any input partition with any output partition is an *I-O* pair for a Moore machine.

$$P_1 = (\{\overline{1, 2, 3, 4}\}, \{\overline{z_1, z_2, z_3}\})$$
$$P_2 = (\{\overline{1, 2, 3}; \overline{4}\}, \{\overline{z_1, z_2}; \overline{z_3}\})$$
$$P_3 = (\{\overline{1, 2, 4}; \overline{3}\}, \{\overline{z_1, z_3}; \overline{z_2}\})$$
$$P_4 = (\{\overline{1, 2}; \overline{3, 4}\}, \{\overline{z_1}; \overline{z_2, z_3}\})$$
$$P_5 = (\{\overline{1}; \overline{2}; \overline{3}; \overline{4}\}, \{\overline{z_1}; \overline{z_2}; \overline{z_3}\})$$

Fig. 3.11.   The $Mm_{S\text{-}O}$ lattice for machine E.

3.4   PARTITION PAIRS AND STATE ASSIGNMENT

In this section we investigate the application of the partition pair algebras on M to the state assignment problem. This application illustrates the usefulness of the partition pairs and it also motivates the more abstract structure results developed later in this chapter. It should be pointed out that the results of this section do not make explicit claims about the economy of the assignments they describe. They only describe necessary and sufficient conditions for the existence of assignments with "reduced" functional dependence. On the other hand, experience suggests that, whenever some degree of variable independence can be achieved, the realizations with the minimal logical dependence generally compare favorably with the best possible.

The next lemma is basic to all partition pair applications. Informally, it says that if a state partition ρ contains enough information to compute the next block of τ from the input and if input partition μ contains enough information to compute the next block of τ from the present state, then ρ and μ jointly (or $\rho \times \mu$) contain enough information to compute the next block of τ. The function f names a block of τ and the condition

$$f[B_\rho(s), B_\mu(x)] = B_\tau(\delta(s, x))$$

tells us that f names the block of τ which contains the next state. (Recall that $B_\rho(s)$ stands for the block of ρ which contains s.) The effect of this lemma is to establish that input dependence and state dependence can be reduced *simultaneously* and to provide a symbolic statement of this fact.

LEMMA 3.3.   Given a machine $M = (S, I, O, \delta, \lambda)$ and partitions ρ and τ on S and μ on I, then

$$\rho \leqslant M_{S\text{-}S}(\tau) \qquad \text{and} \qquad \mu \leqslant M_{I\text{-}S}(\tau)$$

if and only if there exists a function

$$f: \rho \times \mu \longrightarrow \tau$$

such that

$$f[B_\rho(s), B_\mu(x)] = B_\tau[\delta(s, x)]$$

for all s in S and x in I. Furthermore, this f is unique.

Proof. Suppose such a function exists. Then for s, t in S,

$$B_\rho(s) = B_\rho(t)$$

implies for all x in I that

$$B_\tau[\delta(s, x)] = f[B_\rho(s), B_\mu(x)] = f[B_\rho(t), B_\mu(x)] = B_\tau[\delta(t, x)].$$

But this is just another way of saying that

$$s \equiv t \ (\rho) \text{ implies } \delta(s, x) \equiv \delta(t, x) \ (\tau) \text{ for all } x \text{ in } I.$$

Thus (ρ, τ) is a partition pair and by Theorem 3.1 (ix),

$$\rho \leqslant M_{S\text{-}S}(\tau).$$

By a similar argument,

$$\mu \leqslant M_{I\text{-}S}(\tau).$$

Now assume that the two inequalities hold. Then (ρ, τ) is an *S-S* pair and (μ, τ) is an *I-S* pair. Therefore, by definition of these pairs, for all s and t in S and a and b in I,

$$s \equiv t \ (\rho) \qquad \text{and} \qquad a \equiv b \ (\mu)$$

imply

$$\delta(s, a) \equiv \delta(s, b) \equiv \delta(t, b) \ (\tau).$$

Therefore, there is exactly one way to define f, namely

$$f(B_\rho, B_\mu) = B_\tau[\delta(s, x)] = \text{ the unique block of } \tau \text{ containing } \delta(s, x)$$

for all s in B_ρ and x in B_μ. This proves the result. ∎

EXERCISE. Restate Lemma 3.3 in terms of *S-O* and *I-O* pairs.

Next, we in effect generalize Lemma 3.3 to the many variable case by replacing τ by $\{\tau_i\}$ and μ by $\{\mu_j\}$.

LEMMA 3.4. Given a machine $M = (S, I, O, \delta, \lambda)$, a set of partitions $\{\rho_i\}$ on S, a set of partitions $\{\mu_j\}$ on I, and a partition τ on S; then

$$\prod \rho_i \leqslant M_{S-S}(\tau) \qquad \text{and} \qquad \prod \mu_j \leqslant M_{I-S}(\tau)$$

if and only if there exists a function

$$f: (\times \rho_i, \times \mu_j) \longrightarrow \tau$$

such that

$$f[\times B_{\rho_i}(s), \times B_{\mu_j}(x)] = B_\tau[\delta(s, x)]$$

for all s in S and x in I.

Proof. Suppose that f exists. Let f' be the restriction of f to those tuples $(\times B_{\rho_i} \times B_{\mu_j})$ such that

$$\cap B_{\rho_i} \neq \varnothing \qquad \text{and} \qquad \cap B_{\mu_j} \neq \varnothing .$$

Then we may write

$$f' : \rho \times \mu \longrightarrow \tau$$

where

$$\rho = \prod \rho_i = \{ B \,|\, B = \cap B_{\rho_i} \neq \varnothing \}$$

and

$$\mu = \prod \mu_j = \{ B \,|\, B = \cap B_{\mu_j} \neq \varnothing \}.$$

But

$$f'[B_\rho(s), B_\mu(x)] = B_\tau[\delta(s, x)]$$

for all s and x because f' is a restriction of f. Therefore, by Lemma 3.3, we know that

$$\prod \rho_i = \rho \leqslant M_{s\text{-}s}(\tau) \qquad \text{and} \qquad \prod \mu_j = \mu \leqslant M_{i\text{-}s}(\tau).$$

Conversely, if these inequalities hold, we know from Lemma 3.3 that we can define

$$f' : \rho \times \mu \longrightarrow \tau$$

such that

$$f'[B_\rho(s), B_\mu(x)] = B_\tau[\delta(s, x)]$$

for all s and x. This may be interpreted as a function on

$$\{(\times B_{\rho_i}, \times B_{\mu_j}) \text{ in } (\times \rho_i, \times \mu_j) \,|\, \cap B_{\rho_i} \neq \varnothing \neq \cap B_{\mu_j} \}$$

and we let f be any extension of f' to the full set

$$(\times \rho_i, \times \mu_j).$$

Of course,

$$f[\times B_{\rho_i}(s), \times B_{\mu_j}(x)] = f'[B_\rho(s), B_\mu(x)] = B_\tau[\delta(s, x)]$$

for all s and x, and so we have a desired f. ∎

The partition inequalities in the lemma and applications are often referred to as *information flow inequalities*.

EXERCISE. Restate this lemma for *S-O* and *I-O* pairs.

Now we can easily prove the central theorem of variable dependence.

THEOREM 3.4. Suppose that, for a machine M,
state variables $\{y_i\}$ are assigned according to partitions $\{\tau_i\}$,
input variables $\{x_j\}$ are assigned according to input partitions $\{\mu_j\}$,
output variables $\{Z_k\}$ are assigned according to output partitions $\{\omega_k\}$,
and that some P and Q are given such that

$$P \subseteq \{y_i\} \qquad \text{and} \qquad Q \subseteq \{x_j\};$$

then

(i) state variable Y_i can be expressed as a function of the variables in $P \cup Q$ if and only if

$$\prod_P \tau_j \leqslant M_{S\text{-}S}(\tau_i) \quad \text{and} \quad \prod_Q \mu_j \leqslant M_{I\text{-}S}(\tau_i);$$

(ii) output variable Z_k can be expressed as a function of the variables in $P \cup Q$ if and only if

$$\prod_P \tau_j \leqslant M_{S\text{-}O}(\tau_i) \text{ and } \prod_Q \mu_j \leqslant M_{I\text{-}O}(\omega_k).$$

Proof. By definition, we need a function

$$Y_i \colon (\underset{P}{\times} y_l, \underset{Q}{\times} x_j) \longrightarrow y_i$$

such that

$$Y_i[\times y_l(s), \times x_j(\mathrm{a})] = y_i[\delta(s, a)]$$

for all s in S and a in I. The range of the variables correspond in a one-to-one manner with blocks at the partitions according to which they are assigned, and so Y_i may be regarded as a function

$$Y_i \colon (\underset{P}{\times} \tau_l, \underset{Q}{\times} \mu_j) \longrightarrow \tau_i$$

such that

$$Y_i[\underset{P}{\times} B_{\tau_l}(s), \underset{Q}{\times} B_{\mu_j}(a)] = B_{\tau_i}[\delta(s, a)].$$

for all s in S and a in I.

But Lemma 3.4 tells us that Y_i exists if and only if the information inequalities of part (i) hold. (To apply the lemma, let $\rho_i = \tau_i$ for y_i in P, let $\{\mu_j\}$ be for all x_j in Q, and let $\tau = \tau_i$.) Thus part (i) is proved. Part (ii) is proved similarly by using Lemma 3.4 restated for *S-O* and *I-O* pairs. ∎

EXAMPLE. Now we apply our knowledge about the information flow in machine *C* to obtain a good state assignment. For the sake of simplicity, we assume that the input variables have been preassigned as follows:

$$x_1 \ x_2$$
$$a \longrightarrow 0 \ 0$$
$$b \longrightarrow 0 \ 1$$
$$c \longrightarrow 1 \ 1$$
$$d \longrightarrow 1 \ 0.$$

Our objective is to make a three-digit binary state assignment reducing the number of dependences. In terms of partitions, we are looking for three partitions τ_1, τ_2, τ_3 of two blocks each such that

$$\tau_1 \cdot \tau_2 \cdot \tau_3 = 0$$

and $M(\tau_1)$, $M(\tau_2)$, $M(\tau_3)$ are each greater than the product of only a small subset of the partitions τ_1, τ_2, τ_3. Generally speaking, the larger the M partitions, the better chance of this happening. We observe, for instance, that if a variable according to some partition τ is to depend only on a variable according to some other partition τ', then $\tau \leqslant M(\tau')$ and $M(\tau')$ can have at most two blocks. In the case of machine C, the only such M partitions are π_1 and I.

With this in mind, we decide to let $\tau_3 = \pi_1$ and later we choose τ_1 to be a two-block partition that is an enlargement of π_1'; hence, (τ_3, τ_1) is a partition pair and the state variable according to τ_1 depends only on the state variable according to τ_3 and the input. The largest m partition less than τ_3 is π_3', and hence, $M(\tau_3) = \pi_3'$.

We see that if we choose $\tau_2 = \pi_2'$, then

$$\tau_2 \cdot \tau_3 \leqslant M(\tau_3)$$

and we have additional reduced dependence. Finally, we have to choose

$$\tau_1 \geqslant \pi_1' \text{ so that } \tau_1 \cdot \tau_2 \cdot \tau_3 = 0$$

and this can be done if states "1" and "4" are separated. Letting

$$\tau_1 = \{\overline{1,3,5}; \overline{2,4}\},$$

we get the inequality

$$\tau_1 \cdot \tau_2 \leqslant M(\tau_2)$$

and τ_2 is independent of τ_3. This leads to an assignment requiring forty-two diodes.

An alternative choice for τ_2 would be

$$\tau_2 = \{\overline{1,5}; \overline{2,3,4}\}$$

which gives the relation $\tau_2 \cdot \tau_3 \leqslant M(\tau_2)$ and then enlarging

$$\pi_1' \text{ to } \tau_1 = \{\overline{1,3,4,5}; \overline{2}\}$$

which gives

$$\tau_1 \cdot \tau_2 \cdot \tau_3 = 0 \quad \text{and} \quad \tau_1 \cdot \tau_3 \leqslant M(\tau_3).$$

$$(M(\tau_1), \tau_1) = (\{\overline{1,2,4}; \overline{3,5}\}, \{\overline{1,3,4,5}; \overline{2}\})$$
$$(M(\tau_2), \tau_2) = (\{\overline{1}; \overline{2,4}; \overline{3}; \overline{5}\}, \{\overline{1,5}; \overline{2,3,4}\})$$
$$(M(\tau_3), \tau_3) = (\{\overline{1,4}; \overline{3,5}; \overline{2}\}, \{\overline{1,2,4}; \overline{3,5}\})$$

$M(\tau_1) \geq \tau_3$	$y_1 \ y_2 \ y_3$
$M(\tau_2) \geq \tau_2 \cdot \tau_3$	$1 \longrightarrow 0 \ \ 0 \ \ 0$
$M(\tau_3) \geq \tau_1 \cdot \tau_3$	$2 \longrightarrow 1 \ \ 1 \ \ 0$
$\tau_1 \cdot \tau_2 \cdot \tau_3 = 0$	$3 \longrightarrow 0 \ \ 1 \ \ 1$
	$4 \longrightarrow 0 \ \ 1 \ \ 0$
	$5 \longrightarrow 0 \ \ 0 \ \ 1$

Fig. 3.12. Partition pairs, information-flow inequalities, and state assignment for machine C.

This leads to an assignment shown in Fig. 3.12 along with the corresponding
partition pairs and information-flow inequalities. It is interesting to observe
that for either choice the number of dependencies is the same. In the first

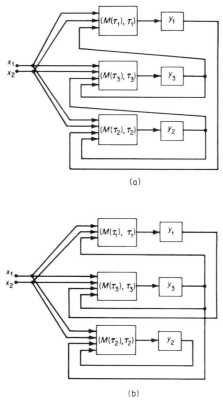

(a)

(b)

Fig. 3.13. (a) Realization for machine C resulting from
first choice of τ_2. (b) Realization for machine C resulting
from assignment of Fig. 3.12.

case the realization has the form shown in Fig. 3.13a and in the second case
the form shown in Fig. 3.13b. Both choices utilize Mm pairs which are high
on the Mm lattice. The actual logical equations for the second assignment are:

$$Y_1 = x_1 \bar{x}_2 \bar{y}_3$$
$$Y_2 = x_1 \bar{y}_3 + x_2 y_3 + \bar{x}_1 y_2 y_3 + \bar{x}_2 \bar{y}_2 \bar{y}_3$$
$$Y_3 = x_1 y_3 + \bar{x}_1 \bar{x}_2 \bar{y}_1 + \bar{x}_1 x_2 y_1$$
$$Z = y_2 y_3.$$

It is seen that this assignment requires only thirty diodes. For the sake of comparison, there is a bad assignment for this machine requiring sixty-five diodes.

EXERCISE. Compute the *Mm* lattices for machine *A* of Fig. 3.1 and derive the information flow inequalities that characterize the assignment of Fig. 3.2.

3.5 ABSTRACT NETWORKS

The purpose of this section is to define a network as an abstract algebraic system. This is somewhat analogous to what was done previously for machines. A sequential machine is really a complex physical computing device, but we isolate its mathematical properties by the simple expedient of saying that a machine is a quintuple $(S, I, O, \delta, \lambda)$. This enables the development of an algebraic analysis without further reference to the "real world." Similarly, we wish to set aside the idea that a circuit is really a connection of wires, delays, and gates, and regard the network as an algebraic system. Such an exercise is hardly necessary for design applications, as the methods are easy to apply without knowledge of such a formalism. For this same reason, it would hardly be worthwhile pursuing a "theory of abstract networks." Nevertheless, there are two good reasons for presenting such a definition here. First, it underscores the fact that machine decomposition and the reduction of variable dependence are virtually identical concepts. Second, it establishes a standard notation for the information associated with a network which is useful in later discussions.

DEFINITION 3.9. An *abstract network* $\mathcal{N}$ of machines consists of:
1. $\{M_i = (S_i, I_i, \delta_i)\}$, $1 \leqslant i \leqslant n$, a set of state machines referred to as *component machines*;
2. I—a nonvoid finite set of external inputs;
3. O—a nonvoid finite set of external outputs;
4. $f_i \colon (\times S_j) \times I \longrightarrow I_i$, $1 \leqslant i, j \leqslant n$, machine connecting rules;
5. $g \colon (\times S_i) \times I \longrightarrow O$, the output function.
The network is said to be in *logic delay form* if and only if for all i,

$$\delta_i(s, x) = \delta_i(t, x) \qquad \text{for all } s, t \text{ in } S_i, \text{ and } x \text{ in } I_i.$$

(That is, the next state of any component machine is not a function of its present state.) The network is said to be in *standard form* if and only if the functions f_i are expressed in the form

$$f_i(s_1, \ldots, s_n, x) = (f_{1,i}(s_1), \ldots, f_{n,i}(s_n), f_{I,i}(x)).$$

The use of state (or Moore) machines in this definition is essential. The use of Mealy machines here is ruled out because of "timing" considerations. Physically, the output of a Mealy machine is a combination of the present state and present input and so its presence in a circuit presupposes that the present input is being applied. This output, therefore, cannot be readily combined with the next input signal. Mathematically, it is impossible to make a formulation of the definition in terms of Mealy machines so that the network can be said to "define a machine." We return to this point shortly.

Note that the state of component machine M_k can govern the behavior of M_k in two ways. The first way is internal, the way the state of a machine usually affects its behavior; the second way is external, affecting the inputs. In other words, s_k appears two places in

$$\delta_k(s_k, f_k(s_1, \ldots, s_k, \ldots, s_n, x)).$$

This allows some freedom in describing a circuit as an abstract net, depending on which wires one chooses to call internal and which external. When all the wires are external, we have the logic delay form.

EXAMPLE. Consider network $\mathcal{N}_F$ and circuit shown in Fig. 3.14. The

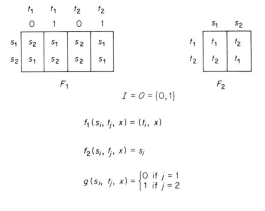

	t_1 0	t_1 1	t_2 0	t_2 1
s_1	s_2	s_1	s_2	s_1
s_2	s_1	s_2	s_2	s_1

F_1

	s_1	s_2
t_1	t_1	t_2
t_2	t_2	t_1

F_2

$$I = O = \{0, 1\}$$

$$f_1(s_i, t_j, x) = (t_j, x)$$

$$f_2(s_i, t_j, x) = s_i$$

$$g(s_i, t_j, x) = \begin{cases} 0 & \text{if } j = 1 \\ 1 & \text{if } j = 2 \end{cases}$$

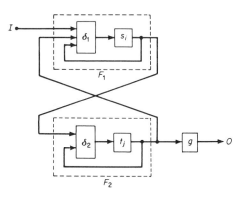

Fig. 3.14. Network $\mathcal{N}_F$ and circuit.

component machines F_1 and F_2 are enclosed in the circuit drawing by a dotted line. The wire from delay s_i to logic δ_1 is *inside* the dotted line because the input to F_1 does not depend on s_i. Thus, the dependence on s_i is kept *internal*. In Fig. 3.15, there is a network $\mathcal{N}'_F$ and circuit. The circuits for

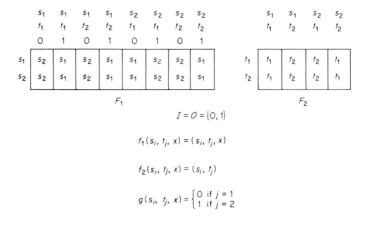

$$I = O = \{0, 1\}$$

$$f_1(s_i, t_j, x) = (s_i, t_j, x)$$

$$f_2(s_i, t_j, x) = (s_i, t_j)$$

$$g(s_i, t_j, x) = \begin{cases} 0 & \text{if } j = 1 \\ 1 & \text{if } j = 2 \end{cases}$$

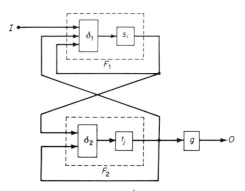

Fig. 3.15. Network $\mathcal{N}'_F$ and circuit.

$\mathcal{N}_F$ and $\mathcal{N}'_F$ are identical except for the placement of the dotted lines. In this case, the wire from s_i to δ_1 appears *outside* the dotted line because it is now considered part of the input. The next state of F_1 can be computed from the input of F_1 without any direct knowledge of the present state, so the dependence on s_i is regarded as *external*. Network $\mathcal{N}'_F$ is in logic delay form.

The network $\mathcal{N}_F$ is regarded as a connection of two machines. Because output of the delay elements is sent to the other component machines without further processing, $\mathcal{N}_F$ is in standard form. Another view of standard form is that the components are supplying Moore-type outputs to each other.

Network $\mathcal{N}'_F$ is pictured as in state assignment applications where the component "machines" are really just the delay elements and the preceding combinational logic. Thus, the terminology "logic delay form." For networks in this form, it is more customary and logical to specify only the combinational logic functions, bypassing the rather trivial component machine flow tables. The flow table representation is used in Fig. 3.15 only to emphasize the basic sameness of the two cases. Again, $\mathcal{N}'_F$ is in standard form.

One final comment on Definition 3.9. It is not the most general definition that could be given, but it is quite sufficient for the purposes here. In fact, this book uses the "standard form" almost exclusively.

Of course, networks are for the realization of machines, and so we give the abstract counterpart of Definition 1.17.

DEFINITION 3.10. An abstract network $\mathcal{N}$ *defines* the machine

$$M_{\mathcal{N}} = (S, I, O, \delta, \lambda)$$

with

$S = \times S_i,$

$I = I$ and $O = O,$

$\delta(s, x) = \delta[(s_1, s_2, \ldots, s_n), x] = \times \delta_i[s_i, f_i(s_1, \ldots, s_n, x)],$

$\lambda(s, x) = g(s_1, \ldots, s_n, x).$

Network $\mathcal{N}$ *realizes* machine M if and only if machine $M_{\mathcal{N}}$ realizes M.

EXAMPLE. Machine F defined by $\mathcal{N}_F$ or $\mathcal{N}'_F$ of Figs 3.14 and 3.15 is shown in Fig. 3.16. Symbolically, $F = M_{\mathcal{N}_F} = M_{\mathcal{N}_F'}.$

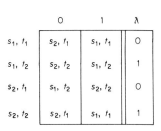

Fig. 3.16. Machine F.

EXAMPLE. Consider the network $\mathcal{N}_G$ of Fig. 3.17. Each of the two component machines have Moore-type outputs which are used as inputs to each other. These outputs determine the connecting functions f_1 and f_2 given in the figure. This network is in standard form if we take $f_{1,2} = \lambda_2, f_{2,1} = \lambda_1,$ and other f's as identity maps. Network $\mathcal{N}_G$ defines machine G of Fig. 3.18.

Suppose one tries to replace Moore machines G_1 and G_2 by similar Mealy machines G'_1 and G'_2. Machine G'_1 would require only two states because rows s_2 and s_3 of the flow table are identical, and G'_2 would, of course, require three states. But any hook-up of G'_1 and G'_2 could not define machine G, since a two-state and a three-state machine can represent at most a six-state reduced machine and reduced machine G has nine states!

G_1

	(b₀,0)		(b₁,0)		λ_1
	(b₀,1)	(b₀,2)	(b₁,1)	(b₁,2)	
s_1	s_1	s_3	s_2	s_1	a_0
s_2	s_2	s_2	s_1	s_3	a_0
s_3	s_2	s_2	s_1	s_3	a_1

G_2

	(a₀,1)		(a₁,1)		λ_2
	(a₀,0)	(a₀,2)	(a₁,0)	(a₁,2)	
t_1	t_2	t_3	t_1	t_2	b_0
t_2	t_3	t_1	t_1	t_3	b_0
t_3	t_1	t_2	t_3	t_2	b_1

$$I = \{0,1,2\} \qquad O = \{0,1\}$$
$$f_1(s_i, t_j, x) = (\lambda_2(t_j), x)$$
$$f_2(s_i, t_j, x) = (\lambda_1(s_i), x)$$
$$g(s_i, t_j, x) = 1 \text{ if and only if } i = j = 3$$

Fig. 3.17. Network $\mathcal{N}_G$.

		0	1	2	g
(s_1, t_1)	1	2	3	9	0
(s_1, t_2)	2	3	1	7	0
(s_1, t_3)	3	4	5	2	0
(s_2, t_1)	4	5	6	6	0
(s_2, t_2)	5	6	4	4	0
(s_2, t_3)	6	1	2	8	0
(s_3, t_1)	7	4	5	5	0
(s_3, t_2)	8	4	6	6	0
(s_3, t_3)	9	3	2	8	1

Fig. 3.18. Machine G.

The next step is to define some information partitions which are induced on M by a network $\mathcal{N}$ in standard form that defines M. These "associated" partitions on M may be thought of as a global characterization (on M) of the information used and computed in a component machine of $\mathcal{N}$. It is this natural correspondence between local and global properties that allows us to approach the structure of machines with partition algebra.

First, recall that any function

$$f: S \longrightarrow B$$

induces a partition π on S by the relationship

$$s \equiv t\,(\pi) \qquad \text{if and only if} \qquad f(s) = f(t).$$

We now use such relationships to define partitions induced by $\mathcal{N}$.

DEFINITION 3.11. Suppose that the state behavior of a machine M is realized by abstract network $\mathcal{N}$ in standard form and suppose that

$$s = \alpha(s_1, s_2, \ldots, s_n) \text{ and } t = \alpha(t_1, \ldots, t_n)$$

are states of M and a and b are inputs to M, then let

(i) $s \equiv t\,(\tau_i)$ if and only if $s_i = t_i$;

(ii) $s \equiv t\,(\rho_{i,j})$ if and only if $f_{i,j}(s_i) = f_{i,j}(t_i)$;

(iii) $a \equiv b\,(\mu_i)$ if and only if $f_{I,i}(\iota(a)) = f_{I,i}(\iota(b))$.

The partitions τ_i, $\rho_{i,j}$ and μ_i for $1 \leqslant i, j \leqslant n$ are called the *associated partitions induced on M by $\mathcal{N}$*.

EXAMPLE. The associated partitions induced on machine G of Fig. 3.18 by network $\mathcal{N}_G$ of Fig. 3.17 are:

$$\tau_1 = \{\overline{1,2,3}; \overline{4,5,6}; \overline{7,8,9}\},$$
$$\tau_2 = \{\overline{1,4,7}; \overline{2,5,8}; \overline{3,6,9}\},$$
$$\rho_{1,1} = \rho_{2,2} = I,$$
$$\rho_{1,2} = \{\overline{1,2,3,4,5,6}; \overline{7,8,9}\},$$
$$\rho_{2,1} = \{\overline{1,2,4,5,7,8}; \overline{3,6,9}\},$$
$$\mu_1 = \{\overline{0,1}; \overline{2}\},$$
$$\mu_2 = \{\overline{0}; \overline{1,2}\}.$$

We can now give a fundamental theorem of machine interconnections.

THEOREM 3.5. Given a machine $M = (S, I, O, \delta, \lambda)$ and partitions τ_i and $\rho_{i,j}$ on S and μ_i on I for $1 \leqslant i, j \leqslant n$; then there exists a network $\mathcal{N}$ in standard form such that $M_{\mathcal{N}}$ realizes the state behavior of M, and $\tau_i, \rho_{i,j},$ μ_i are the associated partitions on M if and only if the following conditions hold:

(i) $\tau_i \prod_j \rho_{j,i} \leqslant M_{S\text{-}S}(\tau_i)$ for all i;

(ii) $\mu_i \leqslant M_{I\text{-}S}(\tau_i)$ for all i;

(iii) $\rho_{i,j} \geqslant \tau_i$ for all i and j;

(iv) $\prod_i \tau_i = 0.$

Proof. Suppose that partitions are given satisfying (i) to (iv). To define a network in standard form, let

$$S_i = \tau_i \quad \text{and} \quad I_i = \mu_i.$$

Because of (iii), we may define

$$f_{i,j}(B_{\tau_i}) = B_{\rho_{i,j}}(B_{\tau_i}).$$

We also define

$$f_{I,i}(x) = B_{\mu_i}(x).$$

Because of Lemma 3.4, we may define a δ_i such that

$$\delta_i(B_{\tau_i}(s), \underset{j}{\times} B_{\rho_{j,i}}(s), B_{\mu_i}(x)) = B_{\tau_i}(\delta(s, x))$$

for all s in S and x in I. Finally, define

$$g(\underset{i}{\times} B_{\tau_i}, x) = \lambda(s, x) \text{ if } \cap B_{\tau_i} = \{s\},$$

arbitrary otherwise. This completes the network. Let

$$\alpha(s) = \underset{i}{\times} B_{\tau_i}(s).$$

Function α is one-to-one because of (iv). Taking ι and ζ to be identity maps, the reader may easily verify that we have a state behavior realization of M.

Conversely, if M, $\mathcal{N}$, and (α, ι, ζ) are given, then δ_i are essentially functions

$$\delta_i : (\tau_i, (\underset{j}{\times} \rho_{j,i}), \mu_i) \longrightarrow \tau_i$$

satisfying Lemma 3.4, and so conditions (i) and (ii) must hold. Condition (iii) is a direct consequence of the definition of associated partitions and condition (iv) must hold for α to be one-to-one. ∎

If one is interested in keeping the wires of the component machine internal, then one always chooses $\rho_{i,i} = I$. Since $\rho_{i,i} \cdot \tau_i = \tau_i$ by (iii), the $\rho_{i,i}$ term could be dropped from the product in (i). If, however, one wants only external feedback wires, then one must drop the τ_i from the product, as stated by the next corollary.

COROLLARY 3.5.1. If the network $\mathcal{N}$ of Theorem 3.5 is to be in standard logic-delay form, then condition (i) must be replaced by:

(i) $\displaystyle\prod_j \rho_{j,i} \leqslant M_{S\text{-}S}(\tau_i)$ for all i.

Proof. Same as the proof of Theorem 3.5 with the B_{τ_i} term dropped from δ_i. ∎

The last theorem and corollary show that a network can be built to certain specifications on what information is to be stored where and what carry information is to be used in computing states. This is a considerable aid in later chapters to understanding and attaching precise meanings to such concepts as "loop-free" and "feedback." One can, of course, define additional associated partitions to study carries to output logics, but there is no need for such concepts in this book. The reader should now be equipped to make these extensions if a need arises.

3.6 DON'T CARE CONDITIONS, FIRST APPROACH

We saw in the previous section how "d.c." conditions can appear even in problems involving completely specified machines. These conditions need not be incidental. It is therefore appropriate that we try to extend the structure theory to the d.c. case. Immediately, we are faced with the problem of defining a pair concept to account for d.c. conditions. We know of two ways of doing this using partitions, both of which seem natural. The approach we take in this section is to call (π, τ) a partition pair whenever the d.c. conditions could be filled to preserve this pair. This is called a weak partition pair. An alternative partition approach is discussed in the next section. A third approach is given in Chapter 5.

DEFINITION 3.12. If $M = (S, I, O, \delta, \lambda)$ is a machine with d.c. conditions and π and τ are partitions on S, we say that (π, τ) is a *weak partition pair* (w.p.p.) if and only if

$$s \equiv t(\pi) \text{ implies } \delta(s, x) \equiv \delta(t, x)(\tau)$$

for all x in I such that $\delta(s, x)$ and $\delta(t, x)$ are specified.

Of course this definition generalizes to I-S, S-O, and I-O pairs. We refer to these concepts without writing out their formal definitions.

To illustrate the w.p.p. concept, consider machine H of Fig. 3.19. Observe that

$$(\pi_1, \tau) = (\{\overline{1}; \overline{2,4}; \overline{3}\}, \{\overline{1}; \overline{2,3}; \overline{4}\})$$

and

$$(\pi_2, \tau) = (\{\overline{1}; \overline{2,3}; \overline{4}\}, \{\overline{1}; \overline{2,3}; \overline{4}\})$$

are both w.p.p.'s. On the other hand,

$$(\pi_1 + \pi_2, \tau + \tau) = (\{\overline{1}; \overline{2,3,4}\}, \{\overline{1}; \overline{2,3}; \overline{4}\})$$

	a	b	c	
1	4	1	3	-
2	-	2	4	0
3	1	3	4	1
4	2	3	-	0

Fig. 3.19.   Machine H.

is *not* a w.p.p. This is one of the major disadvantages of weak partition pairs. The concept of an M partition for H is ruled out because to have $M(\tau) \geqslant \pi_1$ and $M(\tau) \geqslant \pi_2$ ensures that $(M(\tau), \tau)$ is not a w.p.p.

In other words, $\{\pi \,|\, (\pi, \tau) \text{ is a w.p.p.}\}$ contains several maximal elements. Now let us see what algebra can be salvaged.

LEMMA 3.5. If Δ is the set of all weak partition pairs on M with d.c. conditions, then
  (i) (π, I) and $(0, \pi)$ are in Δ.
  (ii) (π, π') and (τ, τ') in Δ imply $(\pi \cdot \tau, \pi' \cdot \tau')$ in Δ.
    (π, π') in Δ implies $(\pi, \pi' + \tau)$ in Δ.

Proof. (i) is obvious and (ii) is proved similar to the corresponding results about partition pairs. ∎

Thus the weak partition pairs satisfy all but the "sum" postulate of a pair algebra, which is now replaced by a weaker form. We generalize to cover weak pairs.

DEFINITION 3.13. Let L_1 and L_2 be finite lattices. Then a subset Δ of $L_1 \times L_2$ is a weak pair algebra on $L_1 \times L_2$ if and only if
    P_1: (x, y) in Δ and y' in L_2 implies that $(x, y + y')$ in Δ
    (x_1, y_1) and (x_2, y_2) in Δ implies that $(x_1 \cdot x_2, y_1 \cdot y_2)$ in Δ
    P_2: for any x in L_1 and y in L_2, (x, I) and $(y, 0)$ are in Δ.
The ordering of Δ is defined component-wise, and again

$$m(x) = \prod \{y \,|\, (x, y) \text{ in } \Delta\}.$$

THEOREM 3.6. Let Δ be a weak pair algebra. Then

(i) $[x, m(x)]$ is in Δ

(ii) $x_1 \geqslant x_2$ implies $m(x_1) \geqslant m(x_2)$

(iii) $m(x_1 + x_2) \geqslant m(x_1) + m(x_2)$

(iv) $m(x_1 \cdot x_2) \leqslant m(x_1) \cdot m(x_2)$.

(v) $\tau \geqslant m(x)$ if and only if (π, τ) in Δ.

Proof. We have merely restated relations which were previously derived without using the summation postulate. $\blacksquare$

We have only five conditions instead of the sixteen conditions of Theorem 3.1, and 3.6 (iii) is weaker than 3.1 (iii). Thus the importance of the summation rule is evident. Even without the M operator, however, many nice properties remain. For example, Δ is easily shown to be a lattice under our ordering, the bounds being given by

g.l.b. $\{(\pi, \pi'), (\tau, \tau')\} = (\pi \cdot \tau, \pi' \cdot \tau')$

and

l.u.b. $\{(\pi, \pi'), (\tau, \tau')\} = (\pi + \tau, \pi' + \tau' + m(\pi + \tau))$.

EXERCISE. Give a proof of the above statement.

Let us now consider the dependence results of the previous section. Of course, the information flow inequalities involve the M operator, but if we replace the conditions of the form "$\prod \tau_i \leqslant M(\pi)$" by the equivalent statement "$(\prod \tau_i, \pi)$ is a p.p.," then we have a formulation suitable for generalization. However, in proving that the conditions of Theorem 3.4 are sufficient for a realization with all the reduced dependences, we assumed that our machine was completely specified. (Specifically, this is vitial to the proof of Lemma 3.3 where $\delta(s, b)$ is assumed to have a value.) Any hope to get around this is shattered by machine J of Fig. 3.20a. For machine J,

$(\{\overline{1,2}\}, \{\overline{1}; \overline{2}\})$ is a weak S-S pair,

and

$(\{\overline{0,1}\}, \{\overline{1}; \overline{2}\})$ is a weak I-S pair.

If Theorem 3.4 were to generalize completely, we would be able to make δ independent of both input and output, contrary to the fact that δ cannot be constant because the table already has transitions to nonequivalent states. We can fill the conditions so that the machine is state independent *or* input independent (as shown in Fig. 3.20 *b* and *c*) but not both.

When we talk about a *realization* or *state behavior realization* of a machine with *d.c. conditions*, we mean the same as Definitions 1.15 and 1.16 where it is understood that the conditions need only hold whenever $\delta(s, a)$ or $\lambda(s, a)$ exist. Thus, machine K of Fig. 3.21 is a state behavior realization of machine J (Fig. 3.20a).

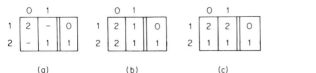

Fig. 3.20.   Machine J with d. c. conditions filled in two different ways.

Fig. 3.21.   Machine K.

We now give our dependence theorem, corresponding to Theorem 3.4, for the d.c. case.

THEOREM 3.7. Suppose that, for a machine M with d.c. conditions, state variables $\{y_i\}$ are assigned according to state partitions $\{\tau_i\}$, input variables $\{x_j\}$ are assigned according to input partitions $\{\xi_j\}$, and output variables $\{Z_k\}$ are assigned according to output partitions $\{\omega_k\}$; and suppose further that

$$\prod_P \tau_i = 0, \qquad \prod_Q \xi_i = 0, \qquad P \subseteq \{y_i\}, \qquad \text{and} \qquad Q \subseteq \{x_i\},$$

then in writing equations to realize M:

(i) variable Y_i can be expressed as a function of $P \cup \{x_j\}$ if and only if $(\prod_P \tau_j, \tau_i)$ is a weak S-S pair;

(ii) variable Y_i can be expressed as a function of $\{y_i\} \cup Q$ if and only if $(\prod_Q \xi_j, \tau_i)$ is a weak I-S pair;

(iii) variable Z_k can be expressed as a function of $P \cup \{x_j\}$ if and only if $(\prod_P \tau_i, \omega_k)$ is a weak S-O pair;

(iv) variable Z_k can be expressed as a function of $\{y_i\} \cup Q$ if and only if $(\prod_Q \xi_i, \omega_k)$ is a weak I-O pair.

Proof. The proof is so similar to previous proofs that we leave it as an exercise. The conditions $\prod \tau_i = 0$ and $\prod \xi_i = 0$ are used to ensure that $\{x_i\}$ and $\{y_i\}$ determine the exact input and state. ∎

Compare Theorem 3.7 with Theorem 3.4. Theorem 3.4 says that state and input dependence can be reduced simultaneously, whereas Theorem 3.7 says that either state or input dependence can be reduced, but not always simultaneously. This is one disadvantage of the first approach, but for applications (such as feedback) when only one kind of dependence is of interest, this approach is most direct.

3.7 DON'T CARE CONDITIONS, SECOND APPROACH

In the first approach, we ignored the occurrences of the d.c. conditions. In the second approach, we give each condition a separate name, and then keep a careful record of it. *A machine with labeled d.c. conditions* is given by a machine table where some values of δ may be from a set of labels C and some values of λ may be from a set of labels D. Given such a machine, the concept of a p.p. extends naturally.

DEFINITION 3.14. Given a machine $M = (S, I, O, \delta, \lambda)$ with labeled d.c. conditions C and D, and given a partition π on S and partition τ on $S \cup C$, then (π, τ) is called an *extended partition pair* (e.p.p.) if and only if

$$s \equiv t\,(\pi) \text{ implies } \delta(s, x) \equiv \delta(t, x)\,(\tau) \text{ for all } x \text{ in } I.$$

	a	b	c	
1	4	1	3	d_1
2	c_1	2	4	0
3	1	3	4	1
4	2	3	c_2	0

Fig. 3.22. Machine L.

Again this definition extends to other pairs.

To illustrate our definitions, we show machine L with extended d.c. conditions in Fig. 3.22 which is just Fig. 3.19 with the conditions labeled. Observe that

$$(\pi_1, \tau_1) = (\{\overline{1}; \overline{2,4}; \overline{3}\}, \{\overline{c_1, 2, 3}; \overline{c_2, 4}; \overline{1}\})$$

and

$$(\pi_2, \tau_2) = (\{\overline{1}; \overline{2,3}; \overline{4}\}, \{\overline{c_1, 1}; \overline{2,3}; \overline{c_2}; \overline{4}\})$$

are extended partition pairs. Partition τ_1 accounts for the fact that any choice of c_1 must be in the same block as 2 and 3. Partition τ_2 says that the choice of c_1 must be in the same block as 1. This fact was overlooked in the previous section when w.p.p.'s were used, and that is why the sum law failed. Here,

$$(\pi_1 + \pi_2, \tau_1 + \tau_2) = (\{\overline{1}; \overline{2,3,4}\}, \{\overline{c_1, 1, 2, 3}; \overline{c_2, 4}\})$$

is also an e.p.p. More generally, we have the following:

LEMMA 3.6. Given a machine M with labeled don't care conditions, the set Δ of all extended partition pairs is a pair algebra.

Proof. The definition of an e.p.p. is the same as a p.p., except that set $S \cup D$ is used instead of S. The proof for p.p. therefore carries over word for word. ∎

We now have the m operator and M operator with all the pair algebra results at our disposal. In addition to our S-$S \cup C$ pairs, we of course have I-$S \cup C$, S-$O \cup D$, and I-$O \cup D$ pairs and the corresponding operators. In our dependence theorem, when we refer to $\bar{\tau}_i$ as the restriction of τ_i to S, we mean

$$s \equiv t\,(\bar{\tau}_i) \text{ for } s, t \text{ in } S \text{ if and only if } s \equiv t\,(\tau_i).$$

THEOREM 3.8. Suppose that, for a machine M with labeled don't care conditions, state variables $\{y_i\}$ are assigned according to partitions $\{\tau_i\}$ on $S \cup C$, input variables $\{x_j\}$ are assigned according to input partitions $\{\xi_j\}$, and output variables $\{Z_k\}$ are assigned according to partitions $\{\omega_i\}$ on $O \cup D$; and suppose further that $P \subseteq \{y_i\}$ and $Q \subseteq \{x_i\}$, then, in writing equations to realize M:

(i) variable Y_i can be expressed as a function of $P \cup Q$ if and only if

$$\prod_P \bar{\tau}_i \leqslant M_{S-S \cup C}(\tau_i) \quad \text{and} \quad \prod_Q \xi_j = M_{I-S \cup C}(\tau_i),$$

where $\bar{\tau}_i$ is the restriction of τ_i to S.

(ii) variable Z_k can be expressed as a function of $P \cup Q$ if and only if

$$\prod_P \bar{\tau}_i \leqslant M_{S-O \cup D}(\omega_k) \quad \text{and} \quad \prod_Q \xi_j \leqslant M_{I-O \cup D}(\omega_k)$$

where $\bar{\tau}_i$ is the restriction of τ_i to S.

Proof. The construction is straightforward and similar to Theorem 3.4. We leave the details to the reader. ∎

Thus we have the analogy to Theorem 3.4 where independence from certain state and input information can be achieved simultaneously. This is the big advantage of the second approach over the first. This is counter-balanced by the need to keep track of the labels, which entails more book keeping than in the first approach. The third approach, which will be investigated later, provides some interesting insights, but is not suitable for systematic use.

3.8   COMPONENT MACHINES AND LOCAL MACHINES

We wish to make a brief consideration of the relationship between the structure of a machine M and the structure of a component machine in a network $\mathcal{N}$ which realizes the state behavior of M. Intuitively, we know that any decomposition of the component machine can be regarded as a further decomposition of the original machine, and might therefore be detectable from the partition structure of the original machine. Such a characterization of component machine structure is impossible, however, since the component machines are usually obtained only after some d.c. conditions are filled, and the partitions on M cannot possibly account for how these conditions are filled. A global characterization of the local struc-ture can be achieved only if we step back and look at the component machines before the d.c. conditions are filled.

Considering the component machine in more detail, the transitions in its flow table are seen to be of two types: those which are used when $\mathcal{N}$ imitates M and those which are not used. The transitions which are used are determined exactly by the transitions of M they help imitate. Those transitions not used can actually be assigned arbitrarily since they lie outside the anticipated use of $\mathcal{N}$. If these arbitrary transitions are regarded as d.c. conditions, then we are left with a unique machine with d.c. conditions. We call this machine a "local machine."

DEFINITION 3.15. Let $M = (S, I, O, \delta, \lambda)$ be a machine and let τ and ρ be partitions on S and μ a partition on I such that

$$\rho \cdot \tau \leqslant M_{S-S}(\tau) \qquad \text{and} \qquad \mu \leqslant M_{I-S}(\tau).$$

The *local machine* $M(\tau; \rho, \mu)$ on M is given by

$$M(\tau; \rho, \mu) = (S', I', \delta')$$

where

$$S' = \tau \qquad \text{and} \qquad I' = \rho \times \mu$$

and δ' is that unique function

$$\delta' : \tau \times \rho \times \mu \longrightarrow \tau$$

such that

$$\delta'(B_\tau(s), B_\rho(s), B_\mu(x)) = B_\tau(\delta(s, x))$$

for all s in S and x in I and

$$\delta'(B_\tau, B_\rho, B_\mu) = \text{"don't care"}$$

whenever

$$B_\tau \cap B_\rho = \varnothing.$$

EXERCISE. Prove that there always is the unique δ' as claimed in Definition 3.15.

The local machine is the skeleton of the component machine and is an intermediate step in constructing a component machine. More formally:

THEOREM 3.9. If $M_{\mathcal{N}}$ realizes the state behavior of M, then every component machine of $\mathcal{N}$ is a state behavior realization of some local machine.

Proof. Left as an exercise. ∎

The next result shows how the weak partition pair m operator for a local machine can be obtained for the m operator on the realized machine.

THEOREM 3.10. If $M(\tau; \rho, \mu)$ is a local machine for $M = (S, I, O, \delta, \lambda)$ and if for any $\pi \geqslant \tau$ we define $\bar{\pi}$ on the blocks of τ by:

$$B_\tau \equiv B'_\tau (\bar{\pi}) \text{ if and only if } s \equiv s' (\pi) \text{ for } s \in B_\tau \text{ and } s' \in B'_\tau;$$

and if we use "m" for the operators on M and "$\bar{m}$" for the w.p.p. operators on $M(\tau; \rho, \mu)$, then the following relationships hold:

(i) $\bar{m}_{S-S}(\bar{\pi}) = \overline{m_{S-S}(\pi \cdot \rho) + \tau}$ for $\pi \geqslant \tau$;

(ii) $\bar{m}_{I-S}[(\sigma, v)] = \overline{m_{I-S}(v) + m_{S-S}(\sigma \cdot \tau) + \tau}$ for $\sigma \geqslant \rho$, where (σ, v) has its obvious interpretation as a partition on $\{B_\rho\} \times \{B_\mu\}$.

Proof. We prove (i) only. Note however that there are partitions on $\{B_\rho\} \times \{B_\mu\}$ which do not have the form (σ, ν) and thus (ii) does not apply to the complete domain of $\bar{m}_{I-s}$.

First we show that $(\bar{\pi}, \overline{m(\pi \cdot \rho) + \tau})$ is a w.p.p. Because of Definition 3.12, we need to show that

$$B_\tau(\delta(s, x)) \equiv B_\tau(\delta(s', x)) \, (\overline{m(\pi \cdot \rho) + \tau})$$

for all s in $B_\rho \cap B_\tau$, s' in $B_\rho \cap B'_\tau$, and x in B_μ whenever $B_\tau \equiv B'_\tau \, (\bar{\pi})$.

Now $B_\tau \equiv B'_\tau \, (\bar{\pi})$ implies by definition that

$$s \equiv s' \, (\pi) \text{ for all } s \text{ in } B_\tau \text{ and } s' \text{ in } B'_\tau.$$

This obviously implies

$$s \equiv s' \, (\pi \cdot \rho) \text{ for all } s \text{ in } B_\rho \cap B_\tau \text{ and } s' \text{ in } B_\rho \cap B'_\tau.$$

By definition of m, this implies

$$\delta(s, x) \equiv \delta(s', x) \, (m(\pi \cdot \rho)) \text{ for all } s \text{ in } B_\rho \cap B_\tau \text{ and } s' \text{ in } B_\rho \cap B'_\tau.$$

This implies

$$t \equiv t' \, (m(\pi \cdot \rho) + \tau) \text{ for all } t \text{ in } B_\tau \, (\delta(s', x)) \text{ and } t' \text{ in } B_\tau(\delta(s', x)).$$

This in turn implies that

$$B_\tau(\delta(s, x)) \equiv B_\tau(\delta(s', x)) \, (\overline{m(\pi \cdot \rho) + \tau})$$

which was to be shown.

Now suppose that $(\bar{\pi}, \bar{\pi}')$ is a w.p.p. on the local machine, where $\pi' \geqslant \tau$. (All state partitions for $M(\tau; \rho, \mu)$ have the form $\bar{\pi}'$ for $\pi' \geqslant \tau$.) Suppose further that

$$B_\tau \equiv B'_\tau \, (\pi').$$

Because $(\bar{\pi}, \bar{\pi}')$ is a w.p.p. and because of Definition 3.12,

$$B_\tau(\delta(s, x)) \equiv B_\tau(\delta(s', x)) \, (\bar{\pi})$$

for all s in $B_\tau \cap B_\rho$, s' in $B'_\tau \cap B_\rho$, and x in I.

This implies that

$$\delta(s, x) \equiv \delta(s', x) \, (\pi') \text{ whenever } s \equiv s' \, (\pi \cdot \rho).$$

Therefore $\pi' \geqslant m(\pi \cdot \rho)$ and since also $\pi' \geqslant \tau$, we have

$$\bar{\pi}' \geqslant \overline{m(\pi \cdot \rho) + \tau}. \quad \blacksquare$$

Of course, we know that there is no $\bar{M}$ operator in general because the local machines have "d.c." conditions. Even in those cases where there are no don't cares, however, the $\bar{M}$ has no formula in terms of M, m, plus, and times. More specifically, this is the case where ρ and τ permute (i.e., $B_\rho \cap B_\tau \neq \varnothing$ for all B_ρ and B_τ) and we know that $\bar{M}(\pi)$ is the largest partition π' greater than τ and such that $m(\rho \cdot \pi') \leqslant \pi$, but we know of no way to obtain $\bar{\pi}'$ without explicitly taking this maximum. One exception to this is the case where $\rho = I$ and τ therefore has S.P. $(m(I \cdot \tau) \leqslant \tau)$. Here we have the following:

COROLLARY 3.10.1. If $M(\tau; I, \mu)$ is a local machine then:

(i) $\bar{m}_{S-S}(\bar{\pi}) = \overline{m_{S-S}(\pi) + \tau}$ for $\pi \geqslant \tau$;

(ii) $\bar{m}_{I-S}(\bar{\nu}) = \overline{m_{I-S}(\nu) + \tau}$ for $\nu \geqslant \mu$;

(iii) $\bar{M}_{S-S}(\bar{\pi}) = \overline{M_{S-S}(\pi)}$ for $\pi \geqslant \tau$;

(iv) $\bar{M}_{I-S}(\bar{\pi}) = \overline{M_{I-S}(\pi)}$ for $\pi \geqslant \tau$.

Proof. (i) Substitute $\rho = I$ in part (i) of theorem. (ii) Substitute $\sigma = I$ in part (ii) and observe $m_{S-S}(I \cdot \tau) \leqslant \tau$. (iii) Obviously $\overline{M(\pi)} \geqslant \tau$, so $M(\pi)$ is well defined and easily seen to be $\bar{M}(\bar{\pi})$. (iv) Obvious. ∎

NOTES

Partition pairs were first introduced for the study of sequential machines by the authors in [28]. The more general concept of the pair algebra and its application to automata theory is discussed in [18]. For related mathematical concepts, see the discussion of Galois connections between partially ordered sets in [3].

4 LOOP-FREE STRUCTURE OF MACHINES

4.1 LOOP-FREE NETWORKS

In the previous chapter we saw how each network may be considered to be an interconnection of its component machines. In this chapter we study various aspects of the "loop-free" case where none of the machines are connected in a circle. Actually, this study was started in Chapter 2 when simple series and parallel decompositions were analyzed. In this chapter we extend this study to arbitrary loop-free decompositions and show that there exists a one-to-one correspondence between "nonredundant" sets of S. P. partitions and loop-free decompositions of the state behavior of a machine. In this correspondence the lattice ordering of the S.P. partitions which define the decomposition is directly reflected in the interconnection of the component machines, and a physical layout for these component machines can be read off directly from the S.P. lattice. Once this basic relationship between lattice structure and machine structure is established, many additional implications of the S.P. lattice are extracted. Thus it is seen that this simplest and most accessible of the information lattices says a great deal about machine structure. We need to develop some preliminary definitions and lemmas before we define a loop-free network.

DEFINITION 4.1. Let M_1, M_2, . . . , M_n be the component machines of some network $\mathcal{N}$. Then we say that M_i is a *predecessor* of M_j if and only if the output of M_i is used directly as an input to M_j. In other words, M_i is a predecessor of M_j if and only if $\rho_{i,j} \neq I$, where $\rho_{i,j}$ is the associated partition of Definition 3.11.

This definition is pragmatic in the sense that we call M_i a predecessor if and only if there is a wire from M_i carrying information to M_j, even though the behavior of M_j may actually be functionally independent of M_i. The only reason for not using functional dependence is that this would later force us to exclude constructions that happen to turn out better (with less dependence) than anticipated.

DEFINITION 4.2. If $\{M_i\}$ is the set of component machines of some network $\mathcal{N}$, then we say that a subset C of $\{M_i\}$ is closed in $\mathcal{N}$ if and only if C contains all the predecessors of machines in C.

LEMMA 4.1. The set $\{C_i\}$ of all closed sets of machines in a network $\mathcal{N}$ is closed under the operation of set intersection and set unions.

Proof. Let C_i and C_j be closed in $\mathcal{N}$. If M_k is in $C_i \cap C_j$, then M_k is in C_i and C_j. But then all predecessors of M_k are in C_i and C_j and are therefore in $C_i \cap C_j$. Thus, $C_i \cap C_j$ is closed.

If M_k is in $C_i \cup C_j$, then M_k is in C_i or C_j and hence C_i or C_j contains all predecessors of M_k. But then $C_i \cup C_j$ contains these predecessors and we conclude that $C_i \cup C_j$ is closed. ∎

This result shows that the set of closed sets forms a lattice under the set operations. Since the set operations are distributive, this lattice of closed sets is distributive.

DEFINITION 4.3. If L is a subset of component machines for network $\mathcal{N}$, then the *closure* $C(L)$ of L in $\mathcal{N}$ is the smallest closed subset containing L. Operator C is referred to as the *closure operator* of $\mathcal{N}$. If L contains exactly one machine M_k, we may write $C(M_k)$ instead of $C(\{M_k\})$.

LEMMA 4.2. The closure operator C of $\mathcal{N}$ satisfies the conditions:
  (i) $C(L) \supseteq L$;
  (ii) $L_1 \subseteq L_2$ implies $C(L_1) \subseteq C(L_2)$;
  (iii) $C[C(L)] = C(L)$;
  (iv) $C(L) = \cap \{C_i \mid C_i \text{ closed set in } \mathcal{N} \text{ and } C_i \supseteq L\}$;
  (v) $C(L_1 \cap L_2) = C(L_1) \cap C(L_2)$;
  (vi) $C(L_1 \cup L_2) = C(L_1) \cup C(L_2)$.

Proof. Routine. ∎

DEFINITION 4.4. An abstract network, $\mathcal{N}$, with component machines $\{M_i\}$ is said to be *loop-free* if and only if there does not exist a pair of machines M_j and M_k, $j \neq k$, such that

$$M_j \text{ is in } C(M_k) \text{ and } M_k \text{ is in } C(M_j).$$

DEFINITION 4.5. If a loop-free network $\mathcal{N}$ of component machines realizes the state behavior of M, then we shall say that $\mathcal{N}$ is a *loop-free realization* or *decomposition* of M.

We now associate a partition with each closed set.

DEFINITION 4.6. Let $\mathcal{N}$ be a network that realizes the state behavior of machine M and that has component machines $\{M_i\}$. For each M_i, let τ_i be the associated partition of Definition 3.11 on the states of M. Then for any $N \subseteq \{M_i\}$, define

$$\varphi(N) = \prod \{\tau_i \mid M_i \in N\}.$$

If N has only one element M_j, we write $\varphi(M_j)$ instead of $\varphi(\{M_j\})$.

Now we come to the main result of this section that says that φ maps the closed sets of $\{M_i\}$ into the S.P. lattice in a systematic way.

THEOREM 4.1. Suppose that network $\mathcal{N}$ with component machines $\{M_i\}$ realizes the state behavior of machine M. Then
   (i) C closed in $\mathcal{N}$ implies that $\varphi(C)$ has S.P.;
   (ii) $C_1 \subseteq C_2$ implies $\varphi(C_1) \geqslant \varphi(C_2)$;
   (iii) $\varphi(C_1 \cup C_2) = \varphi(C_1) \cdot \varphi(C_2)$.

Proof. Let J be the index set such that $\varphi(C) = \prod_{J} \tau_i$. Because the state of M_i is determined by its predecessors $\{M_k\}$ for k in some index set J_i, we know from Theorem 3.5 and Corollary 3.5.1 that

$$\prod_{J_i} \tau_k \leqslant M(\tau_i).$$

Because C is closed, $J_i \subseteq J$ for M_i in C and hence,

$$\varphi(C) = \prod_{i \in J} \tau_i \leqslant \prod_{i \in J} \left(\prod_{k \in J_i} \tau_k \right) \leqslant \prod_{J} M(\tau_i)$$
$$= M\left(\prod_{J} \tau_i \right) = M[\varphi(C)].$$

Therefore $\varphi(C)$ has S.P. by Corollary 3.1.3 and (i) is proven. Now let J_1 and J_2 be index sets such that

$$\varphi(C_1) = \prod_{J_1} \tau_i \text{ and } \varphi(C_2) = \prod_{J_2} \tau_i.$$

If $C_1 \subseteq C_2$, then $J_1 \subseteq J_2$ which implies

$$\varphi(C_1) = \prod_{J_1} \tau_i \geqslant \prod_{J_2} \tau_i = \varphi(C_2).$$

This is just statement (ii). Statement (iii) follows from the equation

$$\varphi(C_1 \cup C_2) = \prod_{J_1 \cup J_2} \tau_i = \left(\prod_{J_1} \tau_i \right) \cdot \left(\prod_{J_2} \tau_i \right) = \varphi(C_1) \cdot \varphi(C_2)$$

and the theorem is proved. ∎

4.2   OBTAINING LOOP-FREE REALIZATIONS

The main objective of this section is to derive a converse of Theorem 4.1. This converse shows how certain sets of S.P. partitions on the states of a machine M determine the loop-free realizations of M. As is the case with all our theory, each such set determines the realization in a constructive manner. In order to obtain a strong converse, we need to pinpoint a certain type of redundancy.

Let the network $\mathcal{N}$ of component machines $\{M_i\}$ realize M. We know from the previous theorem that there exists a mapping, φ, of the closed sets of $\mathcal{N}$ into the set of S.P. partition on M. We now show that if this mapping is not a one-to-one-mapping for closed sets, then there exist redundant machines in the realization $\mathcal{N}$ of M.

Assume that there exist two distinct closed sets C_1 and C_2 in $\mathcal{N}$ such that $\varphi(C_1) = \varphi(C_2) = \pi$. Without loss of generality, we may assume that there exists a machine M_k in C_2 that is not in C_1. By Theorem 4.1 we know that

$$\pi = \prod \{\pi_j \mid \pi_j = \varphi(M_j),\ M_j \text{ in } C_1\}.$$

From $\varphi(M_k) = \pi_k$, we have $\pi \leqslant \pi_k$. This implies that M_k computes some information about the state of M that is also computed by the machines in the set C_1. Since the machine M_k is not in the closed set C_1, we know that the output of M_k is not used as input in any one of the machines in C_1. Thus, the information about the present state of M given by M_k is computed independently at least twice. Thus, there is a machine in $\mathcal{N}$ whose output is independently available elsewhere.

Having seen that only realizations with superfluous component machines are associated with φ that are not one-to-one over the closed sets, we are motivated to establish the corresponding phenomenon for partitions.

DEFINITION 4.7. We say that a set of partitions,

$$T = \{\pi_i\},$$

defined on S, is *nonredundant* if and only if the π_i are distinct and, for all $T' \subseteq T$ and π_k in T,

$$\prod \{\pi_j \mid \pi_j \text{ in } T'\} \leqslant \pi_k \text{ implies } \pi_k \geqslant \pi_i$$

for some π_i in T'.

THEOREM 4.2. If the state behavior of a machine M is realized by a loop-free network $\mathcal{N}$ of component machines $\{M_i\}$ such that φ is one-to-one over closed sets, then the set of partitions $\{\varphi[C(M_i)]\}$ is nonredundant.

Proof. First of all, suppose that the set of partitions is redundant because

$$\varphi[C(M_j)] = \varphi[C(M_k)]$$

for $j \neq k$. Because $\mathcal{N}$ is loop-free,

$$C(M_j) \neq C(M_k)$$

by Definition 4.4 and therefore φ is not one-to-one.

Now suppose the set of partitions is redundant because a set T' and a partition $\varphi[C(M_k)]$ violate the condition. Then M_k is not in $C(M_j)$ for any $\varphi[C(M_j)]$ in T' because

$$\varphi[C(M_k)] \not\geqslant \varphi[C(M_j)].$$

Therefore, letting $C_1 = \underset{T'}{\cup} C(M_j)$, we know that M_k is not in C_1 and thus closed sets C_1 and $C_2 = C_1 \cup C(M_k)$ are distinct. To show that $\varphi(C_1) = \varphi(C_2)$, we know by assumption that

$$\varphi[C(M_k)] \geqslant \prod_{T'} \varphi[C(M_j)] = \varphi(C_1);$$

and multiplying by $\varphi(C_1)$, we get by Theorem 4.1 (iii)

$$\varphi(C_2) = \varphi(C_1) \cdot \varphi[C(M_k)] \geqslant \varphi(C_1).$$

But $\varphi(C_1) \geqslant \varphi(C_2)$ by Lemma 4.2 (ii) and therefore $\varphi(C_1) = \varphi(C_2)$, and φ is not one-to-one over closed sets. ∎

THEOREM 4.3. Let $T = \{\pi_1, \pi_2, \ldots, \pi_n\}$ be a nonredundant set of S.P. partitions on S of M such that

$$\prod \pi_i = 0.$$

Then there exists a loop-free network $\mathcal{N}$ of n machines, $M_1, M_2, \ldots, M_n$, such that:

(i) $\mathcal{N}$ realizes the state behavior of M;
(ii) M_i is in $C(M_j)$ if and only if $\pi_i \geqslant \pi_j$;
(iii) $\varphi[C(M_i)] = \pi_i$;
(iv) φ is one-to-one over closed sets.

Proof. For any π_j in T, let $\pi_j^* = \prod \{\pi_i \in T \,|\, \pi_i > \pi_j\}$. Choose τ_j to be any partition such that $\tau_j \cdot \pi_j^* = \pi_j$. For the sake of obtaining simple realizations, one generally chooses such a τ_j with the minimal number of blocks. Since π_j has S.P.,

$$m(\tau_j \cdot \pi_j^*) = m(\pi_j) \leqslant \pi_j \leqslant \tau_i$$

and so we can let M_j be a machine obtained from $M(\tau_j; \pi_j^*, 0)$ by filling in the "don't cares." Let $f_{i,j}$ be the identity map if $\pi_i \geqslant \pi_j$, and the constant map otherwise. Let $g = \beta(s, x)$ where s is the single element in $\cap B_{\tau_i}$ (arbitrary otherwise). Note that the τ_i defined here are in fact the partitions associated with the M_i, and that for this network, $\rho_{i,j} = \tau_j$ for $\pi_i \geqslant \pi_j$ and $\rho_{i,j} = I$ otherwise. Observing that

$$\pi_j = \tau_j \cdot \pi_j^* = \prod \{\tau_i \,|\, \pi_i \geqslant \pi_j\} = \prod \rho_{i,j},$$

it is easily verified that Theorem 3.5 holds and we have a realization. Furthermore, (ii) holds by construction and (iii) is verified by the previous equation.

To show (iv), assume $\varphi(C_1) = \varphi(C_2)$ for closed sets $C_1 \neq C_2$. We may assume that there is a machine M_k in C_2 that is not in C_1. Choosing $T' = \{\pi_j \mid M_j \in C_1\}$, we know from Definition 4.7 that there is an M_i in C_1 such that $\pi_i \leqslant \pi_k$. By (ii), M_k is in $C(M_i)$. But $C(M_i) \subseteq C_1$ so M_k must be in C_1 contrary to our assumption. Therefore, (iv) holds. ∎

NOTE. In the above construction, one may be more liberal in the choice of carry variables. Any $\rho_{i,j} \geqslant \tau_j$ for $i > j$ may be chosen as long as $\prod_i \rho_{i,j} \leqslant M(\tau_j)$.

As a result of this last theorem, we now know that for one-to-one φ, loop-free state behavior realizations give nonredundant subsets of the S.P. partitions and vice versa. Furthermore, this relationship is constructive. To illustrate the network construction in the proof, let us consider two examples. First, look at machine A in Fig. 4.1.

By an easy computation, we obtain the following list of S.P. partitions:

$$\pi_1 = \{\overline{1}; \overline{2}; \overline{3}; \overline{4}; \overline{5}; \overline{6}; \overline{7}; \overline{8}\} = 0,$$
$$\pi_2 = \{\overline{1,4}; \overline{2,3}; \overline{5,8}; \overline{6,7}\},$$
$$\pi_3 = \{\overline{1,2}; \overline{3,4}; \overline{5,6}; \overline{7,8}\},$$
$$\pi_4 = \{\overline{1,2,7,8}; \overline{3,4,5,6}\},$$
$$\pi_5 = \{\overline{1,2,3,4}; \overline{5,6,7,8}\},$$
$$\pi_6 = \{\overline{1,2,3,4,5,6,7,8}\} = I.$$

The lattice of S.P. partitions for this machine is shown in Fig. 4.2.

	x_1	x_2	x_3	x_4	x_5
1	2	1	5	8	3
2	1	2	6	7	4
3	4	3	6	6	1
4	3	4	5	5	2
5	5	6	3	4	7
6	6	5	4	3	8
7	7	8	4	2	5
8	8	7	3	1	6

Fig. 4.1. Machine A.

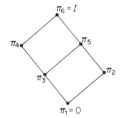

Fig. 4.2. The S. P. lattice L_A for machine A.

Now let us see how all the state behavior realizations involving one-to-one φ are schematically available from the lattice. By inspection, we easily obtain all the sets of nonredundant partitions. Some of these are listed below and the corresponding realizations for these six sets are shown schematically in Fig. 4.3.

$$\{\pi_5, \pi_1\}, \qquad \{\pi_4, \pi_5, \pi_1\},$$
$$\{\pi_4, \pi_3, \pi_1\}, \quad \{\pi_4, \pi_2\},$$
$$\{\pi_3, \pi_2\}, \qquad \{\pi_5, \pi_3, \pi_2\}.$$

In Fig. 4.3, a symbol such as π_1/π_5 indicates that the corresponding machine refines the information in π_5 to π_1. The minimum number of blocks

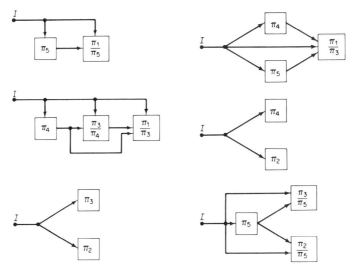

Fig. 4.3.   Information flow in six realizations of machine A.

required in a partition τ such that $\pi_5 \cdot \tau = \pi_1$ is the minimum number of states that the component machine can have.

We now consider in detail a realization of machine A corresponding to the set of partitions $\{\pi_5, \pi_1\}$. Since $\pi_5 > \pi_1$, we have a cascade connection of two machines. The first machine, A_1 defined by π_5, has two states,

$$a = \overline{1,2,3,4} \qquad \text{and} \qquad b = \overline{5,6,7,8},$$

corresponding to the blocks of π_5. Its state behavior can be read off from the state behavior of machine A (Fig. 4.1) and is shown in Fig. 4.4. The output of A_1 is its present state and it will be an additional input of the second machine A_2. To construct A_2 we have to choose a partition τ such that

$$\pi_5 \cdot \tau = 0.$$

Since the blocks of π_5 each contain four states, the partition τ must have four (or more) blocks. It is seen that there are twenty-four such four-block partitions. We choose

$$\tau = \{\overline{1,8}; \overline{2,7}; \overline{3,6}; \overline{4,5}\} = \{A; B; C; D\}.$$

The resulting four-state machine can be determined from the state behavior of machine A and is shown in Fig. 4.5. There are ten possible inputs cor-

	x_1	x_2	x_3	x_4	x_5
a	a	a	b	b	a
b	b	b	a	a	b

Fig. 4.4. Machine A_1.

	ax_1	ax_2	ax_3	ax_4	ax_5	bx_1	bx_2	bx_3	bx_4	bx_5
A	B	A	D	A	C	A	B	C	A	C
B	A	B	C	B	D	B	A	D	B	D
C	D	C	C	C	A	C	D	D	C	A
D	C	D	D	D	B	D	C	C	D	B

Fig. 4.5. Machine A_2.

responding to the pairs of inputs made up from the present external input and the present state variable of machine A_1 although many pairs have the same effect.

Observe also that when the exterior input x is applied, the two machines compute their next states simultaneously since the output of A_1, needed in A_2, is the old state variable of A_1.

The construction of all other loop-free realizations of this machine is similar to the previous illustration.

Later in this chapter we discuss how the choice of the partition τ affects the properties of the second machine in a serial re-alization.

	00	01	10
1	1	4	2
2	1	4	2
3	1	4	2
4	5	1	3
5	5	1	3

Fig. 4.6. Machine B.

Now let us consider machine B of Fig. 4.6.

We see that it has a nonredundant set of S.P. partitions $\{\pi_1, \pi_2, \pi_3\}$, where

$$\pi_1 = \{\overline{1,2,3}; \overline{4,5}\},$$

$$\pi_2 = \{\overline{1,4,5}; \overline{2,3}\},$$

$$\pi_3 = 0.$$

We choose our τ_i as follows:

$$\tau_1 = \pi_1,$$

$$\tau_2 = \pi_2,$$

$$\tau_3 = \{\overline{1,3,5}; \overline{2,4}\}.$$

We expect to get a realization as shown schematically in Fig. 4.7 a with closed sets $\varnothing$, $\{M_1\}$, $\{M_2\}$, $\{M_1, M_2\}$, and $\{M_1, M_2, M_3\}$. Because each τ_i has only two blocks, we assign a variable y_i to be computed by M_i and get the following assignment and equations:

	y_1	y_2	y_3
1	0	0	0
2	0	1	1
3	0	1	0
4	1	0	1
5	1	0	0

$$Y_1 = y_1\bar{x}_1\bar{x}_2 + \bar{y}_1 x_2$$
$$Y_2 = x_1$$
$$Y_3 = \bar{y}_1 x_2 + \bar{y}_1 x_1.$$

We have bypassed making a flow table for M_1, M_2, and M_3 by deriving their realizations (equations) directly. Considering these machines in terms of functional dependence, we see that they hook up schematically as shown

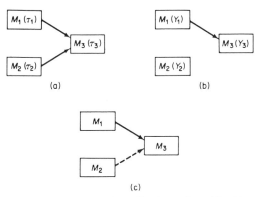

(a)

(b)

(c)

Fig. 4.7. Schematic realizations of machine B.

in Fig. 4.7b. This looks different than the realization we anticipated (Fig. 4.7a). If we recall, however, that we intended M_3 to receive information from M_2 (we chose $\rho_{2,3} = \tau_2$) and add a fictitious wire along the route (Fig. 4.7c), then we see that it also fits the form we intended.

Now let us take our realization at face value and consider it to be in the form of Fig. 4.7b. The closed sets for this realization are $\varnothing$, $\{M_1\}$, $\{M_2\}$, $\{M_1, M_2\}$, $\{M_1, M_3\}$, $\{M_1, M_2, M_3\}$. This list includes the previous list but contains one additional set. This inclusion is to be expected because removing a "wire" must leave the old closed sets intact. Now compute the $\pi'_j = \varphi[C(M_i)]$:

$$\pi'_1 = \{\overline{1,2,3}; \overline{4,5}\};$$
$$\pi'_2 = \{\overline{1,4,5}; \overline{2,3}\};$$
$$\pi'_3 = \{\overline{1,3}; \overline{2}; \overline{4}; \overline{5}\}.$$

Comparing this with the old list, we see that $\pi'_1 = \pi_1$, $\pi'_2 = \pi_2$, but $\pi'_3 \neq \pi_3$. This new set is also nonredundant and one sees that our realization could have been obtained using this new set as the basic set. Thus, this realization is not a surprise bonus, but one that could be found directly starting from the proper nonredundant set. This is always the case when minimal block τ_i are chosen, because this ensures that the information computed by a component is not computed elsewhere, which means that φ must be one-to-one, which means by Theorem 4.2 that the decomposition is associated with a nonredundant set of S.P. partitions.

4.3 IMPLICATIONS OF THE S. P. LATTICE

In the previous section we took steps to eliminate realizations that contained superfluous components. This was done to eliminate an infinite class of uneconomical redundant realizations. It was shown that, to avoid these realizations, one has to start with a nonredundant set of partitions. The big question remaining for the application of this theory is which nonredundant set of partitions to choose. In order to help answer this question, we point out a couple of more subtle forms of "redundancy" that can be spotted from the S.P. lattice. Even though these new forms of redundancy are not as undesirable as the previous form, it is advantageous for a designer to understand them. However, because of the highly specialized nature of these results, and because they are not needed elsewhere in the book, we suggest that *this section can be omitted on first reading*.

First, we consider the case where the computations of two machines partially overlap. For illustration, we compare the two realizations of machine A (Fig. 4.1) defined by the two sets of partitions

$$\{\pi_3, \pi_2\} \qquad \text{and} \qquad \{\pi_5, \pi_3, \pi_2\}.$$

From the set $\{\pi_3, \pi_2\}$ we get a realization of machine A from two parallel machines, each having four states, since π_3 and π_2 are four block partitions. This shows that we use a sixteen-state machine to realize an eight-state machine. It does not necessarily follow that utilization of these two partitions for a realization results in an uneconomical one, because the increase in the number of storage elements may be compensated by a decrease in "logical complexity" of the machines that are used, but there is redundancy here. Since $\pi_5(= \pi_2 + \pi_3)$ is greater than π_2 and π_3, one can look at the state of either component machine and determine which block of π_5 contains the present state of the machine. Thus, the information is computed independently by both components.

Now consider a realization determined from the set $\{\pi_5, \pi_3, \pi_2\}$. Here, the information about π_5 is computed once in a component A_5 and is fed to components A_3 and A_2 that refine this information down to π_3 and π_2, respectively (see Fig. 4.3). In this realization, only two states are required in each of the three components so A is decomposed without using additional memory.

The difference between these realizations is that in the second case, the common calculation has been "factored out" into a single unit that supplies this information to the other machines.

Whenever two component machines in a realization compute S.P. partitions π_1 and π_2, the sum $\pi_1 + \pi_2$ represents a redundant computation and should possibly be factored out; but there are cases where factoring out will cost additional memory. In general, one should pick a subset of S.P. partitions that includes all the partitions possible without enlarging the memory requirements.

Another type of redundancy is using a component for which a smaller reduced version could be used. To illustrate this, consider machine C of Fig. 4.8. It is easily computed that this machine has three nontrivial partitions with S.P., namely:

	a	b	c	d	
0	0	4	6	3	0
1	1	5	7	2	1
2	0	6	4	1	0
3	1	7	5	0	0
4	1	0	1	7	0
5	1	1	0	6	0
6	0	2	3	5	0
7	0	3	2	4	0

Fig. 4.8. Machine C.

$$\pi_1 = \{\overline{0,1}; \overline{2,3}; \overline{4,5}; \overline{6,7}\},$$

$$\pi_2 = \{\overline{0,1,2,3}; \overline{4,5,6,7}\},$$

$$\pi_3 = \{\overline{0,7}; \overline{1,5}; \overline{2,6}; \overline{3,4}\}.$$

Since $\{\pi_1, \pi_3\}$ is nonredundant and $\pi_1 \cdot \pi_3 = 0$, we know that it has a corresponding parallel decomposition into component machines C_{π_1} and C_{π_3} (using appropriate output logic). Furthermore, $\pi_1 + \pi_3 = I$ so nothing can be factored out. The same can be said about $\{\pi_2, \pi_3\}$ and so there is also a parallel decomposition using C_{π_2} and C_{π_3}. Therefore, we see that either C_{π_1} or C_{π_2} can be used in parallel with C_{π_3}.

Since π_2 is greater than π_1, we see that C_{π_1}, when used with C_{π_3}, computes more information than is really necessary. In Fig. 4.9, we show a realization in terms of C_1, C_3 (based on π_1 and π_2) and output logic.

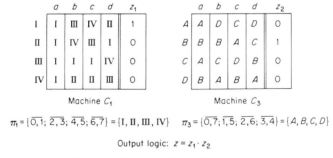

Machine C_1 Machine C_3

$\pi_1 = \{\overline{0,1}; \overline{2,3}; \overline{4,5}; \overline{6,7}\} = \{I, II, III, IV\}$ $\pi_3 = \{\overline{0,7}; \overline{1,5}; \overline{2,6}; \overline{3,4}\} = \{A, B, C, D\}$

Output logic: $z = z_1 \cdot z_2$

Fig. 4.9. Decomposition of machine C.

With this output, C_1 appears irreducible and one might not suspect that it could be replaced by machine C_2 (based on π_2) of Fig. 4.10. This replacement is possible because we could have chosen $\lambda(II) = 1$ for machine C_1, in which case the replacement would be state reduction.

If we look at the S.P. lattice for machine C (Fig. 4.11) we get a graphic picture of what has happened. Both π_1 and π_2 have identical interactions with π_3. The moral is that when confronted with such a choice, the larger partition should generally be chosen.

In lattice theory, those lattices that do not contain any sublattices isomorphic to the lattice in Fig. 4.11 are called modular lattices. Thus we see

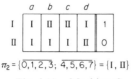

$$\pi_2 = \{\overline{0,1,2,3}; \overline{4,5,6,7}\} = \{\mathrm{I}, \mathrm{II}\}$$

Fig. 4.10. Machine C_2.

Fig. 4.11. S. P. lattice for machine C.

a relationship between a pure lattice theory concept and a pure machine theory concept. More striking correlations will be pointed out later.

Just because a component machine cannot be replaced by a reduced version does not mean that it cannot be replaced by some other machine with fewer states. An example of this is supplied by machine D of Fig. 4.12.

The nontrivial S.P. partitions for machine D are seen to be:

$$\pi_1 = \{\overline{1,2}; \overline{3,4}; \overline{5,6}\},$$
$$\pi_2 = \{\overline{1,4}; \overline{2,5}; \overline{3,6}\},$$
$$\pi_3 = \{\overline{1,6}; \overline{2,3}; \overline{4,5}\},$$
$$\pi_4 = \{\overline{1,3,5}; \overline{2,4,6}\}.$$

Since

$$\pi_1 + \pi_2 = I \quad \text{and} \quad \pi_1 \cdot \pi_2 = 0,$$

we can obtain a parallel decomposition from $\{\pi_1, \pi_2\}$ that cannot be factored. Such a realization is shown in Fig. 4.13. Neither of these components can

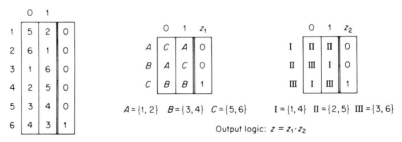

Fig. 4.12. Machine D.   **Fig. 4.13.** Machines D_1 and D_2.

be replaced by a reduced version (ignoring outputs) because they have no nontrivial S.P. partitions. Yet either D_1 or D_2 can be replaced by D_4 (corresponding to π_4) as shown in Fig. 4.14.

The partitions π_1, π_2, π_4 generate the lattice shown in Fig. 4.15. From

	0	1	z_3
α	α	β	0
β	β	α	1

$\alpha = \{1, 3, 5\}$ $\beta = \{2, 4, 6\}$

Fig. 4.14. Machine D_4.

Fig. 4.15. Sublattice of the S. P. lattice L_D.

this lattice, it is obvious that any two of the three partitions give a decomposition, as we have shown.

It is known from lattice theory that lattices which do not contain sublattices isomorphic to the lattices shown in Figs. 4.11 or 4.15 are distributive lattices. Recall the definition from Chapter 0:

L is distributive if and only if for all x, y, z in L,

$$x \cdot (y + z) = x \cdot y + x \cdot z$$

and

$$x + (y \cdot z) = (x + y) \cdot (x + z).$$

If the S.P. lattice is distributive, the last two kinds of component machine substitution cannot occur, and there ought to be a theorem to this effect. Indeed there is, and we state and prove it next. Its narrow hypothesis limits its usefulness to our general theory, but we regard the connection between lattice theory and machine theory as interesting in itself.

THEOREM 4.4. A parallel realization for a machine M based on S.P. partitions π_1 and π_2 is called *prime* if and only if $\pi_1 + \pi_2 = I$, i.e., if no machine can be "factored out." If the S.P. lattice for M is distributive and π is an S.P. partition, then there is at most one partition π_1 such that $\{\pi, \pi_1\}$ gives a prime parallel decomposition.

Proof. Suppose π_1 and π_2 are S.P. partitions such that $\pi \cdot \pi_i = 0$ and $\pi + \pi_i = I$ for $i = 1, 2$. Then

$$\pi_1 = \pi_1 \cdot I = \pi_1 \cdot (\pi_2 + \pi),$$

and applying the distributive laws

$$\pi_1 \cdot (\pi_2 + \pi) = \pi_1 \cdot \pi_2 + \pi_1 \cdot \pi = \pi_1 \cdot \pi_2 + 0 = \pi_1 \cdot \pi_2.$$

Therefore $\pi_1 = \pi_1 \cdot \pi_2$ and $\pi_1 \leqslant \pi_2$. Similarly, $\pi_2 \leqslant \pi_1$ and hence $\pi_1 = \pi_2$. ∎

4.4   PROPERTIES OF A TAIL MACHINE

So far, little has been said about the choice of the state partitions τ_i and those component machines that refine one partition into another. In this section we investigate some aspects of these machines, including the affect of restricting the input or carry information. To keep things simple, we speak in terms of simple serial decompositions of Moore machines, although the principles may be applied more generally.

Throughout this section we assume that, for the machine M under discussion, π is a partition with S.P. and τ is a partition such that $\pi \cdot \tau = 0$. The partitions π and τ are used to design a serial decomposition of M with a "tail machine" that takes carry information from the "front machine" and uses it to compute the block of τ. The carry information from the front machine is designated by $\rho \geqslant \pi$. Of course,

$$\rho \cdot \tau \geqslant m(\tau),$$

since the local tail machine is $M(\tau; \rho, \mu)$, where μ is some input partition satisfying $M_{I\text{-}S}(\mu) \leqslant \tau$. The tail machine is just the local tail machine with the "don't cares" filled.

First, let us get some insight into the structure of the local tail machine. Recalling the notation of Theorem 3.10, we state the first result.

THEOREM 4.5. If π has S.P. and $\rho = \pi$, then $\bar{\gamma}$ for $\gamma \geqslant \tau$ has S.P. for $M(\tau; \pi, \mu)$ if and only if

$$\pi \cdot \gamma \text{ has S.P. on } M.$$

Proof. If $\bar{\gamma}$ has S.P., then by Theorem 3.10,

$$\bar{\gamma} \geqslant \bar{m}(\bar{\gamma}) = \overline{m(\gamma \cdot \pi) + \tau}$$

or

$$\gamma \geqslant m(\gamma \cdot \pi) + \tau \geqslant m(\gamma \cdot \pi).$$

Since π has S.P.,

$$\pi \geqslant m(\pi) \geqslant m(\gamma \cdot \pi).$$

Multiplying the inequalities,

$$\gamma \cdot \pi \geqslant m(\gamma \cdot \pi)$$

and so $\gamma \cdot \pi$ has S.P. Conversely, if $\gamma \cdot \pi$ has S.P., then

$$m(\pi \cdot \gamma) \leqslant \pi \cdot \gamma$$

from which we obtain

$$m(\pi \cdot \gamma) + \tau \leqslant \pi \cdot \gamma + \tau \leqslant (\pi + \tau) \cdot (\gamma + \tau) = (\pi + \tau) \cdot \gamma \leqslant \gamma.$$

And so

$$\bar{\gamma} \geqslant \overline{m(\pi \cdot \gamma) + \tau} = \bar{m}(\bar{\gamma})$$

and $\bar{\gamma}$ has S.P. ∎

If $\rho > \pi$, then this result does not necessarily hold. To illustrate this and to show some interesting properties of "don't care" conditions in serial realizations we consider machine C shown in Fig. 4.8. It can be computed that this machine has three nontrivial partitions with S.P.,

$$\pi_1 = \{\overline{0,1}; \overline{2,3}; \overline{4,5}; \overline{6,7}\},$$
$$\pi_2 = \{\overline{0,1,2,3}; \overline{4,5,6,7}\},$$
$$\pi_3 = \{\overline{0,7}; \overline{1,5}; \overline{2,6}; \overline{3,4}\}.$$

To obtain a serial realization of this machine, we choose the determining partitions to be

$$\pi = \pi_1 \quad \text{and} \quad \tau = \pi_3.$$

Since in this case, τ has S.P., we know that the local tail machine can be operated independent of the front machine, or in other words, we may choose $\rho = I$. When we do this, we get the old parallel realization of Fig. 4.9 with (local) tail machine C_3. But

$$\gamma = \{\overline{A,D}; \overline{B,C}\} = \{\overline{0,7,3,4}; \overline{1,5,2,6}\}$$

does not have S.P. for C_3, even though

$$\gamma \cdot \pi = 0,$$

has S.P. for C. Thus, Theorem 4.5 does not extend.

Now let us choose $\rho = \pi = \pi_1$, even though we do not need all that information. Local machine $C_3' = M(\tau; \pi, 0)$ receives the state of C_1 as part of its input and is shown in Fig. 4.16. Here, γ has S.P. as predicted by the

	I				II				III				IV				z_2
	a	b	c	d	a	b	c	d	a	b	c	d	a	b	c	d	
A	A	D	C	D	–	–	–	–	–	–	–	–	A	D	C	D	1
B	B	B	A	C	–	–	–	–	B	B	A	C	–	–	–	–	0
C	–	–	–	–	A	C	D	B	–	–	–	–	A	C	D	B	0
D	–	–	–	–	B	A	B	A	B	A	B	A	–	–	–	–	0

Fig. 4.16. Local machine C_3'.

theorem. The difference between C_3 and C_3' is that C_3 is C_3' with "d.c." condition filled and equivalent inputs identified. In filling these conditions, the S.P. partition is destroyed.

In regard to reducing input information, we know that $M_{I\text{-}S}(\pi)$ is the least amount of information needed to run the front machine and $M_{I\text{-}S}(\tau)$ is the minimal amount needed to run the tail machine. Let us put all our knowledge together and derive a good serial decomposition of machine E of Fig. 4.17.

Computing the S.P. partitions for E, we find that there is only one that is nontrivial, namely

$$\pi = \{\overline{0,3}; \overline{1,2}; \overline{4,7}; \overline{5,6}\}.$$

Thus, we can realize machine E from two machines E_1 and E_2 connected in series. Machine E_1 will require four states and E_2 will require two states.

We therefore plan to assign two binary variables y_1 and y_2 to distinguish between the states of E_1 and a variable y_3 to distinguish between the two states of E_2. In the worst case, y_3 would depend on all three state variables and both inputs. However, we still have some freedom in assigning y_3 (we can use any two block partition that refines π to 0) and the input variables, so we continue to look for ways to reduce the dependence.

In order to reduce the input information to E_2, we start looking at I-S pairs. Soon we discover that

$$M_{I\text{-}S}(I) = \{\overline{0,1,4,5};\, \overline{2,3,6,7}\} = \pi_I$$

and

$$\pi \cdot \pi_I = 0$$

Therefore, we choose $\tau = \pi_I$, which means assigning y_3 according to π_I, and the state of the tail machine will now be independent of the external inputs.

	a	b	c	d	
0	1	0	4	5	0
1	7	3	3	7	0
2	4	0	0	4	1
3	2	3	7	6	1
4	6	2	6	7	0
5	5	5	1	0	0
6	6	6	2	3	1
7	5	1	5	4	1

Fig. 4.17. Machine E.

	y_1	y_2	y_3
0 →	0	0	0
1 →	1	0	0
2 →	1	0	1
3 →	0	0	1
4 →	1	1	0
5 →	0	1	0
6 →	0	1	1
7 →	1	1	1

Fig. 4.18. State assignment and information flow for a realization of machine E.

In order to reduce the number of carry variables from two to one, we must find a partition ρ which is suitable for defining y_1 and which contains enough information to compute τ. This means that we must look for a $\rho > \pi$ that has two four state blocks such that $(\rho \cdot \tau, \tau)$ is a partition pair. Potential ρ are created by identifying two pairs of blocks of π. It is easily seen that the partitions

$$\{\overline{0,3,1,2};\, \overline{4,7,5,6}\}$$

and

$$\{\overline{0,3,4,7};\, \overline{1,2,5,6}\}$$

obtained this way do not yield the required partition pair. On the other hand

$$\rho = \{\overline{0,3,5,6};\, \overline{1,2,4,7}\}$$

is such that $(\rho \cdot \tau, \tau)$ is a p.p. If we assign y_1 according to ρ, then the tail machine needs only y_1 as a carry. Finally, y_2 is assigned according to a partition τ_2 such that $\rho \cdot \tau_2 = \pi$. The resulting assignment and schematic realization is shown in Fig. 4.18. The reader is invited to work out the equations or machines if further verification is needed.

4.5   CLOCKS IN SEQUENTIAL MACHINES

We now apply the previously developed results to the study of clocks in sequential machines.

DEFINITION 4.8. A sequential machine M with only one input symbol is called an *autonomous sequential machine* or a *clock*.

The next result justifies the name "clock."

LEMMA 4.3. Let M be an autonomous sequential machine. Then, for any starting state s_1, its output sequence is ultimately periodic.

Proof. Let M have n states. And denote the sequence of states M goes through by

$$s_1, s_2, \ldots$$

Since there are only n distinct states, there is a state among the first $(n + 1)$ states in this sequence that occurs twice. Let s_k be the first state that occurs twice. Then, since there is only one input symbol, the state sequence must repeat after it enters state s_k. Therefore, its output sequence is an ultimately periodic sequence. ∎

We refer to the period of this sequence as the *period* of M.

LEMMA 4.4. A strongly connected autonomous machine M has a periodic output sequence.

Proof. Since M is a clock, the state sequence it goes through is ultimately periodic. Since it is strongly connected, the periodic part must include all states. Thus, the output sequence is periodic. ∎

The strongly connected clocks are characterized by their periods, and their S.P. lattices are easily described by our next result.

LEMMA 4.5. Let M be a strongly connected clock with period k and let K be the set of all integers that divide k. Then:
   (i) For each j in K, there is a unique j block partition π_j with S.P. on the states of M. Furthermore, there are no other S.P. partitions for M;
   (ii) $\pi_i \geqslant \pi_j$ for i and j in K if and only if i divides j;
   (iii) The machine M_{π_j} is a strongly connected clock with period j;
   (iv) The S.P. lattice, L_M, is distributive.

Proof. (i) Let $s_0, s_1, \ldots, s_{k-1}$ be the set of states in the order that the machine goes through them, starting with some given s_0. We define for j in K

$$s_{i_1} \equiv s_{i_2} \ (\pi_j) \qquad \text{if and only if} \qquad i_1 \equiv i_2 \ (\text{mod } j).$$

Since

$$\delta(s_i, x) = s_{i+1 \ (\text{mod } k)}$$

and since

$$k \equiv 0 \ (\text{mod } j),$$

π_j has S.P. on M. The partition π_j obviously has j blocks.

Now let π be any S.P. partition for M and let B_π be any block of π. Let j be the smallest number of inputs that carries some state of B_π into another. It is easily seen that j inputs must carry each state of B_π into another state of B_π and that furthermore, each block of π must have this same property and so,

$$s_{i_1} \equiv s_{i_2} \ (\pi) \qquad \text{if and only if} \qquad i_1 \equiv i_2 \ (\text{mod } j),$$

and since π has S.P.,

$$k \equiv 0 \ (\text{mod } j)$$

which proves that j is in K and $\pi = \pi_j$.

(ii) i divides j implies that

$$i_1 \equiv i_2 \ (\text{mod } j) \text{ implies } i_1 \equiv i_2 \ (\text{mod } i)$$

which implies from the definition that $\pi_i \geqslant \pi_j$. If $\pi_i \geqslant \pi_j$, the uniformity of π_i and π_j implies that each block of π_i contains an equal number of blocks of π_j which implies i divides j.

(iii) M_{π_j} is strongly connected because M is strongly connected, it has only one input by construction, and has j states because π_j has j blocks.

(iv) L_M is isomorphic to K under the ordering relation "i divides j." This lattice is a well-known distributive lattice. ∎

The clock is such a simple device that one is naturally led to the problem of obtaining decompositions which have a clock as one component. In the state behavior case, this is a very easy problem.

THEOREM 4.6. The state behavior of a machine M_1 can be realized by a serial decomposition of the form $M_1 \ominus M_2$ where M_1 is a clock if and only if M_1 is isomorphic to a machine $M(\pi; I, I)$ where π is an S.P. partition satisfying

$$\pi \geqslant m_{I\text{-}S}(I).$$

Proof. Since, by definition, the clock M_1 receives no inputs or carries, it must derive from a local machine of the form $M(\pi; I, I)$ for some π. Since $M(\pi; I, I)$ has no d.c. conditions, M_1 must be isomorphic to $M(\pi; I, I)$. Since $M(\pi; I, I)$ is a local machine, π must satisfy the equations

$$\pi \geqslant m(I \cdot \pi) = m(\pi) \qquad \text{and} \qquad \pi \geqslant m_{I\text{-}S}(I).$$

The first equation implies that π has S.P. and the theorem is proved. ∎

NOTATION. The partition $m_{I\text{-}s}(I)$ of the theorem appears often in various sections of the book so we abbreviate with the symbol π_I and write

$$\pi_I = m_{I\text{-}s}(I).$$

Intuitively, π_I is the partition on S of M that shows how much can be computed about the next state of M if we do not know which input symbol was used. Partition π_I is easily computed by making a block of all the states of M that are contained in the same row of the flow table, and then combining those blocks with common elements.

The clocks for state behavior realizations are thus determined by those S.P. partitions greater than π_I. These obviously form a sublattice of the S.P. lattice in the same manner that the output consistent partitions did in Section 2.5. One obvious choice of π for a clock is the smallest S.P. partition π greater than π_I, as this gives the clock with the most states. This smallest π can be characterized algebraically:

COROLLARY 4.6.1. Given an n-state machine M, there is a largest clock M_1 that can be used in a state behavior decomposition of M. This is the clock $M(\pi; I, I)$ where

$$\pi = \sum_0^n m^i(\pi_I).$$

This clock is the largest in the sense that any other such clock must be a homomorphic image of M_1.

Proof. The formula is a direct consequence of Corollary 3.1.5 and the discussion which follows it. The last statement holds because other clocks are determined by S.P. partitions larger than π. ∎

	0	1	z
0	5	4	0
1	4	4	1
2	1	0	0
3	0	1	1
4	7	7	0
5	6	7	1
6	3	2	0
7	3	3	1

Fig. 4.19. Machine F.

To illustrate these results, consider machine F of Fig. 4.19. A short computation shows that for this machine,

$$\pi_I = \{\overline{0,1}; \overline{2,3}; \overline{4,5}; \overline{6,7}\}.$$

Furthermore,

$$m(\pi_I) = \pi_I,$$

and thus we conclude that π_I has S.P. and the maximal clock of F is defined by π_I. It is seen that the machine

$$F_{\pi_I}$$

is strongly connected and thus is a clock of period four. We choose

$$\tau = \{\overline{0,2,4,6}; \overline{1,3,5,7}\}$$

to determine the second machine in the realization of F. Figure 4.20 shows an assignment determined by π_I and τ. This assignment leads to the following logical equations:

$$Y_1 = \bar{y}_2$$
$$Y_2 = y_1$$
$$Y_3 = \bar{y}_3\bar{x} + y_2y_3x + y_1y_2y_3 + y_1\bar{y}_2x.$$

The corresponding realization is shown in Fig. 4.21.

0 →	0	0	0
1 →	0	0	1
2 →	0	1	0
3 →	0	1	1
4 →	1	0	0
5 →	1	0	1
6 →	1	1	0
7 →	1	1	1

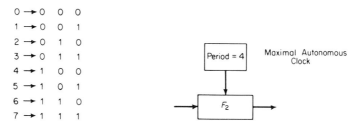

Fig. 4.20. State assignment for machine *F*.

Fig. 4.21. Realization of machine *F*.

Since F_{π_I} has period four, we know from Lemma 4.5 that there exists an S.P. partition on F_{π_I} and therefore an S.P. partition on F that defines a clock of period two. This partition is given by

$$\pi_2 = \{\overline{0,1,6,7}; \overline{2,3,5,4}\}.$$

An assignment using

$$\pi_I, \pi_2 \text{ and } \tau$$

is shown in Fig. 4.22. This leads to the equations

$$Y_1 = \bar{y}_1$$
$$Y_2 = y_1\bar{y}_2 + \bar{y}_1y_2$$
$$Y_3 = \bar{y}_3\bar{x} + y_1\bar{y}_2x + y_2y_3x + \bar{y}_1y_2y_3,$$

0 →	0	0	0
1 →	0	0	1
2 →	1	1	0
3 →	1	1	1
4 →	1	0	0
5 →	1	0	1
6 →	0	1	0
7 →	0	1	1

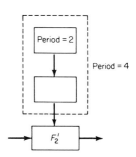

Fig. 4.22. Second assignment for machine *F*.

Fig. 4.23. Second realization of machine *F*.

The realization is shown in Fig. 4.23.

> **EXERCISE.** Show that machine G of Fig. 4.24 can be realized by a nontrivial parallel connection of a clock and an input dependent machine.

As a final example, we consider machine H of Fig. 4.25 which is not strongly connected. We compute that

$$\pi_I = \{\overline{1,3,14,16}; \overline{2,13}; \overline{4,15}; \overline{5,7,9,11}; \overline{6}; \overline{8,10,12}\}$$

and

$$\pi_1 = \sum_0^n m^i(\pi_I) = \{\overline{1,3,14,16}; \overline{2,4,13,15};$$
$$\overline{5,7,9,11}; \overline{6}; \overline{8,10,12}\}$$

$$= \{B_1; B_2; B_3; B_4; B_5\}.$$

The state diagram of machine H_{π_1} is shown in Fig. 4.26 and it is seen not to be strongly connected. There is, though, a partition on H_{π_1}

$$\pi_2 = \{\overline{B_1}; \overline{B_2}; \overline{B_3}; \overline{B_4,B_5}\}$$

that yields a strongly connected clock (see Fig. 4.27).

Clocks which are not strongly connected can only occur in state behavior realizations when the original machine is not strongly connected. However, as the next result states, the existence of a nonstrongly connected clock for a machine guarantees a suitable strongly connected clock with the same period.

	0	1	z
1	6	4	0
2	5	3	0
3	2	6	0
4	1	5	0
5	4	2	0
6	3	1	1

Fig. 4.24. Machine G.

	0	1	z
1	5	11	1
2	10	8	1
3	11	7	1
4	8	8	0
5	13	2	0
6	3	16	0
7	4	15	0
8	14	3	0
9	2	13	0
10	16	1	0
11	15	4	0
12	3	14	0
13	8	12	0
14	9	5	1
15	12	12	0
16	7	5	0

Fig. 4.25. Machine H.

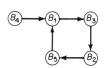

Fig. 4.26. Machine H_{π_1}.

Fig. 4.27. Machine H_{π_2}.

COROLLARY 4.6.2. If S.P. partition π on the states S of a machine M determines a clock $M(\pi; I, I)$ for M with period k, then there is an S.P. partition π' on S such that

$$\pi' \geqslant \pi$$

and $M(\pi'; I, I)$ is a strongly connected clock with period k.

Proof. Exercise. ∎

NOTES

The study of multiple decomposition of machines and the relation of these decompositions to the properties of the S.P. lattice of the machine were first investigated by one of the authors in [14] and some further results were obtained in [16]. Clocks in sequential machines were studied in [13].

5 STATE SPLITTING

5.1 STRUCTURE AND STATE REDUCTION

In the previous chapters we were concerned almost exclusively with state behavior realizations. This was done because this case is conceptually and computationally easier, and the use of many codes in a realization to represent one state increases the memory requirement if done very extensively. Nevertheless, these state behavior realizations do have limitations, and there are machines shown in this chapter for which the most economical realizations are not state behavior realizations. In this chapter we abandon the state behavior restriction and investigate techniques which allow one to enlarge machines for multiple coding. We call these "state-splitting" techniques.

First, we investigate the effects state reduction has on machine structure to underscore those aspects of reduced machines we want to overcome. Then we generalize the partition concept to over-lapping partitions or set systems and show that these methods can recover many of the realizations destroyed by state reduction. The set systems and their algebraic properties developed in this chapter are also used in the subsequent chapters to study feedback in machines and to relate the structure of a machine to its semigroup of state mappings.

In Sections 1.2 and 2.6, we considered state reduction as the process of obtaining the reduced machine. Here we use the term to mean the process of obtaining realizations by any sort of state identification.

First, we establish a special notation for the reduced realizations that can be obtained by machine homomorphism.

119

DEFINITION 5.1. Let π be an output consistent S.P. partition on the set of states of the machine

$$M = (S, I, O, \delta, \lambda).$$

Then we write

$$M_\pi^o = (\{B_\pi\}, I, O, \delta_\pi, \lambda_\pi)$$

where

$$\delta_\pi(B_\pi, x) = B_\pi' \qquad \text{if and only if } \delta(B_\pi, x) \subseteq B_\pi'$$

and

$$\lambda_\pi(B_\pi, x) = \lambda(s, x) \qquad \text{for any (all) } s \text{ in } B_\pi.$$

Machine M_π^o is just the image machine M_π of Definition 2.2 with an output added. This natural extension of M_π is only possible when π is output consistent. In the case $\pi = \pi_R$, $M_{\pi_R}^o$ is the reduced machine equivalent to M cited in Theorem 2.6.

These machines M_π^o are now used to generalize the concept of a state behavior realization.

DEFINITION 5.2. Machine M' is a *reduced realization* of machine M if and only if, for some output consistent S.P. partition π on the set of states S of M, M' realizes the state behavior of M_π^o.

Note that any state behavior realization of M is trivially a reduced realization by letting $\pi = 0$. On the other hand, for all other partitions, this definition admits realizations by (sub) machines which have fewer states than M. Thus, the reduced realization is indeed a generalization of the state behavior realization. In terms of assignment mappings, the reduced realizations are characterized by the following elementary result.

THEOREM 5.1. Machine M' is a reduced realization of machine M if and only if M' realizes M with an assignment (α, ι, ζ) such that α maps each state of M onto a single state of M'.

Proof. Exercise. ∎

Comparing Theorem 5.1 with Definition 1.16, one sees that the only difference between a state behavior realization and a reduced realization is that the α mapping for a reduced realization need not be one-to-one.

The primary objective of the remainder of this section is to demonstrate that the structure of all reduced realizations of a machine M can be obtained directly from the structure of M itself. This leads to the conclusion that, in reducing a machine before analyzing its structure, one can only obscure some potential reduced dependence realization. Conversely, we see that it might even be advantageous to "unreduce" or "split" a machine in order to obtain a best realization.

This loss of structure can be dramatically illustrated for the S.P. lattices, so we consider this case first. To do this, we recall some notation. If π is a partition on a set S and τ is a partition greater or equal to π, then τ can be considered as a partition $\bar{\tau}$ on the set of blocks of π and

$$\tau \longrightarrow \bar{\tau}$$

is a one-to-one mapping of

$$\{\tau \mid \tau \geqslant \pi\} \text{ into } \{\bar{\tau} \mid \bar{\tau} \text{ partition on } \{B_\pi\}\}.$$

Thus, $\tau \longrightarrow \bar{\tau}$ is the mapping of $\tau \geqslant \pi$ into its quotient with respect to π.

THEOREM 5.2. Let π be an output consistent S.P. partition on the set of states of machine M. Then the S.P. lattice of M_π^0 is given by

$$L_{M_\pi^0} = \{\bar{\tau} \mid \tau \text{ has S.P. on } M \text{ and } \tau \geqslant \pi\}.$$

Proof. (A more complete proof is given in the next theorem). If τ has S.P. on M, and $\tau \geqslant \pi$, then blocks of $\bar{\tau}$ obviously behave as the corresponding blocks of τ and $\bar{\tau}$ has S.P. on M_π. Conversely, if $\bar{\tau}$ has S.P. on M_π, then for s, t in S

$$s \equiv t\,(\bar{\tau}) \qquad \text{if and only if } B_\pi(s) \equiv B_\pi(t)\,(\bar{\tau})$$

and therefore

$$B_\pi[\delta(s, x)] \equiv B_\pi[\delta(t, x)]\,(\bar{\tau}).$$

But then

$$\delta(s, x) \equiv \delta(t, x)\,(\tau)$$

and τ has S.P. on M. Note that this argument applies equally well to any L_{M_π}, even when π is not output consistent. ∎

EXAMPLE. Consider machine A together with its S.P. lattice as shown in Fig. 5.1. We see that π_3 is the only nontrivial output consistent S.P. partition and hence $\pi_R = \pi_3$. A glance at the lattice tells us that the partitions for $A_{\pi_3}^0$ are $\bar{\pi}_3$, $\bar{\pi}_4$, $\bar{\pi}_6$, and $\bar{I}$ as shown in Fig. 5.2.

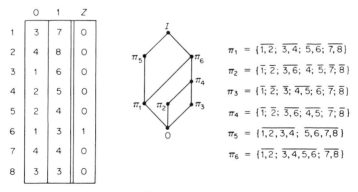

	0	1	Z
1	3	7	0
2	4	8	0
3	1	6	0
4	2	5	0
5	2	4	0
6	1	3	1
7	4	4	0
8	3	3	0

$\pi_1 = \{\overline{1,2};\ \overline{3,4};\ \overline{5,6};\ \overline{7,8}\}$

$\pi_2 = \{\overline{1};\ \overline{2};\ \overline{3,6};\ \overline{4};\ \overline{5};\ \overline{7};\ \overline{8}\}$

$\pi_3 = \{\overline{1};\ \overline{2};\ \overline{3};\ \overline{4,5};\ \overline{6};\ \overline{7};\ \overline{8}\}$

$\pi_4 = \{\overline{1};\ \overline{2};\ \overline{3,6};\ \overline{4,5};\ \overline{7};\ \overline{8}\}$

$\pi_5 = \{\overline{1,2,3,4};\ \overline{5,6,7,8}\}$

$\pi_6 = \{\overline{1,2};\ \overline{3,4,5,6};\ \overline{7,8}\}$

Fig. 5.1. Machine A and S. P. lattice L_A.

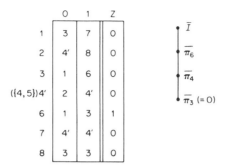

	0	1	Z
1	3	7	0
2	4'	8	0
3	1	6	0
({4,5})4'	2	4'	0
6	1	3	1
7	4'	4'	0
8	3	3	0

Fig. 5.2. Machine A_{π_3} and S. P. lattice.

It is interesting to compare the usefulness of the two structures. Since $\pi_5 > \pi_1 > 0$, we know that there is a three-machine serial realization of A based on π_5, π_1, and 0. The uniformity of these blocks makes the realization especially suitable for binary assignments since each component machine needs but two states. Such a realization is shown in Fig. 5.3 where

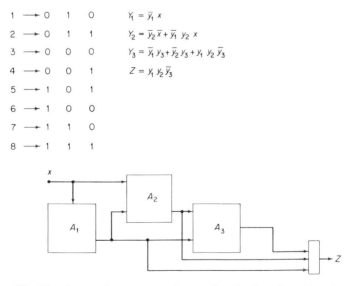

$$Y_1 = \bar{y}_1 \, x$$
$$Y_2 = \bar{y}_2 \bar{x} + \bar{y}_1 \, y_2 \, x$$
$$Y_3 = \bar{y}_1 \, y_3 + \bar{y}_2 \, y_3 + y_1 \, y_2 \, \bar{y}_3$$
$$Z = y_1 \, y_2 \, \bar{y}_3$$

Fig. 5.3. State assignment, equations, and realization of machine A.

the assignment, Boolean equations, and schematic diagrams are given. The state behavior equations require nineteen diodes. The partitions on $A_{\pi_3}^0$, however, do not lend themselves to realizations because their irregular makeup requires four binary variables to exploit. The best known binary assignment for machine $A_{\pi_3}^0$ was found by an anonymous referee and requires twenty-two diodes using shared logic. Thus, we see that even the most useful structure may be lost under state reduction.

The next two theorems give a complete description of the effect of state reduction on the various information lattices. This is followed by an exact statement of our claim that the reduced dependence decompositions using reduced realizations can be detected from the unreduced structure. Finally, we give some special conditions under which state reduction is safe. The main point, however, has already been illustrated once by the previous theorem and example. Consequently, *the remainder of this section can be omitted on first reading.*

THEOREM 5.3. Let π be an output consistent S.P. partition on the states of machine M and let

$$L'_M = \{\tau \in L_M \mid \tau \geqslant \pi\},$$
$$P'_M = \{(\tau, \tau') \in P_M \mid \tau \geqslant \pi \text{ and } \tau' \geqslant \pi\},$$
$$Q'_M = \{(\tau, \tau') \in Q_M \mid \tau = M(\tau' + \pi)\}.$$

Then the mappings

$$h_1 = \tau \longrightarrow \bar{\tau} : L'_M \longrightarrow L_{M_\pi},$$
$$h_2 = (\tau, \tau') \longrightarrow (\bar{\tau}, \bar{\tau}') : P'_M \longrightarrow P_{M_\pi},$$
$$h_3 = (\tau, \tau') \longrightarrow (\bar{\tau}, \overline{\tau' + \pi}) : Q'_M \longrightarrow Q_{M_\pi}$$

are lattice isomorphisms.

Proof. Because $\tau \longrightarrow \bar{\tau}$ is a one-to-one mapping which preserves the lattice operations, we need only show that the h_i map onto the sets that we claim they are.

Let m be the operator for M and let $\bar{m}$ be the operator for M_π. Because M_π^o is the same as $M(\pi; 0, I)$ except for outputs, we know from Corollary 3.10. that

$$\bar{m}(\bar{\tau}) = \overline{m(\tau) + \pi} \qquad \text{for } \tau \geqslant \pi.$$

Now τ in L'_M implies

$$\tau \geqslant m(\tau)$$

which implies

$$\tau + \pi \geqslant m(\tau) + \pi$$

which implies because $\tau \geqslant \pi$ that

$$\tau \geqslant m(\tau) + \pi$$

which implies

$$\bar{\tau} \geqslant \overline{m(\tau) + \pi} = \bar{m}(\bar{\tau})$$

which implies $\bar{\tau} \in L_{M_\pi}$ and so h_1 is indeed a mapping into L_{M_π}. Conversely, $\bar{\tau} \in L_{M_\pi}$ implies

$$\bar{\tau} \geqslant \bar{m}(\bar{\tau}) = \overline{m(\tau) + \pi}$$

which implies because $\pi \geqslant m(\pi)$

$$\tau \geqslant m(\tau) + \pi \geqslant m(\tau) + m(\pi) = m(\tau + \pi) = m(\tau)$$

which implies that h_1 is onto.

The reasoning for h_2 is the same except that we have τ' on the left-hand side of the inequalities (i.e., (τ, τ') in P_M' implies $\tau' \geqslant m(\tau)$, etc.)

To prove that h_3 does map into $Q_{M\pi}$, we again appeal to Corollary 3.10.1 and obtain the following equations for (τ, τ') in Q_M:

$$\bar{m}(\bar{\tau}) = \overline{m(\tau) + \pi} = \overline{\tau' + \pi} = \bar{\tau}';$$

$$\bar{M}(\overline{\tau' + \pi}) = \overline{M(\tau' + \pi)} = \bar{\tau}.$$

This shows that $(\bar{\tau}, \overline{\tau' + \pi})$ is in $Q_{M\pi}$. Given any (τ, τ') in $Q_{M\pi}$,

$$\bar{\tau} = \bar{M}(\bar{\tau}') = \overline{M(\tau')}$$

and so $\tau = M(\tau')$. Furthermore,

$$\bar{\tau}' = \bar{m}(\bar{\tau}) = \overline{m(\tau) + \pi}$$

and so $\tau' = m(\tau) + \pi$. By substitution, we have $\tau = M(\tau') = M(m(\tau) + \pi)$ and so $(\tau, m(\tau))$ is in Q_M'. Since h_3 maps this pair onto $(\bar{\tau}, \bar{\tau}')$, h_3 is onto. ∎

COROLLARY 5.3.1. If the partition π in Theorem 5.3 satisfies the equation

$$\pi = m(\pi),$$

then

$$Q_M' = \{(\tau, \tau') \in Q_M \mid \tau \geqslant \pi \text{ and } \tau' \geqslant \pi\}$$

and

$$h_3: Q_M' \longrightarrow Q_{M\pi} = (\tau, \tau') \longrightarrow (\bar{\tau}, \bar{\tau}').$$

Proof. $\tau = M(\tau' + \pi)$ implies $\tau \geqslant M(\pi) \geqslant \pi$ which implies

$$\tau' = m(\tau) \geqslant m(\pi) = \pi.$$

This justifies the alternate formulation of Q_M' for this case. It also follows that $\tau' = \tau' + \pi$ and the simplified formulation of h_3 is justified. ∎

The advantage of analyzing M is now evident. The structure of M reveals all the structure of M_π^o. The disadvantage is that the analysis of M must involve more bookkeeping.

EXAMPLE. Consider machine B and its Mm lattice Q_B as shown in Fig. 5.4. Looking for all Mm pairs (π, π') such that $\pi \geqslant \pi'$, we soon discover that

$$I \geqslant I, \quad \pi_4 \geqslant \pi_4', \quad \text{and} \quad 0 \geqslant 0.$$

The S.P. partitions are thus seen to be

$$I, \pi_4, \pi_4', \text{ and } 0.$$

Checking the outputs, we see that π_4, π_4', and 0 are all output consistent and thus

$$\pi_R = \pi_4.$$

	00	01	11	10	Z
1	5	2	1	4	0
2	5	1	2	4	0
3	1	5	4	3	1
4	2	5	4	3	1
5	4	3	1	5	1

$$(\pi_1, \pi_1') = (\{\overline{1,4};\ \overline{2};\ \overline{3};\ \overline{5}\},\ \{\overline{1,3,4};\ \overline{2,5}\})$$

$$(\pi_2, \pi_2') = (\{\overline{1,5};\ \overline{2};\ \overline{3};\ \overline{4}\},\ \{\overline{1};\ \overline{2,3};\ \overline{4,5}\})$$

$$(\pi_3, \pi_3') = (\{\overline{1,2,5};\ \overline{3,4}\},\ \{\overline{1,2,3};\ \overline{4,5}\})$$

$$(\pi_4, \pi_4') = (\{\overline{1,2};\ \overline{3,4};\overline{5}\},\ \{\overline{1,2};\ \overline{3};\ \overline{4};\ \overline{5}\})$$

$$(\pi_5, \pi_5') = (\{\overline{1,2};\ \overline{3,4,5}\},\ \{\overline{1,2,4};\ \overline{3,5}\})$$

$$(\pi_6, \pi_6') = (\{\overline{1};\ \overline{2};\ \overline{3,5};\overline{4}\},\ \{\overline{1,4};\ \overline{2};\ \overline{3,5}\})$$

$$(\pi_7, \pi_7') = (\{\overline{1};\overline{2,3};\ \overline{4};\ \overline{5}\},\ \{\overline{1,5};\ \overline{2,3,4}\})$$

Fig. 5.4. Machine B and lattice Q_B.

Machine $B_{\pi_R}^o$ and Mm lattice are shown in Fig. 5.5. Note that (π_3, π_3') is not in Q_B' [because $\pi_3 \neq M(\pi_3' + \pi_R)$] even though it is above (π_4, π_4')

	00	01	11	10	Z
$\{1,2\} = 1'$	5	1'	1'	3'	0
$\{3,4\} = 3'$	1'	5	3'	3'	1
5	3'	3'	1'	5	1

$\bullet (\overline{I}, \overline{I})$

$\bullet (\overline{\pi_4}, \overline{\pi_4})$

Fig. 5.5. Machine B_{π_4} and lattice $Q_{B_{\pi_4}}$.

in Q_B. The partition $\overline{\pi_3' + \pi_R}$ is necessarily an $\bar{m}$ partition [namely, $\bar{m}(\bar{\pi}_3)$], but it belongs to an $\bar{M}$ partition larger than $\bar{\pi}_3$ (namely $\bar{I}$).

Suppose we wish to find the $Q_{B\pi}^o$ for

$$\pi = \pi_4'.$$

Since $m(\pi_4') = \pi_4'$, Corollary 5.3.1 applies, and we know the $\overline{Mm}$ pairs must be:

$$(\bar{I}, \bar{I}), (\bar{\pi}_3, \bar{\pi}_3'), (\bar{\pi}_5, \bar{\pi}_5'), (\bar{\pi}_4, \bar{\pi}_4').$$

Not only is the *S-S* information flow for M_π^o easily determined from the *S-S* flow for M; but the *I-S*, *S-O*, and *I-O* information is also available. The next result says this formally.

THEOREM 5.4. Given a machine $M = (S, I, O, \delta, \beta)$ and output consistent S.P. partition π, let τ, μ, ω represent partitions on S, I, O respectively and define:

$$h_1 : (\mu, \tau) \longrightarrow (\mu, \bar{\tau}) \text{ for } \tau \geqslant \pi ;$$

$$h_2 : (\mu, \tau) \longrightarrow (\mu, \overline{\tau + \pi}) \text{ for } \mu = M_{I\text{-}S}(\tau + \pi);$$

$$h_3 : (\tau, \omega) \longrightarrow (\bar{\tau}, \omega) \text{ for } \tau \geqslant \pi .$$

Then the following statements are true.

    (i) h_1 is a lattice isomorphism between a sublattice of the *I-S* lattice for M and the *I-S* lattice for M_π^o.

    (ii) h_2 is a lattice isomorphism between a sublattice of the $Mm_{I\text{-}S}$ lattice for M and the $Mm_{I\text{-}S}$ lattice for M_π^o.

    (iii) h_3 is a lattice isomorphism between a sublattice of the *S-O* lattice for M and the *S-O* lattice for M_π^o.

    (iv) h_3 is a lattice isomorphism between the $Mm_{S\text{-}o}$ lattice for M and the $Mm_{S\text{-}o}$ lattice for M_π^o.

    (v) The *I-O* lattices for M and M_π^o are identical.

Proof. The proof is so similar to the proof of Theorem 5.3 that we leave it as an exercise. Note that (iv) says that the entire $Mm_{S\text{-}o}$ lattice for M is mapped onto the lattice for M_π^o. This is because π is output consistent which is equivalent to the equation:

$$\pi \leqslant M_{S\text{-}o}(0);$$

and so all $M_{S\text{-}o}$ partitions are greater than π. ∎

As further exercise, the reader may prove this analogy to Corollary 5.3.1, as follows.

COROLLARY 5.4.1. If in Theorem 5.4, π is an $m_{I\text{-}S}$ partition, then h_2 is h_1 restricted to $Mm_{I\text{-}S}$ pairs.

We have seen that the information lattices for M leads to an easy calculation of the lattices for the various M_π^o. This relationship is in fact so direct that one does not have to calculate these lattices at all to look for a good reduced realization. One just has to look for enough desirable partitions and information flow inequalities to compute the output. Stated more formally:

THEOREM 5.5. Suppose there is a machine M and a set of partitions which satisfies all the conditions of Theorem 3.5 except that condition

$$\prod \tau_i = 0$$

is replaced by
$$\prod \tau_i \leqslant M_{S-O}(0);$$
then π,
$$\pi = \prod \tau_i,$$
has S.P., all the conditions of Theorem 3.5 hold with τ_i and $\rho_{i,j}$, replaced by $\bar{\tau}_i$ and $\bar{\rho}_{i,j}$ (bar with respect to π) and this leads to a corresponding state behavior realization of M_π^ϱ which is also a reduced realization of M.

Proof. Intuitively, this theorem is obvious, one just writes the equations corresponding to the information flow inequalities and the resulting circuit cannot help but give the desired reduced realization. Proceeding formally, and using conditions (i) and (iii) of Theorem 3.5, we see that

$$\pi = \prod_i \tau_i \leqslant \prod_i \tau_i (\prod_j \rho_{j,i}) \leqslant \prod_i M(\tau_i) = M(\prod_i \tau_i) = M(\pi)$$

and so π has S.P. Since the τ_i are greater than π, condition (iii) also tells us that the $\rho_{i,j}$ are larger than π and so the quotients $\bar{\tau}_i$ and $\bar{\rho}_{i,j}$ may be formed. Of course,

$$\prod_i \bar{\tau}_i = \overline{\prod_i \tau_i} = \bar{\pi} = \text{zero quotient partition,}$$

which is just condition (iv). Inequalities (i) and (ii) are shown to be preserved under the quotient operation by judicious application of Theorems 5.3 and 5.4. Theorem 3.5 now tells us that the state behavior of M_π^ϱ is realized, and thus we have a reduced realization of M. ∎

EXAMPLE. We wish to find a realization of machine B of Fig. 5.4. If some variable is to depend on only one state variable, we must use Mm pair (π_3, π_3') since $\{\overline{1,2,5}; \overline{3,4}\}$ is the only two block M partition. Therefore, we choose

$$\tau_1 = \{\overline{1,2,3}; \overline{4,5}\}$$
$$\tau_2 = \{\overline{1,2,5}; \overline{3,4}\}$$

and we get information flow inequality

$$\tau_2 \leqslant M(\tau_1).$$
We observe that
$$\tau_1 \cdot \tau_2 \leqslant M(\tau_1)$$

and so we may write equations for the corresponding variables y_1 and y_2 using assignment $1 = 2 = 00$, $3 = 01$, $4 = 11$, $5 = 10$:

$$Y_1 = y_2 x_2 + \bar{y}_2 \bar{x}_2$$
$$Y_2 = x_1 y_2 + y_1 \bar{y}_2 \bar{x}_1 + \bar{y}_1 x_1 \bar{x}_2.$$

Because $\tau_1 \cdot \tau_2$ is output consistent, we can express the output as a function of y_1 and y_2, namely,

$$z = y_1 + y_2.$$

Thus we have realized B in spite of the fact that

$$\tau_1 \cdot \tau_2 = \{\overline{1, 2}; \overline{3}; \overline{4}; \overline{5}\} > 0.$$

We have actually realized the state behavior of B_π^o where $\pi = \pi_4'$, even though we made no conscious effort to do so. Since no further dependence reduction is possible for B, none further is possible for B_π^o because its structure is contained in the structure of B. The overall result is that we did not need to look at the structure of B_π^o at all.

We have seen now how state reduction destroys structure and how the analysis of a big machine automatically takes in an analysis of its reduced forms. If, however, one is only interested in parallel realizations, there is a condition under which state reduction is safe.

THEOREM 5.6. Suppose that machine M has a distributive S.P. lattice L_M. Then for any parallel state behavior realization of M with component machines $\{M_i\}$, there exists a corresponding parallel state behavior realization of $M_{\pi_R}^o$ with component machines $\{M_i'\}$ such that M_i' is a reduced form of M_i.

Proof. We know from Chapter 4 that each M_i is some M_{π_i} for some π_i in L_M. Let

$$M_i' = M'_{\overline{\pi_i + \pi_R}}.$$

Using equation

$$\prod \pi_i = 0,$$

and the distributive law, we get

$$\prod \overline{\pi_i + \pi_R} = \overline{(\prod \pi_i) + \pi_R} = \overline{\pi_R} = \text{zero quotient partition},$$

so the M_i' can be used in a parallel decomposition of $M_{\pi_R}^o$. Of course, M_i' is just M_i reduced by $\overline{\pi_i + \pi_R}$ (where the quotient is with respect to π_i). ∎

EXAMPLE. The principles of the last proof apply whenever the partitions in question distribute and do not depend on the fact that the whole lattice L_M distributes. Machine C of Fig. 5.6 has many S.P. partitions, including:

$$\pi_1 = \{\overline{1,6}; \overline{2,5}; \overline{3,8}; \overline{4,7}\},$$

$$\pi_2 = \{\overline{1,2,3,4}; \overline{5,6,7,8}\},$$

$$\pi_3 = \{\overline{1,3,5,7}; \overline{2,4,6,8}\},$$

$$\pi_R = \{\overline{1,2}; \overline{3}; \overline{4}; \overline{5,6}; \overline{7}; \overline{8}\}.$$

Notice that C can be realized by C_{π_1} operating in parallel with either C_{π_2} or C_{π_3}. Notice also that

$$(\pi_1 + \pi_R) \cdot (\pi_2 + \pi_R) = \pi_1 \cdot \pi_2 + \pi_R = \pi_R$$

and so $C_{\pi_R}^o$ may be realized by $C_{\pi_1 + \pi_R}$ and $C_{\pi_2 + \pi_R}$ operating in parallel. But

	x_1	x_2	x_3	x_4	x_5	Z
1	2	5	5	1	8	0
2	1	6	6	1	8	0
3	4	7	5	3	6	0
4	3	8	6	1	6	1
5	6	1	1	1	8	1
6	5	2	2	1	8	1
7	8	3	1	1	6	0
8	7	4	2	3	6	1

Fig. 5.6. Machine C.

$$(\pi_1 + \pi_R)\cdot(\pi_3 + \pi_R) > \pi_1\cdot\pi_3 + \pi_R$$

and so the parallel connection of $C_{\pi_1+\pi_R}$ and $C_{\pi_3+\pi_R}$ does not realize $C^o_{\pi_R}$. The distributivity of these partitions used is now easily seen as a necessary and sufficient condition for component-wise reduction.

	0	1	Z
1	4	2	0
2	3	2	1
3	2	3	1
4	1	4	0

EXAMPLE. Consider machine D of Fig. 5.7. It has two nontrivial S.P. partitions, namely;

$$\pi = \{\overline{1,2};\,\overline{3,4}\},$$
$$\pi_R = \{\overline{1};\,\overline{2,3};\,\overline{4}\}.$$

Fig. 5.7. Machine D.

Lattice L_D is seen to be distributive. The state behavior of D is realized by a parallel connection of M_π and M_{π_R}. Applying our result, we know that the state behavior of $D^o_{\pi_R}$ is realized by

$$D_{\pi_R} = D_{\pi_R+\pi_R} \qquad \text{and}$$
$$D_I = D_{\pi_R+\pi}$$

in parallel. But D_I is trivial and can be discarded whereas D_{π_R} is actually the desired machine. Thus, a nontrivial decomposition is mapped into a trivial one. This is no great loss, however, as the trivial one is better than the original, and discarding the trivial component only makes it better. The point is that the theorem does not guarantee that the reduced decomposition cannot be further simplified. Notice also that the distributivity of L_D does not guarantee against destroying serial decompositions. Take the realization of D obtained from π and

$$\tau = \{\overline{1,4};\,\overline{2,3}\}.$$

This realization is destroyed under state reduction because τ, not constrained by the distributivity of L_D (τ is not in L_D) does not distribute; that is,

$$(\pi + \pi_R)\cdot(\tau + \pi_R) > \pi\cdot\tau + \pi_R = \pi_R.$$

5.2 THE STATE-SPLITTING PROBLEM

We saw in the last section that state behavior realizations of a reduced machine are not always "best," both from the point of view of having rich structure and from the point of view of requiring the fewest diodes. The state-splitting problem is just this: *Given a reduced machine M, how does one find the larger (unreduced) machine M' whose state behavior realization is the "best" possible realization of M?* Machine M' may generally have several states equivalent to one state of M, which suggests that this state has been "split."

Of course, the difficulty of this problem depends on what we mean by "best." If we mean "fewest diodes," then the state-splitting problem becomes the state assignment problem which probably never will be perfectly solved in a practical sense. On the other hand, if by "best," we mean a state behavior realization with the most nonredundant parallel components, it is easily solved by inspecting the S.P. lattice and applying the techniques of the previous chapter.

In general, the more restrictive we interpret the word "best," the easier the solution becomes and the less practical significance the solution has. The purpose of this section is to compare some limitations one might place on our problems.

Let us consider the problem of finding serial decompositions of a machine M into two machines M_1 and M_2. If we restrict ourselves to state behavior realizations whose component machines have no unused states or inputs, we can find all possible decompositions by choosing all combinations of π with S.P. and τ such that $\pi \cdot \tau = 0$, and by filling d.c. conditions of $M(\tau; \pi, 0)$ in all possible ways.

We know, however, that a reduced machine may have a nice serial decomposition which is not a state behavior realization. In the last example for instance, we saw that the three-state machine $D^o_{\pi_R}$ could be realized by a two-state front machine and a two-state tail machine, but this was not a state behavior realization. Somehow, we would like to relax the state behavior condition to include such decompositions; but at the same time, we still want to exclude from consideration a host of decompositions which are obviously unsatisfactory. Ideally, this should be done by forbidding component machines which are in some sense too "big" or "complex."

Fig. 5.8. Machine *E*.

Now consider machine E of Fig. 5.8. This machine is sometimes called a "flip-flop." At first glance one might think of this machine as indecomposable. Yet this machine has an infinite number of serial decompositions which one would hesitate to call "unac-

	0	1
s_1	s_2	s_3
s_2	s_3	s_1
s_3	s_1	s_2

E_3

	s_1	s_2	s_3
t_1	t_2	t_1	t_2
t_2	t_3	t_3	t_2
t_3	t_3	t_1	t_1

E_3'

$Z=0$	$Z=1$	
$s_1 t_1$	$s_1 t_2$	$s_1 t_3$
$s_2 t_2$	$s_2 t_1$	$s_2 t_3$
$s_3 t_3$	$s_3 t_1$	$s_3 t_2$

Output logic

Fig. 5.9. Serial realization of machine E.

ceptable," except on the grounds that the components have too many states. One of these decompositions is shown in Fig. 5.9. Observe that neither E_3 or E_3' alone realize E. Secondly, all the inputs and states to E_3 and E_3' occur repeatedly under some input sequence so that the component machines cannot be replaced by submachines. And thirdly, E_3 and E_3' have no non-trivial S.P. partitions and thus they cannot be replaced by reduced forms, even allowing for renaming of outputs. The only satisfactory objection one can raise against this realization is that E_3 and E_3' each have three states, which is more than machine E which they realize. We can in fact define an infinity of such decompositions as follows. For any prime number p, we define

$$E_p = (S_1, I_1, O_1, \delta_1, \lambda_1) \text{ and}$$
$$E_p' = (S_2, I_2, O_2, \delta_2, \lambda_2)$$

where

$$S_1 = O_1 = S_2 = I_2 = O_2 = \{0, 1, \ldots, p-1\};$$
$$I_1 = \{0, 1\};$$
$$\delta_1(i, 0) = i + 1 \pmod{p},$$
$$\delta_1(i, 1) = i - 1 \pmod{p};$$
$$\delta_2(j, i) = i + 1 \pmod{p} \text{ if } i = j,$$
$$\delta_2(j, i) = i - 1 \pmod{p} \text{ if } i \neq j;$$
$$\lambda_1(i) = i;$$
$$\lambda_2(j) = j.$$

Let the output logic for $E_p \ominus E_p'$ be given by

$$Z(i, j) = 0 \text{ if } i = j,$$
$$Z(i, j) = 1 \text{ if } i \neq j.$$

The reader may verify that $E_p \ominus E_p'$ realizes E and that the same remarks we made for E_3 and E_3' apply equally well to E_p and E_p'.

We have seen that a machine can have an infinite number of decompositions whose components are all distinct and cannot be used to replace one another. The concepts of submachine, equivalence, and realization therefore are not enough to bound the number of realizations. Therefore, any time a finite approach is taken to the state-splitting problem, some essentially different realizations are bound to be overlooked. Some limitation must therefore be inherent in any finite approach, just as the partition approach gives only the state behavior realizations. The trick then is not to try for all realizations but to analyze a class that includes those realizations we might consider practical.

5.3 SET SYSTEMS

The intuitive principle behind serial decompositions is that some "information" about the machine can be calculated from itself. So far, we have approximated the vague concept of information by the precise concept of a partition; i.e.,

$$\text{information} \approx \text{partition}.$$

Because one always deals with finite sets of partitions, the partition analysis of a machine is conveniently bounded and gives precisely the state behavior decompositions. In this section, we introduce a new and more general information concept that gives access to other decompositions but still leads to finite lattices and bounded calculations.

Fig. 5.10.   Machine F.

First, let us consider state machine F of Fig. 5.10 and the serial decomposition of F shown in Fig. 5.11. This is not a state behavior realization, but this serial connection of F_1 and F_2 is certainly

	0	1
s	s	t
t	s	t

F_1

	Os	Ot	1s	1t
s'	t'	s'	s'	t'
t'	s'	s'	s'	s'

F_2

$\alpha(1) = \{(s, s')\}$
$\alpha(2) = \{(t, t'), (s, t')\}$
$\alpha(3) = \{(t, s')\}$

Fig. 5.11.   Decomposition of machine F.

an acceptable decomposition of three-state machine F. Let us look at the front machine F and see what "information" about the state of F is given by the states of F_1. We see that if F_1 is in state s, then F may be in states 1 or 2, and if F_1 is in state t, then F may be in states 2 or 3. Symbolically, we write

$$s \longleftrightarrow \{1, 2\},$$

$$t \longleftrightarrow \{2, 3\}.$$

We might say that the information is given by the "partition"

$$\phi = \{\overline{1,2}; \overline{2,3}\},$$

except that this really is not a partition, because state 2 belongs to two blocks. This suggests the following generalization of a partition.

DEFINITION 5.3. A collection of subsets

$$\phi = \{B_i\},$$

of S is called a *set system* on S if and only if

(i) $\cup B_i = S$;

(ii) $B_i \subseteq B_j$ implies $i = j$.

Condition (ii) ensures that finite sets have only a finite number of set systems and enables us to order these set systems.

DEFINITION 5.4. If ϕ and ψ are set systems on a set S, we write

$$\phi \geqslant \psi$$

if and only if for each B_ψ in ψ, there exists a B_ϕ in ϕ such that

$$B_\phi \supseteq B_\psi.$$

EXAMPLES.

$$\{\overline{1,2,3}; \overline{2,3,4}\} \geqslant \{\overline{1,2}; \overline{2,3}; \overline{3,4}\},$$

$$\{\overline{1,2,3}; \overline{1,3,4}; \overline{2,4}\} \geqslant \{\overline{1,2}; \overline{3,4}\}.$$

Note that, unlike the partition case, the smaller set system may have fewer blocks.

Next we define an operation which is used in set system computations.

DEFINITION 5.5. Let $\{S_i\}$ be an arbitrary collection of subsets of set S. Then we define

Max $\{S_i\} = \{B \subseteq S \mid S_i = B$ for some i and $S_j \supseteq B$ implies $S_j = B\}$.

EXAMPLE. Max $\{\overline{1}; \overline{1,2}; \overline{2,3}; \overline{2,3}\} = \{\overline{1,2}; \overline{2,3}\}$.

We now prove that the set systems form a lattice and the Max operation enables us to give an explicit description of the lattice operations.

THEOREM 5.7. The set of all set systems on a finite set S forms a distributive lattice under the ordering of Definition 5.4. The lattice operations are given by:

$$\phi \cdot \psi = \text{Max}\,\{B_\phi \cap B_\psi \mid B_\phi \in \phi \text{ and } B_\psi \in \psi\};$$

$$\phi + \psi = \text{Max}\,(\phi \cup \psi).$$

Proof. First, we must show that $\geqslant$ is a partial ordering. Obviously $\phi \leqslant \phi$. If

$$\phi \leqslant \psi \text{ and } \psi \leqslant \phi,$$

then for each B_ϕ in ϕ, there must be B_ψ and B'_ψ in ψ such that

$$B_\psi \subseteq B_\phi \subseteq B'_\psi.$$

But by condition (ii) of Definition 5.4,

$$B_\psi = B'_\psi$$

and so

$$B_\psi = B_\phi$$

and it follows that

$$\phi = \psi.$$

If

$$\phi_1 \leqslant \phi_2 \quad \text{and} \quad \phi_2 \leqslant \phi_3,$$

then for each B_1 in ϕ_1, there must be a B_2 in ϕ_2 and a B_3 in ϕ_3 such that

$$B_1 \subseteq B_2 \subseteq B_3$$

and therefore

$$\phi_1 \leqslant \phi_3$$

and $\geqslant$ is indeed a partial ordering.

Second, we must show that arbitrary systems ϕ and ψ have a greatest lower bound and that this bound is

$$\phi' = \text{Max}\{B_\phi \cap B_\psi\}.$$

Set ϕ' is a set system because for each s in S, there are B_ϕ and B_ψ such that s is in $B_\phi \cap B_\psi$ and because of Definition 5.5, there must be a block B in ϕ' such that

$$s \in B_\phi \cap B_\psi \subseteq B.$$

Condition (ii) of Definition 5.4 holds automatically by Definition 5.5 and so ϕ' is a set system.

Since any $B_\phi \cap B_\psi$ in ϕ' is contained in B_ϕ and B_ψ, ϕ' is a lower bound for ϕ and ψ. To show that it is the greatest lower bound, assume that ψ' is any other lower bound and that $B_{\psi'}$ is some block of ψ'. Because ψ' is a lower bound, there exist B_ϕ and B_ψ such that

$$B_{\psi'} \subseteq B_\phi \quad \text{and} \quad B_{\psi'} \subseteq B_\psi$$

or

$$B_{\psi'} \subseteq B_\phi \cap B_\psi$$

and so $B_{\psi'}$ is contained in some block of ϕ'. Therefore, $\psi' \leqslant \phi'$ and ϕ' is the greatest lower bound.

Third, we must show that arbitrary systems ϕ and ψ have a least upper bound and that this bound is

$$\phi' = \text{Max}(\phi \cup \psi).$$

Set ϕ' is easily verified to be a set system on S in a manner similar to the second part of this proof. The proof that ϕ' is an upper bound is also easily proved similarly to the g.l.b case. Suppose that ψ' is any other upper bound and that $B_{\psi'}$ is a block of ψ'. Let B_ϕ and B_ψ be blocks of ϕ and ψ such that

$$B_{\psi'} \supseteq B_\phi \quad \text{and} \quad B_{\psi'} \supseteq B_\psi,$$

and let B in ϕ' be such that

$$B \supseteq B_\psi.$$

Because of Definition 5.4, either

$$B = B_\psi \quad \text{or} \quad B \in \phi,$$

and in the latter case,

$$B = B_\phi.$$

In either case,

$$B_{\psi'} \supseteq B$$

and so $\psi' \geqslant \phi'$ and ϕ' is the l.u.b.

Finally, we must show that the lattice is distributive, and this is done by verifying the following steps:

$$\phi_1 \cdot (\phi_2 + \phi_3)$$
$$= \text{Max} \{ B_{\phi_1} \cap B_\psi \mid B_\psi \in \text{Max} (\{B_{\phi_2}\} \cup \{B_{\phi_3}\}) \}$$
$$= \text{Max} (\{B_{\phi_1} \cap B_{\phi_2}\} \cup \{B_{\phi_1} \cap B_{\phi_3}\})$$
$$= \phi_1 \cdot \phi_2 + \phi_1 \cdot \phi_3. \blacksquare$$

EXAMPLES.

$$\{\overline{1,2,3}; \overline{3,4,5}\} \cdot \{\overline{1,3,4}; \overline{1,5}; \overline{2,3,4}\} = \{\overline{1,3}; \overline{2,3}; \overline{3,4}; \overline{5}\}$$
$$\{\overline{1,2,3}; \overline{1,5}; \overline{3,4}\} + \{\overline{1,2}; \overline{2,3,4}; \overline{3,5}\} = \{\overline{1,2,3}; \overline{1,5}; \overline{2,3,4}; \overline{3,5}\}.$$

Note that

$$\phi = \{\overline{1,2}; \overline{3}\} \quad \text{and} \quad \psi = \{\overline{1}; \overline{2,3}\}$$

can be regarded as set systems or partitions. As partitions,

$$\phi + \psi = \{\overline{1,2,3}\},$$

but as set systems,

$$\phi + \psi = \{\overline{1,2}; \overline{2,3}\}.$$

Thus the "+" operation must always be taken in the context of the lattice under discussion. The "·" operation for set systems is an extension of the "·" operation for partitions.

We have seen that our expanded concept of information, namely, the set system, has all the nice lattice properties that partitions have. One might expect that this new concept might be useful in analyzing "information flow." We now show this to be the case.

DEFINITION 5.6. If ϕ and ψ are set systems on the set of states of a machine M, we say that

(ϕ, ψ) is a *system pair* for M

if and only if for all B in ϕ and x in I,

$$\delta(B, x) \subseteq B' \text{ for some } B' \text{ in } \psi.$$

In other words, (ϕ, ψ) is a system pair if and only if blocks of ϕ go into blocks of ψ under all inputs.

THEOREM 5.8. The set of all system pairs for a machine M is a pair algebra.

Proof. Obviously $(0, \psi)$ and (ϕ, I) are system pairs for all ψ and ϕ. Now suppose that (ϕ_1, ψ_1) and (ϕ_2, ψ_2) are system pairs. Let x be some arbitrary element of I and let B_1 and B_2 be arbitrary blocks of ϕ_1 and ϕ_2, respectively. Finally, let B_1' and B_2' be blocks of ψ_1 and ψ_2 such that

$$\delta(B_1, x) \subseteq B_1' \qquad \text{and} \qquad \delta(B_2, x) \subseteq B_2'$$

(B_1' and B_2' exist by Definition 5.6).

If $B_1 \cap B_2$ is a block of $\phi_1 \cdot \phi_2$, then obviously

$$\delta(B_1 \cap B_2, x) \subseteq \delta(B_1, x) \cap \delta(B_2, x) \subseteq B_1' \cap B_2' \subseteq B',$$

where B' is some block of $\psi_1 \cdot \psi_2$; therefore,

$$(\phi_1 \cdot \phi_2, \psi_1 \cdot \psi_2)$$

is a system pair.

If B_1 is a block of $\phi_1 + \phi_2$, then obviously

$$\delta(B_1, x) \subseteq B_1' \subseteq B'$$

for some B' in $\psi_1 + \psi_2$ and similarly for B_2; therefore,

$$(\phi_1 + \phi_2, \psi_1 + \psi_2)$$

is a system pair and Definition 3.3 is satisfied. ∎

System pairs can be used to make decompositions in a manner similar to partition pairs. Various aspects of these constructions will be discussed in the next section. The generation of Mm partition pairs from $\pi_{s,t}$ partitions was established by Theorem 3.3 and a similar result can be established here.

Another interesting aspect of this algebra is that the M operator is an extension of the partition pair M operator. In other words, they give the same result when applied to partitions. The reader may prove this as an exercise.

DEFINITION 5.7. If $M = (S, I, O, \delta, \lambda)$ is a sequential machine and T is a subset of S, then we define the partition ϕ_T by

$$s \equiv t \, (\phi_T)$$

if and only if

$$s = t \text{ or } \{s, t\} \subseteq T.$$

THEOREM 5.9. If (ϕ, ψ) is an Mm system pair for a machine M, then

$$\psi = \sum \{m(\phi_T) \mid \phi_T \leqslant \phi\}.$$

Proof. For $\phi_T \leqslant \phi$, (ϕ_T, ψ) is a system pair and therefore

$$m(\phi_T) \leqslant \psi.$$

Hence

$$\sum \{m(\phi_T) \mid \phi_T \leqslant \phi\} \leqslant \psi.$$

But

$$(\sum \phi_T, \sum m[\phi_T]) = (\phi, \sum m[\phi_T])$$

is a system pair and so

$$\sum m(\phi_T) \geqslant m(\phi) = \psi.$$

The two inequalities give the result. ∎

Note that the proof depended only on the special properties of a set system lattice (namely, $\phi = \sum_{\phi_T \leqslant \phi} \phi_T$) and the properties of a pair algebra, but *not* on the properties of a system pair. Therefore, this result holds for all pair algebras in which the first lattice is a set system lattice.

For an n-state sequential machine, the number of ϕ_T is given by the formula

$$2^n - n - 1,$$

which grows rapidly with n. In comparison with the partition pair case, there is more of a tendency for the $m(\phi_T)$ to be distinct and a tendency for the $m(\phi_T)$ to generate large quantities of m set systems. Thus, the hand calculation of the Mm set system lattice becomes a very unpleasant task. Although this concept is helpful in formulating and thinking about machine problems, and although we will later develop some specialized applications, it will very seldom be a practical tool for exhaustive analysis.

5.4 SET SYSTEM DECOMPOSITIONS

In the last section, we fit the system pair into the same algebraic mold as the partition pair. It is to be expected, therefore, that our previous circuit constructions go through when the analogous information flow inequalities hold. Nevertheless, the differences between set systems and partitions enter the theory in many ways. The purpose of this section is to acquaint the reader with some of the special aspects of set system constructions.

Consider a set system ϕ with S.P. on the states of some machine, that is, a ϕ which satisfies

$$m(\phi) \leqslant \phi$$

Intuitively, we interpret this inequality to mean that ϕ can be computed from itself and the input. Thus, as stated in the next theorem, we expect this to lead to a serial decomposition. However, note in the construction of the decomposition that:

(1) The front machine is not necessarily unique;
(2) The tail machine need not compute a set system.

THEOREM 5.10. If ϕ is a set system with S.P. on the states of a machine $M = (S, I, O, \delta, \lambda)$, then there exists a serial decomposition of M such that:

(i) The front machine has one state corresponding to each block of ϕ;
(ii) The number of states in the tail machine is the same as the number of states in the largest block of ϕ.

Proof. First we define the front machine $M_1 = (S_1, I_1, O_1, \delta_1, \lambda_1)$. Let

$$S_1 = \phi,$$
$$I_1 = I,$$
$$O_1 = S_1 \times I_1,$$
$$\delta_1(B, a) = \text{some } B' \text{ in } \phi \text{ such that } \delta(B, a) \subseteq B',$$
$$\lambda_1(B, a) = (B, a).$$

Such a δ_1 can be defined because of the S.P. condition

$$\phi \geqslant m(\phi).$$

Let S_2 be some set with the same number of elements as the largest block of ϕ. For each B in ϕ, let

$$f_B : S_B \longrightarrow B$$

be some map of a subset S_B of S_2 *onto* B. This is possible because of the size of B. (This map is a generalization of the map defined by τ for the state behaviour realizations of M using the partitions π and τ; see proof of Theorem 2.4).

To define $M_2 = (S_2, I_2, O_2, \delta_2, \lambda_2)$, let

$$I_2 = O_1,$$
$$\delta_2(t, (B, a)) = \text{some } t' \text{ such that } f_{\delta_1(B,a)}(t') = \delta(f_B(t), a)$$

whenever $f_B(t)$ is defined, arbitrary otherwise,

$$\lambda_2(t, (B, a)) = \lambda(f_B(t), a).$$

This definition of δ_2 is possible because $f_{\delta_1(B,a)}$ is an onto map. Let

$$M' = (S', I', O', \delta', \lambda')$$

be the serial connection of M_1 and M_2. This completes what we call the "standard construction." When making such a construction, we usually define $f_B(t)$ by a *connection table* whose columns are labeled by the possible

B, the rows by possible t, and the entries give the value $f_B(t)$. All that remains is to show that M' realizes M. Let

$$\alpha(s) = \{(B, t) \mid f_B(t) = s\},$$
$$\iota = \text{identity map},$$
$$\zeta = \text{identity map}.$$

Suppose (B, t) is in $\alpha(s)$ (i.e., $f_B(t) = s$). Then

$$\delta'((B, t), \iota(a))$$

because ι is identity

$$= \delta'((B, t), a)$$

by definition of δ'

$$= [\delta_1(B, a), \delta_2(t, (B, a))]$$

by construction

$$= (B', t')$$

where

$$f_{B'}(t') = \delta(f_B(t), a) = \delta(s, a)$$

and so

$$(B', t') \text{ is in } \alpha(\delta(s, a))$$

which establishes (i) of Definition 1.14. To verify (ii):

$$\zeta(\lambda'[(B, t), \iota(a)])$$
$$= \lambda'[(B, t), a]$$
$$= \lambda_2[t, (B, a)]$$
$$= \lambda(f_B(t), a)$$
$$= \lambda(s, a). \ \blacksquare$$

	0	1	Z
1	2	5	0
2	3	4	0
3	1	4	1
4	3	2	1
5	4	3	1

EXAMPLE. Machine G of Fig. 5.12 has

$$\phi = \{\overline{1,2,3}; \overline{2,3,4}; \overline{4,5}\} = \{B_1; B_2; B_3\}$$

Fig. 5.12. Machine G.

as a set system with S.P. A construction as specified by the proof is shown in Fig. 5.13. The construction of the front machine G_1 was not unique and one could write

$$\delta_1(B_3, 1) = B_1 \quad \text{or} \quad \delta_1(B_3, 1) = B_2.$$

This is because

$$\delta_1(B_3, 1) = \{2, 3\} \subseteq B_1 \cap B_2.$$

We choose $\delta_1(B_3, 1) = B_1$ and proceeded to define the f_B which may be read from the connection table, i.e.,

$$f_{B_1}(t_1) = 1, f_{B_3}(t_2) = 5, \text{ etc.}$$

We did not choose to define an $f_{B_3}(t_3)$ and this led to the d.c. conditions in G_2. In this (Moore)case, the connection table converts to an output table by replacing each state by its output.

Machine G_1

	0	1
$\{1,2,3\} = B_1$	B_1	B_3
$\{2,3,4\} = B_2$	B_1	B_2
$\{4,5\} = B_3$	B_2	B_1

Connection table

	B_1	B_2	B_3
t_1	1	3	4
t_2	2	2	5
t_3	3	4	–

Machine G_2

	$B_1 0$	$B_1 1$	$B_2 0$	$B_2 1$	$B_3 0$	$B_3 1$
t_1	t_2	t_2	t_1	t_3	t_1	t_2
t_2	t_3	t_1	t_3	t_3	t_3	t_3
t_3	t_1	t_1	t_3	t_2	–	–

Output logic

	B_1	B_2	B_3
t_1	0	1	1
t_2	0	0	1
t_3	1	1	–

Fig. 5.13. A standard decomposition of machine G.

Notice that the states of G have automatically been split. State 2 is now replaced by (B_1, t_2) and (B_2, t_2), state 3 by (B_1, t_3) and (B_2, t_1), etc.

If we also defined $f_{B_3}(t_3) = 5$, the d.c. conditions would vanish, but other alternatives would present themselves, e.g., $\delta_2(t_1, (B_1, 1))$ could be made equal to t_3 instead of t_2.

If one looks at the state of G_2, one can tell which block of

$$\psi = \{\overline{1,3,4}; \overline{2,5}\}$$

contains the present state of G. Even though

$$\phi \cdot \psi > 0,$$

G_1 and G_2 operating together determine the state of G which is more information than is contained in the product of ϕ and ψ. Thus there is little analogy with the tail machine of a state-behavior realization.

There are a variety of cases using set systems where a combination of two component machines yields more "information" than one would expect by taking the product of the component information. It is somewhat startling that this can occur even when the two components operate independently.

EXAMPLE. State machine H and its lattice of S.P. set systems is shown in Fig. 5.14. Figure 5.15 shows a parallel realization of H. Both machines H_1 and H_2 are based on the set system

$$\phi = \{\overline{1,2}; \overline{2,3}\},$$

but the non uniques of such constructions (in this case for transititions under input 2) enables us to construct nonisomorphic H_1 and H_2. Thus, although H_1 and H_2 both compute ϕ, they do it differently and this difference somehow gives perfect state information, not just the information in ϕ alone.

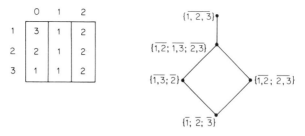

Fig. 5.14. Machine H and S. P. set systems.

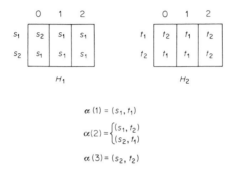

Fig. 5.15. Parallel realization of machine H.

The remainder of this section is used to elaborate on these peculiar properties of set systems by studying the relationship between partition pairs on an expanded machine and system pairs on a reduced machine. These results are not explicitly used elsewhere and *the remainder of this section can be omitted on first reading.*

NOTATION. If S is a set and π_R is some specified partition on S, then for all $B \subseteq S$, we write

$$\check{B} = \{B' \text{ in } \pi_R \mid B' \cap B \neq \varnothing\}.$$

For any other partition π on S, we let $\tilde{\pi}$ be the set system on π_R defined by

$$\tilde{\pi} = \text{Max}\,\{\check{B} \mid B \text{ in } \pi\}.$$

One might say that $\tilde{\pi}$ is the reduced form of π when S is reduced by π_R. We now look at the structural effect of such a reduction.

THEOREM 5.11. Suppose that π_R is an output consistent S.P. partition on the states of a machine $M = (S, I, O, \delta, \lambda)$. Letting $\tilde{M}$ and $\tilde{m}$ be the state partition operators for M and letting M and m be the state set system operators for $M_{\pi_R}^o$, the following relations hold for partitions π and τ on S'.

    (i) $\widetilde{\pi \cdot \tau} \leqslant \tilde{\pi} \cdot \tilde{\tau}$;

(ii) if $\pi \geqslant \pi_R$ then $\widetilde{\pi \cdot \tau} = \tilde{\pi} \cdot \tilde{\tau}$;

(iii) $\widetilde{\pi + \tau} \geqslant \tilde{\pi} + \tilde{\tau}$;

(iv) if (π, τ) is a partition pair, then

   $(\tilde{\pi}, \tilde{\tau})$ is a system pair;

(v) $\widetilde{m(\pi)} \geqslant \tilde{m}(\tilde{\pi})$;

(vi) $\widetilde{M(\pi)} \leqslant \tilde{M}(\tilde{\pi})$.

Proof. (i) Obviously, for all B_π in π and B_τ in τ,

$$\widetilde{B_\pi \cap B_\tau} \subseteq \tilde{B}_\pi \quad \text{and} \quad \widetilde{B_\pi \cap B_\tau} \subseteq \tilde{B}_\tau,$$

and hence

$$\widetilde{B_\pi \cap B_\tau} \subseteq \tilde{B}_\pi \cap \tilde{B}_\tau.$$

Therefore,

$$\text{Max}\,\{\widetilde{B_\pi \cap B_\tau}\} \subseteq \text{Max}\,\{\tilde{B}_\pi \cap \tilde{B}_\tau\}$$

and (i) follows.

(ii) if $\pi_R \leqslant \pi$, then for all B' in π_R,

$B' \cap B_\pi \neq \varnothing$ implies $B' \cap B_\pi = B'$.

This means that

$$
\begin{aligned}
\tilde{B}_\pi \cap \tilde{B}_\tau \\
&= \{B' \in \pi_R \,|\, B' \cap B_\pi \neq \varnothing \text{ and } B' \cap B_\tau \neq \varnothing\} \\
&= \{B' \in \pi_R \,|\, B' \cap B_\pi = B' \text{ and } B' \cap B_\tau \neq \varnothing\} \\
&= \{B' \in \pi_R \,|\, B' \cap B_\pi \cap B_\tau \neq \varnothing\} \\
&= \widetilde{B_\pi \cap B_\tau};
\end{aligned}
$$

and (ii) follows.

(iii) Any block of $\tilde{\pi} + \tilde{\tau}$ must have the form

$$\tilde{B} \text{ for some } B \text{ in } \pi \cup \tau.$$

This implies that B is contained in some block of $\pi + \tau$ and (iii) follows.

(iv) Letting δ_o be the transition function for $M_{\pi_R}^o$, we observe that for all B_π in π and a in I,

$$\delta_o(\tilde{B}_\pi, a) =$$

by definition

$$\{B \in \pi_R \,|\, \delta(s, a) \in B \text{ for some } s \text{ such that } B_{\pi_R}(s) \cap B_\pi \neq \varnothing\} =$$

since $s \equiv t\,(\pi_R)$ implies $\delta(s, a) \equiv \delta(t, a)\,(\pi_R)$

$$\{B \in \pi_R \,|\, \delta(t, a) \in B \text{ for some } t \text{ in } B_{\pi_R}(s) \cap B_\pi \text{ for some } s\} =$$

since one can always choose $s = t$

$$\{B \in \pi_R \,|\, \delta(t, a) \in B \text{ for some } t \text{ in } B_\pi\} = \widetilde{\delta(B_\pi, a)}.$$

Assuming (π, τ) is a p.p., let B_τ be a block of τ such that

$$\delta(B_\pi, a) \subseteq B_\tau.$$

Clearly,

$$\delta_o(\tilde{B}_\pi, a) = \widetilde{\delta(B_\pi, a)} \subseteq \tilde{B}_\tau$$

and since $\tilde{B}_\tau$ is contained in a block of $\tilde{\tau}$, $(\tilde{\pi}, \tilde{\tau})$ is a system pair by definition,

(v) This holds because $(\tilde{\pi}, \widetilde{m(\pi)})$ is a system pair.

(vi) This holds because $(\widetilde{M(\pi)}, \tilde{\pi})$ is a system pair. ∎

The inequalities in this theorem cannot be strengthened and we leave it as an exercise for the reader to find appropriate counterexamples. The fact that information flow inequalities in terms of set systems are only sufficient conditions for a realization may be attributed to the failure of condition (i) to strengthen. More specifically, if τ's and ρ's represent partitions on some expanded version of a machine which reduces under π_R, then

$$\rho_{i,j} \leqslant M(\tau_j)$$

does *not* imply

$$\prod \tilde{\rho}_{i,j} \leqslant \tilde{M}(\tilde{\tau}_j);$$

but if $\widetilde{\pi \cdot \tau} = \tilde{\pi} \cdot \tilde{\tau}$ always held, we would have

$$\prod \tilde{\rho}_{i,j} = \widetilde{\prod \rho_{i,j}} \leqslant \widetilde{M(\tau_j)} \leqslant \tilde{M}(\tilde{\tau}_j).$$

So far, we have just pointed out some peculiar features of system pairs without giving any class of realizations for which set systems are sufficient. This is in sharp contrast to the partition pair case where we could always state necessary and sufficient conditions for state behavior realizations. Now we give a result which says that set systems are sufficient for simple serial decompositions when we wish to restrict ourselves to the case where one cannot replace one component by a fewer-state machine without replacing the other component with a larger machine.

THEOREM 5.12. Let $M_1 \ominus M_2$ be a serial decomposition of machine $M = (S, I, O, \delta, \lambda)$ such that for any other serial decomposition $M_1' \ominus M_2'$,

$$|S_1'| < |S_1| \text{ implies } |S_2| < |S_2'|$$

and

$$|S_2'| < |S_2| \text{ implies } |S_1| < |S_1'|.$$

Then $M_1 \ominus M_2$ is obtained in the standard way from an S.P. set system on the reduced form M_R of M.

Proof. $M_1 \ominus M_2$ may be thought of as a realization of M_R. Without loss of generality, we assume

$$I_1 = I, O_1 = S_1 \times I, \text{ and } O_2 = O$$

(i.e., we assume ι and ζ are identity maps); the general case is achieved by renaming.

To distinguish between the given δ_1 and δ_2 and our choice of δ_1 and δ_2 constructed in the standard way of Theorem 5.10, we represent the latter by δ_1' and δ_2'. Our object is of course to show that these pairs of δ functions are the same after some appropriate renaming of states.

For each s_1 in S_1, let

$$B_{s_1} = \{s \in S_R \mid (s_1, s_2) \in \alpha(s) \text{ for some } s_2 \in S_2\}$$

and let

$$\phi = \text{Max} \{B_{s_1}\}.$$

First we consider the case where

$$\phi = \{B_{s_1}\}.$$

In this case, the M_1 constructed in the proof of Theorem 5.10 is isomorphic to the M_1 here if the δ_1' is chosen such that

$$\delta_1'(B_{s_1}, a) = B_{\delta_1(s_1, a)}.$$

If B_{s_1} is a block of ϕ of maximal size, then

$$|B_{s_1}| \leqslant |S_2|$$

because each s_R in B_{s_1} corresponds to some (s_1, s_2) and hence to some s_2. On the other hand,

$$|B_{s_1}| \geqslant |S_2|$$

for otherwise, the construction of Theorem 5.10 would give a tail machine with fewer states, contrary to our hypothesis. Thus

$$|B_{s_1}| = |S_2|$$

and the set S_2 itself may be used as the S_2 in the standard construction. To do this, we need suitable f_B and we choose

$$f_{B_{s_1}}(s_2) = s_R \qquad \text{if and only if } (s_1, s_2) \in \alpha(s_R).$$

These f_B are definitely functions of a subset of S_2 onto B since

$$(s_1, s_2) \in \alpha(s_R) \cap \alpha(t_R)$$

implies

$$s_R \text{ equivalent to } t_R$$

which, because M_R is reduced, implies

$$s_R = t_R$$

and therefore s_2 can be mapped into at most one s_R under $f_{B_{s_1}}$. The map is of course onto since each s_R in B_{s_1} is determined by some (s_1, s_2). Now we must choose a δ_2' consistent with our choice of f_B and we choose

$$\delta_2'(s_2, (B_{s_1}, a)) = \delta_2(s_2, (s_1, a)).$$

This obviously gives a tail machine isomorphic M_2. This is seen to be consistent with the definition of f_B if we show that this definition of δ_2' satisfies the condition of the proof of Theorem 5.10, i.e., if

$$\delta_R(f_{B_{s_1}}(s_2), a) = f_{\delta_1(B_{s_1}, a)}(\delta_2'[s_2, (B_{s_1}, a)])$$

whenever $f_{B_{s_1}}(s_2)$ is defined. By definition of f_B, this is equivalent to the condition

$$(\delta_1(s_1, a), \delta_2[s_2, (s_1, a)]) \in \alpha(\delta_R(s_R, a))$$

whenever (s_1, s_2) is in $\alpha(s_R)$.

Letting δ^* be the transition function for $M_1 \ominus M_2$, this condition is equivalent to

$$\delta^*((s_1, s_2), a) \in \alpha(\delta_R(s_R, a)) \qquad \text{for} \qquad (s_1, s_2) \in \alpha(s_R).$$

This last condition must hold because α is part of an assignment map; i.e., this is condition (i) of Definition 1.14.

Now we consider the case

$$\phi \neq \{B_{s_1}\}.$$

Here the standard construction gives a front machine M_1' with fewer states than M_1. Again there are at least as many states in S_2 as there are states in the maximal block of ϕ and so the standard construction gives a tail machine M_2' with no more than $|S_2|$ states. Thus we have

$$|S_1'| < |S_1| \qquad \text{and} \qquad |S_2'| \leqslant |S_2|$$

contrary to our hypothesis. The second case is thus ruled out and the theorem established. ∎

COROLLARY 5.12.1. A necessary and sufficient condition that $M_1 \ominus M_2$ satisfy Theorem 5.12 is that the decomposition be constructed from a set system ϕ on S_R with S.P. such that for any other set system ψ on S_R with S.P.

$$|\psi| < |\phi| \qquad \text{implies} \qquad \#|\phi| < \#|\psi|$$

and

$$\#|\psi| < \#|\phi| \qquad \text{implies} \qquad |\phi| < |\psi|,$$

where $\#|\phi|$ and $\#|\psi|$ represent the number of elements in the largest block of the respective set systems.

Proof. If ψ violated one of these conditions, the standard construction on ψ would give an $M_1' \ominus M_2'$ which violated the conditions of the theorem. ∎

Thus we may only be interested in finding S.P. set systems ϕ with small values for $|\phi|$ and $\#|\phi|$. In this case, the next result says that the search can be restricted to some sublattice of the S.P. lattice.

THEOREM 5.13. If

$$M = (S, I, O, \delta, \lambda)$$

is an n-state sequential machine and L is its lattice of set systems with S.P., then for $1 \leqslant k \leqslant n$, the set

$$L_k = \{\phi \text{ in } L \mid \# \mid \phi \mid \leqslant k\}$$

is a sublattice of L and has l.u.b. ("identity" element)

$$\phi_k = \{B \subseteq S \mid |B| = k\}.$$

Proof. Obviously, the sum and product systems $\phi + \psi$ and $\phi \cdot \psi$ cannot have blocks which are larger than the blocks of ϕ and ψ. Thus L_k is a sublattice of L. System ϕ_k has S.P. because blocks of size k always go into blocks of size k or less and these image blocks must be contained in some block of size k (some block of ϕ_k). Furthermore, ϕ_k is obviously larger than any system in L_k and is the least upper bound because it is itself in L_k. ∎

This theorem may be illustrated by machine H and its S.P. set system lattice as shown in Fig. 5.14. Here we have

$$\phi_3 = \{\overline{1,2,3}\},$$
$$\phi_2 = \{\overline{1,2}; \overline{2,3}; \overline{1,3}\},$$
$$\phi_1 = \{\overline{1}; \overline{2}; \overline{3}\}$$

The L_k consists of all the systems less than or equal to the respective ϕ_k.

COROLLARY 5.13.1. Every n-state machine M has at least n distinct set systems with S.P; namely, the systems ϕ_k of Theorem 5.13.

These ϕ_k are generally not very useful because they all have n or more blocks (except $\phi_n = I$) and so the front machines they define are at least as big as M. Nevertheless, there is a theoretical application for them as explained in the last chapter.

5.5 DON'T CARE CONDITIONS, THIRD APPROACH

It should be obvious that the concept of a weak partition pair can be generalized to system pairs.

DEFINITION 5.8. If ϕ and ψ are set systems on the states of a machine M with d.c. conditions, we say that

$$(\phi, \psi) \text{ is a } weak \ system \ pair \text{ for } M$$

if and only if, for all B in ϕ and x in I,

$$\{s \mid s = \delta(t, x) \text{ for some } t \text{ in } B\} \subseteq B' \text{ for some } B' \text{ in } \psi.$$

Notice that this definition is semantically the same as Definition 5.6

of a system pair. The only difference is that in the previous case, each t in B determined a state $s = \delta(t, x)$, whereas in this case it does not.

This accounts for the next result.

THEOREM 5.14. The set of all system pairs for a machine M with d.c. conditions is a pair algebra.

Proof. The proof of Theorem 5.7 carries over word for word when we write

$$\delta(B, x) = \{s \mid s = \delta(t, x) \text{ for some } t \in B\}. \blacksquare$$

This is a striking contrast to the w.p.p. case where we failed to get a pair algebra. Because we already have a pair algebra, it would be rather pointless to go on and define an "extended system pair." It is generally the case that whenever we develop a pair algebra using system pairs, the theory goes through for d.c. conditions. The underlying reason for this is that partition addition with its extra identification required by transitivity was the real villain, and set system addition has eliminated these extra identifications.

As an illustration, recall the discussion in Section 3.6 about the machine in Fig. 3.19. It was observed that one could not find an M partition for

$$\pi = \{\overline{1}; \overline{2,3}; \overline{4}\}.$$

Treating π as a set system, however, we get

$$M(\pi) = \{\overline{1}; \overline{2,3}; \overline{2,4}\}.$$

Again, weak system pairs are too numerous for exhaustive analysis, and its real usefulness is in special applications or as a theoretical tool. One common application is to state reduction. Reduced realizations of a machine with d.c. conditions can be constructed from the output consistent set systems with S.P. Because these output consistent set systems are closed under the lattice operations, one can find a largest output consistent S.P. set system. Unfortunately, this set system does not necessarily determine a realization with the fewest possible states, as some smaller set system might have fewer blocks. In the worst case, a minimal state realization may not correspond to any set system. These remarks are just set system formulations of the early observations of Paull and Unger on state reduction [27].

NOTES

The negative effects of state reduction on machine realization were discussed by the authors in [15]. The problem of state splitting and the use of overlapping partitions for machine decomposition and state assignment are discussed by M. Yoeli [31], Z. Kohavi [21], H.P. Zeiger [33] and the authors [18]. Overlapping partitions have been also used for the study of state reduction of incompletely specified machines by M.C. Paull and S.H. Unger [27].

6 FEEDBACK AND ERRORS

6.1 FEEDBACK DEFINED BY PARTITIONS

In the previous chapters we have emphasized the interpretation of state partitions and set systems as information to be stored, either as the state of a component machine or as the value of a state variable. There are, however, aspects of machine design and behavior which can be interpreted as state information not directly associated with specific memory locations. Perhaps the most basic concept of this type is feedback. One reason for this is that feedback determines the propagation of errors in a circuit, as is shown in the later sections of this chapter. Secondly, the study of feedback information can be applied to obtain desirable machine decompositions and state assignments, even though the feedback information itself is not stored in any single location. Finally, the solutions of various feedback problems demonstrate the full power and versatility of the pair algebra techniques and illustrate a variety of interpretations of the information and information flow concepts. With these techniques, the reader should be able to handle any number of related information problems.

In this section, we apply the partition algebra of Chapter 3 to study feedback in state behavior realizations. First, we need to give a precise mathematical meaning to our intuitive notion of feedback.

Intuitively, we say that a realization of a sequential machine M is feedback-free if the realization does not contain any "closed loops"; or, in other words, if all delay elements and logical elements in the realization can be so arranged that the signals in this circuit propagate only from, say, left to right. If the machine M cannot be realized without feedback, then some of the "wires" in the realization will have to carry signals going from right

to left. Thus in Fig. 6.1 which shows a schematic diagram of the realization of a machine, the information which flows from right to left on the two lower

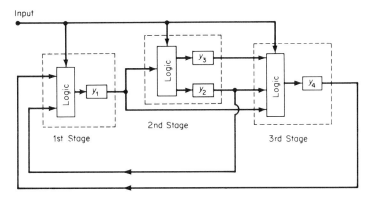

Fig. 6.1.   A schematic circuit diagram for machine M.

wires is considered as feedback. We see that what is considered to be feedback information depends on the state assignment used in the realization of M and on how we look at the circuit (i.e., which wires we consider as feedback). Since we cannot tell from a state table what state assignment will be used and how the resulting realization will be viewed, we cannot say what is *the* feedback in the machine. What we wish to accomplish is to detect from the state table of M the possibility of using certain information for feedback. To accomplish this we now examine the nature of this feedback information. In the case of Fig. 6.1, the values of the state variables y_2 and y_4 are used in the feedback. These two variables define a partition π_f which identifies exactly those states of M which have the same y_2 and y_4 values. Note that in this case the feedback information can be identified with a partition on the set of states S of M. The more general case when feedback information is a function of the input and the state of M is discussed in the next section.

To make this intuitive description of feedback precise, we give our definition in terms of a realization of M by an abstract network in standard logic delay form.

For this application, we introduce a linear ordering of the component machines which simply describes the "arrangement" of the components in our realization and gives precise meaning to the concept "information flowing to the right" and "information flowing to the left."

DEFINITION 6.1. Let the state behavior of M be realized by an abstract network $\mathcal{N}$ in standard logic-delay form and let its component machines M_i, $1 \leqslant i \leqslant n$ be ordered according to i. Then the *feedback partition* π_f of this realization is given by:

$$\pi_f = \prod_{i > j} \rho_{i,j},$$

where the $\rho_{i,j}$ are the associated partitions.

If one imagines the component machines ordered from left to right, each M_i representing the "ith stage" of the realization, the partition π_f describes exactly the information which is "fed back" from right to left.

The question we ask at this point is how can one test a partition π_f on the set of states of M to see if there is a realization that uses π_f for feedback? Theorem 6.1 gives such a test and the proof tells us how to construct such a realization. It is necessary at this point to introduce some more algebra. In the next definition, the partition $A^i(\pi)$ represents the information available for the calculation at the ith stage. The partition $m[A^i(\pi)]$ is the information calculated by the first i stages.

DEFINITION 6.2. If π is a partition on the set of states of the machine M, let

$$A^1(\pi) = \pi$$

and let

$$A^{i+1}(\pi) = \pi \cdot m[A^i(\pi)]$$

for $i \geqslant 1$.

LEMMA 6.1. If π is a partition on a machine M with n states, then

$$A^i(\pi) \geqslant A^j(\pi) \qquad \text{for } i \leqslant j$$

and

$$A^k(\pi) = A^n(\pi) \qquad \text{for } k \geqslant n.$$

Proof. Clearly,

$$\pi \geqslant \pi \cdot m(\pi) \qquad \text{or} \qquad A^1(\pi) \geqslant A^2(\pi).$$

If

$$A^i(\pi) \geqslant A^{i+1}(\pi),$$

then

$$m[A^i(\pi)] \geqslant m[A^{i+1}(\pi)]$$

by the monotonicity of the m operator and hence

$$\pi \cdot m[A^i(\pi)] \geqslant \pi \cdot m[A^{i+1}(\pi)]$$

or

$$A^{i+1}(\pi) \geqslant A^{i+2}(\pi).$$

Thus the first statement follows by induction. Since a partition on n states can be refined at most $n - 1$ times,

$$A^l(\pi) = A^{l+1}(\pi)$$

for some $0 \leqslant l \leqslant n - 1$ and

$$A^i(\pi) = A^{i+1}(\pi)$$

for all $i \geqslant l$ and the lemma follows. ∎

Thus we see that our iteration in the computation of $A^i(\pi)$ settles down by the nth time and our next definition makes good sense.

DEFINITION 6.3. If π is a partition on a machine M with n states, let

$$A(\pi) = A^n(\pi).$$

We can now state our main result.

THEOREM 6.1. The state behavior of a machine M can be realized using the partition π_f for feedback if and only if

$$A(\pi_f) = 0.$$

Proof. Let the state behavior of M be realized by an abstract network in standard logic-delay form with the component machines $M_1, M_2, \ldots, M_k$. Then the feedback partition is

$$\pi_f = \prod_{i \leqslant j} \rho_{j,i}.$$

Let

$$\pi_i = \prod_{j \leqslant i} \tau_j, \qquad \text{for} \qquad 1 \leqslant i \leqslant k.$$

Then π_i defines the state information contained in the first i stages of this realization. The information available at the ith stage from which π_i is computed is given by

$$\prod_{j=1}^{k} \rho_{j,i} = \left(\prod_{i \leqslant j} \rho_{j,i} \right) \cdot \left(\prod_{j < i} \rho_{j,i} \right) \geqslant \pi_f \cdot \prod_{j < i} \rho_{j,i}.$$

Therefore

$$\left(\pi_f \cdot \prod_{j < i} \rho_{j,i}, \pi_i \right)$$

is a partition pair on M. Since

$$\prod_{j < i} \rho_{j,i} \geqslant \pi_{i-1}$$

we can refine the front component of the partition pair to show that

$$(\pi_f \cdot \pi_{i-1}, \pi_i)$$

is a partition pair on M for $1 \leqslant i \leqslant k$ (recall that $\pi_0 = I$, the one-block partition). In particular, it follows from Theorem 3.1 (v) that

$$\pi_1 \geqslant m(\pi_f) = m[A^1(\pi_f)].$$

Suppose that

$$\pi_i \geqslant m[A^i(\pi_f)].$$

Then

$$\pi_f \cdot \pi_i \geqslant \pi_f \cdot m[A^i(\pi_f)] = A^{i+1}(\pi_f),$$

and again by Theorem 3.1 (v) and (ii),

$$\pi_{i+1} \geqslant m(\pi_f \cdot \pi_i) \geqslant m[A^{i+1}(\pi_f)].$$

Thus, by induction, we have that

$$\pi_k \geqslant m[A^k(\pi_f)].$$

Since the network realizes the states behavior of M,

$$\pi_k = 0,$$

which implies that

$$m[A^k(\pi_f)] = 0$$

and therefore

$$A^{k+1}(\pi_f) = 0.$$

But this means that

$$A(\pi_f) = 0.$$

Now suppose that

$$A(\pi_f) = 0.$$

We can build an abstract network that realizes M using π_f for feedback as follows. The first stage is built to calculate

$$m(\pi_f) \text{ from } A^1(\pi_f) = \pi_f.$$

The ith stage calculates a partition

$$\tau_i \text{ from } A^i(\pi_f),$$

such that

$$\tau_i \cdot m[A^{i-1}(\pi_f)] = m[A^i(\pi_f)].$$

This is possible since

$$\tau_i \geqslant m[A^i(\pi)]$$

implies that

$$[A^i(\pi_f), \tau_i]$$

is a partition pair on M. Since

$$A(\pi_f) = 0,$$
$$m[A^k(\pi_f)] = 0$$

for some k and we are through. The information π_f is now available for feedback. ∎

	00	01	11	10
0	0	5	7	2
1	6	1	7	2
2	7	6	1	4
3	7	6	5	4
4	7	0	1	4
5	5	2	3	6
6	1	2	3	6
7	5	2	3	0

Fig. 6.2. Machine A.

EXAMPLE. Let us consider the machine A of Fig. 6.2. We wish to test the partition $\pi_f = \{0,1,2,3,4; \overline{5,6,7}\}$ to see if it can be used for feedback. These calculations are shown below.

$$A^1(\pi_f) = \pi_f = \{\overline{0,1,2,3,4}; \overline{5,6,7}\};$$
$$m(A^1) = \{\overline{0,1,5,6,7}; \overline{2,4}; \overline{3}\};$$
$$A^2 = \pi_f \cdot m(A^1) = \{\overline{0,1}; \overline{2,4}; \overline{3}; \overline{5,6,7}\};$$
$$m(A^2) = \{\overline{0,6}; \overline{1,5}; \overline{2}; \overline{3}; \overline{4}; \overline{7}\};$$
$$A^3 = \pi_f \cdot m(A^2) = \{\overline{0}; \overline{1}; \overline{2}; \overline{3}; \overline{4}; \overline{5}; \overline{6}; \overline{7}\} = 0.$$

Since
$$A^3(\pi_f) = 0,$$
we know that
$$A^3(\pi_f) = A^4(\pi_f) = 0 \quad \text{and} \quad A(\pi_f) = 0;$$
hence, π_f can be used for feedback. Notice that the number of iterations necessary was far less than the theoretical maximum $n - 1 = 7$, and this is almost always the case. We now build a realization for machine A using the procedure of the proof.

To begin with, we let y_f be a variable assigned according to π_f; that is, $y_f = 0$ for states 0, 1, 2, 3, 4 and $y_f = 1$ for states 5, 6 and 7. We do not know in advance if there is a state variable corresponding to this variable. We are now ready to design the first stage.

Stage 1. We wish to build a stage to compute the block of $m(A^1)$. Since this has three blocks we need two binary variables y_1 and y_1^* to distinguish them. We let $y_1 = y_1^* = 0$ for states 0, 1, 5, 6, 7; $y_1 = 0$ and $y_1^* = 1$ for state 3; and $y_1 = 1$ and $y_1^* = 0$ for states 2 and 4. We know that these variables can be computed from the input variables x_1 and x_2 and the feedback variable y_f. With proper use of some "don't care" conditions, we get the equations:

$$Y_1 = x_1 \bar{x}_2 \bar{y}_f + \bar{x}_1 x_2 y_f$$
$$Y_1^* = x_1 x_2 y_f.$$

Thus we have designed the first stage. In order for the reader to keep track of the assignment as we go along, the final assignment may be referred to as shown in Fig. 6.3.

Stage 2. First of all we must choose a partition τ_2 that refines $m(A^1)$ to $m(A^2)$. Partition τ_2 must have at least three blocks because $\overline{0,1,5,6,7}$ must be divided into three blocks. We choose

$$\tau_2 = \{\overline{0,2,6}; \overline{1,5,4}; \overline{3,7}\}.$$

It takes two more binary variables y_2 and y_2^* to distinguish these blocks, and these variables are assigned as shown in Fig. 6.3. This leads to the following equations involving only the inputs, feedback, and stage 1 variables:

$$Y_2 = x_1 x_2 \bar{y}_1 \bar{y}_1^* + \bar{x}_1 \bar{x}_2 y_1 + \bar{x}_1 \bar{x}_2 y_1^*$$
$$Y_2^* = \bar{x}_1 x_2 \bar{y}_1 \bar{y}_1^* \bar{y}_f + x_1 y_1^* + x_1 y_1 + \bar{x}_1 \bar{x}_2 y_f.$$

The second stage is completed.

Stage 3. Here we need a partition τ_3 to refine $m(A^2)$ to $m(A^3) = 0$. Now π_f is such a partition, and so it is convenient to choose $\tau_3 = \pi_f$ and use this stage to compute y_f. The equation

	y_1	y_1^*	y_2	y_2^*	y_f
0	0	0	0	0	0
1	0	0	0	1	0
2	1	0	0	0	0
3	0	1	1	0	0
4	1	0	0	1	0
5	0	0	0	1	1
6	0	0	0	0	1
7	0	0	1	0	1

Fig. 6.3. First assignment for machine A.

	y_1	y_2	y_2^*	y_f
0	0	0	0	0
1	0	0	1	0
2	1	0	0	0
3	1	1	0	0
4	1	0	1	0
5	0	0	1	1
6	0	0	0	1
7	0	1	0	1

Fig. 6.4. Second assignment for machine A.

$$Y_f = \bar{x}_1\bar{x}_2 y_1 + \bar{x}_1\bar{x}_2 y_2 + \bar{x}_1\bar{x}_2 y_2^* + x_2 y_1^* y_2 + x_1 x_2 \bar{y}_1 \bar{y}_f + x_1\bar{x}_2 \bar{y}_2 y_f + x_2 \bar{y}_2 \bar{y}_2^* \bar{y}_f$$

completes the design.

This design used five variables for a machine which could be built using three. It is natural to ask if there is a better design using π_f. In the previous design, at each stage we computed as much information (the finest partition) as possible, namely $m(A^i)$. It is possible, however, to design some stages to compute less information and be more efficient. This is done as follows.

For the first stage, we compute

$$\tau_1 = \{\overline{0,1,5,6,7}; \overline{2,3,4}\}$$

instead of the finer partition $m(\pi_f)$. The important property of τ_1 is that

$$m(\tau_1 \cdot \pi_f) < m(\pi_f)$$

and so more information can be computed at the second stage than at the first. In fact, we can compute as much information here as in the first assignment. The important partitions and partition pairs for the second assignment are shown below:

$$\pi_f = \{\overline{0,1,2,3,4}; \overline{5,6,7}\},$$
$$\tau_1 = \{\overline{0,1,5,6,7}; \overline{2,3,4}\},$$
$$\tau_2 = \{\overline{0,2,6}; \overline{1,4,5}; \overline{3,7}\},$$
$$\tau_3 = \pi_f,$$
$$(\pi_f, \tau_1), (\tau_f \cdot \tau_1, \tau_2), (\pi_f \cdot \tau_1 \cdot \tau_2, \tau_3).$$

This leads us to the assignment of Fig. 6.4 and equations of the form:

$$Y_1 = f_1(y_f, x_1, x_2),$$
$$Y_2 = f_2(y_1, y_f, x_1, x_2),$$
$$Y_2^* = f_3(y_1, y_f, x_1, x_2),$$

$$Y_f = f_4(y_1, y_2, y_2^*, y_f, x_1, x_2).$$

This second assignment requires four variables and this can be shown to be the minimum using π_f for feedback. The two morals to this example are that the canonical construction of the proof need not use the minimum number of storage elements, and even the realization using the minimum may use more than a realization with more feedback.

There is one other point we wish to make in this section before generalizing these results and we illustrate it with machine B of Fig. 6.5. The following computation shows that

$$A(\pi_f) = 0 \qquad \text{for } \pi_f = \{\overline{1,2,3}; \overline{4}\};$$
$$A^1 = \pi_f = \{\overline{1,2,3}; \overline{4}\};$$
$$m(A^1) = \{\overline{1,2}; \overline{3,4}\};$$
$$A^2 = \pi_f \cdot m(A^1) = \{\overline{1,2}; \overline{3}; \overline{4}\};$$
$$m(A^2) = \{\overline{1}; \overline{2}; \overline{3}; \overline{4}\} = 0 = A(\pi_f).$$

Hence, π_f can be used for feedback. If our realization is to be built with two storage elements, we cannot store a variable assigned according to π_f. This does not stop us from making a two-variable realization with π_f for feedback, because we can use the assignment and equations of Fig. 6.6.

	0	1
1	1	4
2	1	4
3	2	3
4	3	1

Fig. 6.5. Machine B.

	y_1	y_2	(y_f)
1	0	1	(0)
2	0	0	(0)
3	1	0	(0)
4	1	1	(1)

$$Y_1 = \bar{x}y_f + x\bar{y}_f$$
$$Y_2 = \bar{y}_1 + xy_f$$
$$Y_f = y_1 y_2$$

Fig. 6.6. Assignment and equations for machine B.

The variable y_f is assigned according to π_f and is not stored and is not part of the assignment. To see that the feedback is confined to a single wire which carries a single bit according to π_f, we show the corresponding circuit diagram in Fig. 6.7

We close this section with a final observation. In general, there is no largest feedback partition for a given machine M. The only algebraic relation useful in finding feedback partitions is the monotonicity of the A-operator:

$$\pi \geqslant \tau \text{ implies } A(\pi) \geqslant A(\tau).$$

In particular, if

$$\pi_{a,b} \leqslant m(\pi_{a,b}),$$

then

$$A(\pi_{a,b}) > 0$$

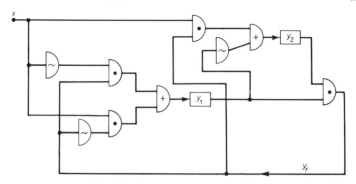

Fig. 6.7.   Realization of machine B.

and we know that any π_f must separate the states a and b. By considering large M partitions and refining them to separate these $\pi_{a,b}$, one is likely to find a large feedback partition if there is any.

6.2 FEEDBACK

In this section we show how the A-operator may be used to characterize feedback independently of the network concept. This approach to feedback generalizes the methods of the preceding section and leads to a variety of applications.

THEOREM 6.2. For a sequential machine M, $A(\pi_f) = 0$ if and only if for some n, the state of M is a function F of the last n inputs and the last n blocks of π_f that contained the state of M. That is, $A(\pi_f) = 0$ if and only if one can write

$$s(t+1) = F\{x(t), x(t-1), \ldots, x(t-n+1),$$
$$B[s(t)], B[s(t-1)], \ldots, B[s(t-n+1)]\}.$$

Proof. If the state of M is only a function of the last n inputs and the last n blocks of π_f, then clearly the machine can be built with only π_f for feedback, and therefore $A(\pi_f) = 0$. One such realization is shown schematically in Fig. 6.8.

Conversely,

$$A(\pi_f) = 0$$

implies that the state of M is only a function of the last n inputs and last n blocks of π_f which contained the state of M. ∎

The previous result suggests our next definition which describes the general feedback concept.

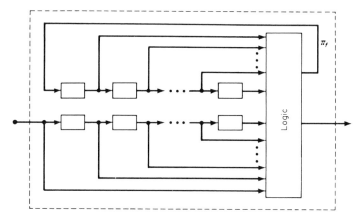

Fig. 6.8. Canonical form of the realization of M using π_f for feedback.

DEFINITION 6.4. The reduced machine M has a realization *using f*,

$$f: S \times I \longrightarrow U$$

as feedback if and only if for some n the state of M is a function of the last n inputs and last n values of f, that is,

$$s(t + 1) = g\{x(t), x(t - 1), \ldots, x(t - n + 1), f[s(t), x(t)],$$
$$f[s(t - 1), x(t - 1)], \ldots, f[s(t - n + 1), x(t - n + 1)]\}.$$

In order to apply this more general feedback concept to the study of information flow, we define a new pair algebra.

DEFINITION 6.5. Given $M = (S, I, O, \delta, \lambda)$, a function f,

$$f: S \times I \longrightarrow U,$$

and the lattice L of all set systems on S, let Δ_f be the subset of $L \times L$ such that (ϕ, ϕ') is in Δ_f if and only if, for all B in ϕ and $C \subseteq B$ such that

$$f(s, x) = f(t, x) \qquad \text{for all } s, t \text{ in } C,$$

there exists a B' in ϕ' such that

$$\delta(C, x) \subseteq B'.$$

LEMMA 6.2. Set Δ_f is a pair algebra.

Proof. The elements of Δ_f satisfy the postulates P_1 and P_2 of a pair algebra (Definition 3.3). ∎

Again the m and M operators in Δ_f on M have a simple intuitive interpretation and are used to formulate and solve a number of problems. For a given set system ϕ, the operator $m(\phi)$ yields the smallest system, or the largest amount of "information" about the next state of M, that can be computed from the block of ϕ that contained the present state of M, the input, and the f value. Similarly, for a given ϕ, the M operator gives the largest system $M(\phi)$ or least amount of "information" needed to compute the block of ϕ containing the present state of M from the block of $M(\phi)$ that contained the state of M, the input, and the f value.

THEOREM 6.3. For a reduced sequential machine M, the following three statements are equivalent:
(i) M can be realized in k stages using f for feedback;
(ii) $m^k(I) = 0$ in Δ_f;
(iii) $M^k(0) = I$ in Δ_f.
This theorem only asserts that there exists a realization of M with f as feedback, not necessarily a realization of the state behavior of M.

Proof. In any pair algebra

$$m^k(I) = 0 \text{ if and only if } M^k(0) = I,$$

by Corollary 3.1.9 and thus, we only have to show the equivalence of conditions (i) and (ii). If

$$m^k(I) = 0,$$

then by definition of the m operator we know that from any input sequence of length k and the corresponding k values of f, we can compute the state of M. Thus condition (ii) implies condition (i).
Conversely, if

$$m^k(I) = \phi > 0,$$

then there exist two states s and t, and an input sequence $\bar{x} = x_1 x_2 \ldots x_k$ such that

$$\bar{\delta}(s, \bar{x}) \neq \bar{\delta}(t, \bar{x})$$

and the corresponding sequence of f values is identical for both transitions, i.e.,

$$f(s, x_1) = f(t, x_1)$$
$$f[\delta(s, x_1), x_2] = f[\delta(t, x_1), x_2]$$
$$\ldots$$
$$f[\bar{\delta}(s, x_1 \ldots x_{k-1}), x_k] = f[\bar{\delta}(t, x_1 \ldots x_{k-1}), x_k].$$

Thus the state of M is not a function of only the last k inputs and f values. Thus condition (i) implies condition (ii). Combining the two implications we have the equivalence of (i) and (ii). ∎

	0	1	0	1
1	5	3	1	0
2	3	4	0	0
3	3	4	0	1
4	2	5	0	0
5	1	3	0	0

Fig. 6.9. Machine C.

To illustrate some of these ideas, consider machine C of Fig. 6.9. In this case let $f(s, a)$ be the output function $\lambda(s, a)$. Then in Δ_f

$$m(I) = \{\overline{1,2,3}; \overline{3,4,5}\} > m^2(I) = \{\overline{1,2,3}; \overline{3,5}; \overline{3,4}\} > m^3(I)$$
$$= \{\overline{3,4}; \overline{1,3}; \overline{2,3}; \overline{5}\} > m^4(I) = \{\overline{2,3}; \overline{1}; \overline{4}; \overline{5}\} > m^5(I) = 0,$$

from which we conclude that machine C can be realized by a five-stage realization using its output for feedback. From this we see that this realization of C will be at least a 32-state machine since each stage has two or more states.

EXERCISE. Give explicitly the state assignment and logical equations for the realization of machine C when its output is used as feedback.

6.3 FEEDBACK-FREE MACHINES

We now derive some results about feedback-free machines that are related in later sections to machine decomposition and error behavior.

First note that if the state partition π has S.P. on M, then the computation of $A(\pi)$ is simplified.

LEMMA 6.3. If π is an S.P. partition on an n-state machine M then

$$A^i(\pi) = m^{i-1}(\pi)$$

and

$$A(\pi) = m^n(\pi).$$

Proof. If π has S.P. then

$$m(\pi) \leqslant \pi.$$

By repeated application of this result, we have

$$m^i(\pi) \leqslant \cdots \leqslant m^2(\pi) \leqslant m(\pi) \leqslant \pi.$$

Clearly,

$$A^1(\pi) = m^0(\pi) = \pi.$$

If

$$A^k(\pi) = m^{k-1}(\pi),$$

then

$$A^{k+1}(\pi) = \pi \cdot m[A^k(\pi)] = \pi \cdot m^k(\pi) = m^k(\pi)$$

and the result follows by induction. ∎

LEMMA 6.4. If π_f has S.P. on M, then the state behavior of M can be realized using π_f for feedback if and only if

$$m^n(\pi_f) = 0.$$

Proof. Follows from Theorem 6.1 and Lemma 6.3. ∎

The next result gives two simple tests for feedback-free machines.

THEOREM 6.4. For an n-state sequential machine M the following statements are equivalent:

(i) M can be realized without feedback;

(ii) $m^n(I) = 0$;

(iii) $M^n(0) = I$.

Proof. From Theorem 6.3, condition (i) is possible if and only if $M^k(0) = I$ in Δ_f for some k where f is a constant (no feedback) function. For constant f, we see from Definition 6.5 that Δ_f is just the set system algebra Δ. But $M^k(0)$ can be assumed to be over the algebra of partiton pairs since the set system M operator and the partition pair M operator coincide over partitions. If (ii) holds for some k, it certainly must hold when $k = n$. Therefore condition (i) is equivalent to condition (iii) and the theorem is proved since the equivalence of (ii) and (iii) was established for all pair algebras. ∎

COROLLARY 6.4.1. If a machine has a feedback-free realization, it has a feedback-free state behavior realization.

Proof. Follows directly from the proof of the theorem. ∎

It should be observed that these tests not only describe an algorithm for testing whether a sequential machine M has a feedback-free realization but also specify a feedback-free realization of M if it exists, and this realization has the minimal number of stages. The next example illustrates the use of these tests and the corresponding realizations.

EXAMPLE. Consider the machine D shown in Fig. 6.10. For this machine

$$m(I) = \{\overline{0,1,3,6}; \overline{2,4,5,7}\},$$

$$m^2(I) = \{\overline{0,3}; \overline{1,6}; \overline{2,4}; \overline{5,7}\},$$

$$m^3(I) = 0,$$

$$M(0) = \{\overline{0,3}; \overline{1,6}; \overline{2,4}; \overline{5,7}\},$$

$$M^2(0) = \{\overline{0,1,3,6}; \overline{2,4,5,7}\},$$

$$M^3(0) = I.$$

Thus this machine has a feedback-free realization that consists of three stages as defined by the partitions

$$m(I) > m^2(I) > m^3(I)$$

which in this example are the same as

$$M^2(0) > M(0) > M^0(0).$$

Using the assignment shown in Fig. 6.11, we obtain the realization of Fig. 6.12.

	0	1	0	1
0	0	2	0	1
1	3	4	1	0
2	6	7	0	1
3	0	2	1	0
4	6	7	1	0
5	1	5	1	0
6	3	4	0	1
7	1	5	0	1

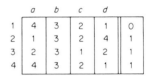

	y_1	y_2	y_3
0 $\rightarrow$	0	0	0
1 $\rightarrow$	0	1	1
2 $\rightarrow$	1	0	0
3 $\rightarrow$	0	0	1
4 $\rightarrow$	1	0	1
5 $\rightarrow$	1	1	1
6 $\rightarrow$	0	1	0
7 $\rightarrow$	1	1	0

Fig. 6.10. Machine D.   **Fig. 6.11.** Assignment for machine D.

Our next example shows that the feedback-free realization of a machine may require the use of more memory (or states) then a realization with feedback.

EXAMPLE. Consider machine E of Fig. 6.13.

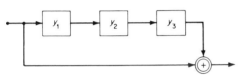

	a	b	c	d	
1	4	3	2	1	0
2	1	3	2	4	1
3	2	3	1	2	1
4	4	3	2	1	1

Fig. 6.12. Feedback-free realization   **Fig. 6.13.** Machine E.
of machine D.

The computations for this machine are shown below:

$$m(I) = \{\overline{1,2,4}; \overline{3}\},$$
$$m^2(I) = \{\overline{1,4}; \overline{2}; \overline{3}\},$$
$$m^3(I) = 0.$$

Thus, to realize this machine in a feedback-free form, we need three stages each containing a two-state component machine. Thus the machine can be realized as a submachine of a feedback-free machine that has eight states.

6.4 DECOMPOSITIONS WITH FEEDBACK-FREE COMPONENTS

If a sequential machine M does not have a feedback-free realization, then we still may be able to decompose M into two component machines so that one of the component machines is feedback-free. Such realizations are investigated in this section. Some of the results are used in the next section to characterize errors that can occur in sequential machines and to relate them to machine structure.

First, we give results about state behavior realizations since these results are computationally simpler than the corresponding results for general realizations.

THEOREM 6.5. Let the state behavior of an n-state machine M be realized by the serial connection,

$$M_1 \ominus M_2,$$

and let M_1 be associated with the S.P. partition π. Then M_1 has a feedback-free realization if and only if

$$\pi \geqslant m^n(I).$$

Furthermore, the largest such front machine M_σ is given by the partition

$$\sigma = m^n(I).$$

Proof. The state behavior of M_1 is isomorphic to the state behavior of the image machine M_π. The machine M_π is feedback-free if and only if (Theorem 6.4)

$$\bar{\pi} = \bar{m}^n(\bar{I})$$

which implies (Corollary 3.10.1)

$$\bar{\pi} = \overline{m^n(I) + \pi}$$

which means

$$\pi = m^n(I) + \pi$$

or

$$\pi \geqslant m^n(I).$$

Finally, since the partition $m^n(I)$ has S.P., we conclude that it defines the largest feedback-free front machine. In other words $m^n(I)$ defines the largest feedback-free homomorphic image of M. ∎

THEOREM 6.6. Let π be an S.P. partition on the n-state machine M. Then the state behavior of M can be realized by a serial connection of M_π to a feedback-free tail machine M_2 if and only if

$$m^n(\pi) = 0.$$

Furthermore, the smallest such front machine (largest S.P. partition σ) that contains all the feedback is given by the partition

$$\sigma = M^n(0).$$

Proof. The machine M_π can contain all the feedback of a realization of M if and only if there exists a feedback partition π_f of M such that

$$\pi_f \geqslant \pi.$$

By the monotonicity of the A operator and Lemma 6.3 we conclude that this is possible if and only if

$$0 = A(\pi_f) \geqslant A(\pi) = m''(\pi),$$

which proves the first part of the theorem. We know by Corollary 3.1.7 that

$$m''(\pi) = 0 \quad \text{if and only if} \quad M''(0) \geqslant \pi.$$

Since

$$\sigma = M''(0)$$

has S.P., we conclude that the smallest front machine containing all feedback is given by M_σ. ∎

We indicate schematically the fact that a machine is feedback-free by a straight double arrow and the existence of feedback by a circular double arrow as shown in Fig. 6.14.

The realization described in Theorem 6.5 is schematically described in Fig. 6.15.

Correspondingly, Fig. 6.16 shows the realization of M described in Theorem 6.6.

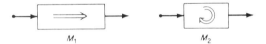

Fig. 6.14. Schematic representation of feedback-free machine, M_1, and a machine with feedback, M_2.

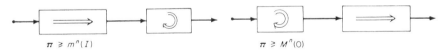

$\pi \geqslant m''(I)$

Fig. 6.15. Realization of M using a feedback-free front machine.

$\pi \geqslant M''(0)$

Fig. 6.16. Realization of M using a feedback-free tail machine.

To illustrate these results and their respective computations, consider machine F shown in Fig. 6.17. For this machine

$$M(0) = 0.$$

Thus the state behavior of machine F cannot be decomposed nontrivially into two serially connected machines so that the tail machine is feedback-free. On the other hand,

	0	1
0	1	7
1	0	6
2	5	2
3	4	3
4	1	6
5	0	7
6	4	2
7	5	3

	a	b	c
1	8	3	7
2	7	4	8
3	6	2	5
4	6	2	5
5	7	4	6
6	8	3	6
7	5	1	8
8	5	1	8

Fig. 6.17. Machine F.   **Fig. 6.18.** Machine G.

$$m(I) = \{\overline{0,1,4,5}; \overline{2,3,6,7}\},$$

$$m^2(I) = \{\overline{0,1}; \overline{2,3}; \overline{4,5}; \overline{6,7}\},$$

$$m^3(I) = m^2(I) = m^n(I),$$

which shows that F can be realized from a four-state, two-stage feedback-free front machine connected to a two-state machine with feedback.

Next consider machine G shown in Fig. 6.18.

For machine G

$$m(I) = \{\overline{1,2,3,4}; \overline{5,6,7,8}\},$$

$$m^2(I) = m(I),$$

$$M(0) = \{\overline{3,4}; \overline{7,8}; \overline{1}; \overline{2}; \overline{5}; \overline{6}\},$$

$$M^2(0) = \{\overline{1,2}; \overline{3,4}; \overline{5,6}; \overline{7,8}\},$$

$$M^3(0) = M^2(0).$$

Thus this machine has the realization shown schematically in Fig. 6.19. The corresponding S.P. partitions of this realization are shown below each of the four stages.

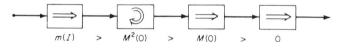

$$m(I) \qquad > \qquad M^2(0) \qquad > \qquad M(0) \qquad > \qquad 0$$

Fig. 6.19. Realization of machine G according to the S. P. partitions $m(I)$, $M^2(0)$, and $M(0)$.

We now give some results about feedback-free decompositions without the restriction to state behavior realizations.

Our first result gives the fewest state machine M_2 which can be connected in series to a feedback-free machine M_1 to realize M. We can think of such realizations as storing the last k inputs (say, in a shift register) in order to reduce the number of states in the tail machine M_2 that contains all the feedback of the system.

NOTATION. We use the symbol $\#|\phi|$ to indicate the number of elements in the largest block of set system ϕ.

THEOREM 6.7. Given a reduced machine M for which

$$I > m(I) > m^2(I) > \cdots > m^k(I) = m^{k+1}(I) = \phi,$$

where m is the S-S set system operator, then M can be realized by a serial connection of a k-stage feedback-free machine M_1 and a $\#|\phi|$ state machine M_2; and no fewer state machine, M_2' exists which can be connected to a feedback-free machine M_1' to realize M.

Proof. Since set system ϕ is such that

$$m(\phi) \leqslant \phi$$

it defines a ϕ image of M, say, M_ϕ. For M_ϕ we have

$$m^k(I) = \phi (= \text{zero partition for } M_\phi)$$

and thus M_ϕ is feedback-free. The largest block of ϕ contains $\#|\phi|$ states and we know that there exists a $\#|\phi|$ state machine M_2, which does this (see Theorem 5.10). To see that no fewer state machine can be used, observe that if B in ϕ and $|B| = \#|\phi|$, then by definition of $m^k(I)$ there exists an input sequence of arbitrary length which transforms $\#|\phi|$ distinct starting states of M onto the states of B. Thus, since M is reduced, none of these states can be equivalent and we need an $\#|\phi|$ state machine to distinguish them. ∎

To illustrate this theorem consider machine G of Fig. 6.18. For this machine the set system operator m yields

$$I > m(I) = \{\overline{1,2,3,4}; \overline{5,6,7,8}\} > m^2(I) = \{\overline{6,7,8}; \overline{5,7,8}; \overline{2,3,4}; \overline{1,3,4}\}$$
$$> m^3(I) = \{\overline{5,8}; \overline{1,3}; \overline{6,8}; \overline{5,7}; \overline{1,4}; \overline{6,7}; \overline{2,4}; \overline{2,3}\} = m^4(I) = \phi.$$

Since $\#|\phi| = 2$ we know that this machine can be realized by the serial connection of a three-stage feedback-free machine to a two-state machine with feedback. To achieve this we have to split states and we will have a 16-state machine. Recall that if we restricted ourselves to state behavior realizations, then we could only have a one-stage, two-state feedback-free front machine, since

$$m(I) = \{\overline{1,2,3,4}; \overline{5,6,7,8}\} = m^2(I).$$

Thus, as was to be expected, we see that state splitting permits us to obtain larger feedback-free front machines and fewer state tail machines that contain all the feedback of the system. If we consider the same problem for serial decompositions with feedback-free tail machines, then the situation is different and state splitting does not gain us anything because, as we observed in Section 5.3 for any partition π, $M(\pi)$ computed on the lattice of set system pairs is the same as $M(\pi)$ computed on the lattice of partition pairs.

The next theorem gives a corresponding result for the case when one stores the last k inputs and the last k outputs of the machine M.

THEOREM 6.8. The reduced machine M for which

$$I > m(I) > \ldots > m^k(I) = m^{k+1}(I) = \phi \text{ in } \Delta_\lambda,$$

can be realized by a $\#|\phi|$ state machine M_2, whose inputs are the last k inputs and last k outputs of this machine, and no fewer state machine can be used in such a realization. This realization is shown schematically in Fig. 6.20.

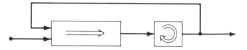

Fig. 6.20. The realization of M described in Theorem 6.8.

Proof. Similar to Theorem 6.7. ■

We now define a new pair algebra which is used in our next result.

DEFINITION 6.6. For a machine M, let the set system pair (ϕ, ϕ') be in Δ^* if and only if for all B in ϕ, x in I, and z in O, there exists a B' in ϕ' such that

$$\{s \mid s = \delta(t, x), t \text{ in } B \text{ and } \lambda(t, x) = z\} \subseteq B'.$$

LEMMA 6.5. For a machine M, Δ^* is a pair algebra.

Proof. Δ^* satisfies P_1 and P_2 of Definition 3.3. ■

THEOREM 6.9. The reduced machine M for which

$$I > m(I) > \ldots > m^k(I) = m^{k+1}(I) = \phi \text{ in } \Delta^*$$

can be realized by an $\#|\phi|$ state machine M_2 whose input is the input of M and the last k outputs of M_2, and no fewer state machine can be used in such a realization. A schematic representation of this realization is shown in Fig. 6.21.

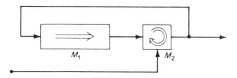

Fig. 6.21. The realization of M described in Theorem 6.9.

Proof. Similar to proof of Theorem 6.7. ■

From the last two theorems we can obtain some special cases.

COROLLARY 6.8.1. For a reduced machine M, the following three conditions are equivalent:

    (i) the state of M is only a function of the last k inputs and outputs;

(ii) $m^k(I) = 0$ in Δ_λ;
(iii) $M^k(0) = I$ in Δ_λ.

COROLLARY 6.9.1. For a reduced machine M, the following three conditions are equivalent:
(i) the state of M is only a function of the last k outputs;
(ii) $m^k(I) = 0$ in Δ^*;
(iii) $M^k(0) = I$ in Δ^*.

Proof. Similar to proof of Theorem 6.7. ∎

In the corresponding realizations of these machines, the machines M_2 of Figs. 6.20 and 6.21 have only one state and thus are combinational circuits.

6.5 STATE ERRORS

In this and the following section we analyze and classify errors which can occur in the state transitions of sequential machines, and relate these results to feedback. We imagine the following situation.

A machine M is monitoring some arbitrary input sequence over which we have no control. At some time when the machine is supposed to enter state s, an error occurs and the machine enters state t instead. We assume that this accident is not due to some permanent equipment failure, and we expect that the next time the machine is supposed to make this transition it will do it correctly. We now single out the errors of this kind that cannot be perpetuated indefinitely.

DEFINITION 6.7. The error in a sequential machine M of storing state t instead of state s is said to be *within a partition* π if and only if $\pi_{s,t} \leqslant \pi$, where $\pi_{s,t}$ is the partition that identifies only s and t. We say that the *error is $\pi_{s,t}$*.

DEFINITION 6.8. An error $\pi_{s,t}$ in machine M is said to be *temporary* if and only if there is an integer k such that for any input sequence $\bar{x}$ of length k,
$$\bar{\delta}(s, \bar{x}) = \bar{\delta}(t, \bar{x}).$$
If an error is not temporary, it is said to be *permanent*.

We now derive some algebraic results about temporary errors that relate them to the structure of the machine.

LEMMA 6.6. For a sequential machine M, the following statements are equivalent:

(i) Error $\pi_{p,q}$ must be corrected within k time units;

(ii) $m^k(\pi_{p,q}) = 0$;

(iii) $\pi_{p,q} \leqslant M^k(0)$.

Proof. It is easily verified that

$$m^k(\pi_{p,q}) = \sum \{\pi_{s,t} \mid s = \bar{\delta}(p, \bar{x}), t = \bar{\delta}(q, \bar{x}), \bar{x} \text{ of length } k\}.$$

Condition (i) says that

$$\bar{\delta}(p, \bar{x}) = \bar{\delta}(q, \bar{x}) \qquad \text{for } \bar{x} \text{ of length } k$$

and

$$\pi_{s,t} = 0,$$

hence (ii). On the other hand, (ii) says that

$$m^k(\pi_{p,q}) = 0,$$

or

$$\bar{\delta}(p, \bar{x}) = \bar{\delta}(q, \bar{x})$$

which is (i). The equivalence of (ii) and (iii) was shown to hold in any pair algebra. ∎

This next theorem enables us to find all temporary errors.

THEOREM 6.10. If M is a machine with n states, then the partition,

$$\pi_e = M^n(0)$$

has S.P. and an error $\pi_{s,t}$ is temporary error in M if and only if

$$\pi_{s,t} \leqslant \pi_e.$$

Proof. Clearly

$$M(0) \geqslant 0$$

and by induction and the monotonicity of the M operator

$$M^{i+1}(0) \geqslant M^i(0).$$

Since the zero partition cannot be enlarged more than $n - 1$ times,

$$M^n(0) = M^{n+i}(0)$$

for all positive integers i. By Lemma 6.6

$$\pi_e = M^n(0)$$

must contain precisely the temporary errors. Since

$$M(\pi_e) = \pi_e,$$

π_e has S.P. ∎

This theorem has interesting implications for machine design. We envision the following type of decomposition of a machine M. The partition

π_e, having S.P., can be used to make a component machine that operates independently of the other components and determines the block of π_e which contains the state of M. This machine must be made reliable since all its errors are permanent. The errors made by the other components (with a little care in design) cause errors only within the block of π_e and hence only cause temporary errors. It is therefore not so important that these components always function properly. Since π_e is the largest partition with S.P. such that

$$m^n(\pi_e) = 0,$$

π_e defines, by Theorem 6.10, the smallest front machine in a decomposition of M which can contain all the feedback of the realization. The next example illustrates an interesting relation between feedback and errors. Consider machine H shown in Fig. 6.22.

	0	1
1	4	2
2	3	2
3	1	4
4	1	4

	0	1
$B_1 = \{1, 2\}$	B_2	B_1
$B_2 = \{3, 4\}$	B_1	B_2

H_1

	$(0, B_1)$	$(0, B_2)$	$(1, B_1)$	$(1, B_2)$
$C_1 = \{1,3\}$	C_2	C_1	C_2	C_2
$C_2 = \{2,4\}$	C_1	C_1	C_2	C_2

H_2

Fig. 6.22. Machine H.   **Fig. 6.23.** Decomposition of machine H.

It is easily verified that

$$\pi_e = \{\overline{1,2}; \overline{3,4}\}.$$

Thus, we can realize H from two two-state machines H_1 and H_2, so that H_2 makes only temporary errors. In Fig. 6.23 we show H_1 and H_2, when H_2 is defined by the partition

$$\tau = \{\overline{1,3}; \overline{2,4}\}.$$

Observe that H_2 cannot be realized without feedback $[m^2(I) > 0]$, and if operated independently of H_1; it could have permanent errors, because of the first column. In the whole system though, H_2 can have only temporary errors since the first input to H_2 cannot occur twice in a row. After input $(0, B_1)$, machine H_1 will enter state B_2 thereby insuring a different input to H_2 at the next time interval.

The reason this works out so well is that every combination of states in H_1 and H_2 represents a state of H, and an error in H_2 must cause a temporary error. In the more general cases where π_e may not be uniform, there may be memory configurations which do not correspond to states of M, and these extra states lead to "don't care" conditions in M_2. Although these states are not accessible to the machine operating properly, these could be entered as a result of an error. It is only with the proper filling of the d.c. conditions that errors in M_2 are all made to be temporary in the system.

It is sufficient to fill the conditions so that all transitions are to memory configurations corresponding to states in M. This can be accomplished by filling the conditions with states of M_2 which already appear elsewhere in the column. Another possible approach is to let several memory configurations correspond to the same state of M. Thus, with "don't care" conditions filled accordingly, any choice of tail machine will only have errors which are temporary in the system.

From Theorems 6.4 and 6.10, we obtain Corollary 6.10.1.

COROLLARY 6.10.1. A sequential machine M has only temporary errors, ($\pi_e = I$) if and only if M can be built without feedback.

One final observation.

COROLLARY 6.10.2. If $\pi_e \neq 0$, then there are two states s and t such that for any input x,

$$\delta(s, x) = \delta(t, x).$$

Proof. Since $M(0)$ must not be 0, it must have two elements s and t, in the same block and these must satisfy the corollary. ∎

NOTE. When working with unreduced machines, it might be more appropriate to study the partition

$$\sigma_e = M^n(\pi_R)$$

for which a similar theory holds; where π_R is the largest output consistent partition with S.P. The partition σ_e contains precisely those errors that always give the same output after some finite length of time k, even though some harmless error persists in the states. Thus σ_e is invariant under state reduction.

There are some state errors that may persist indefinitely and yet only cause a finite number of false outputs. Consider, for example, the machine J of Fig. 6.24 and the associated *error graph*. The error graph has a node

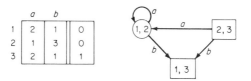

Fig. 6.24.   Machine J with error graph.

for each distinct pair of states. The node is indicated with a circle if the output of the two states is the same and with a rectangle if they are different. If an input leads from one error to another, this is indicated with a directed edge. The error "1,3" has no edges leaving, for each transition from states 1 and 3 leads to identical states. There are no cycles in this graph which contain rectangular nodes and hence all input sequences cause only a finite number of false outputs. The error $\pi_{1,2}$ is permanent, for it can stay in the machine indefinitely; but the only output error it causes is after input b occurs, and this leads to a correction of the error. Contrast this to machine K of Fig. 6.25 where the error $\pi_{2,3}$ leads to a false output every time input a is applied. We now develop these ideas formally.

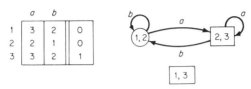

Fig. 6.25. Machine K with error graph.

DEFINITION 6.9. An error $\pi_{s,t}$ in a machine M is said to be *inessential* if and only if, for any infinite input sequence

$$x_1 x_2 x_3 \ldots$$

there is only a finite set J of integers such that there are different outputs associated with the states

$$\bar{\delta}(s, x_1\, x_2 \ldots x_k) \text{ and } \bar{\delta}(t, x_1 x_2 \ldots x_k), k \text{ in } J.$$

For Mealy machines, we refer to the outputs associated with the transitions from

$$\bar{\delta}(s, x_1\, x_2 \ldots x_{k-1}) \text{ to } \bar{\delta}(s, x_1\, x_2 \ldots x_k)$$

and from

$$\bar{\delta}(t, x_1 x_2 \ldots x_{k-1}) \text{ to } \bar{\delta}(t, x_1 x_2 \ldots x_k).$$

THEOREM 6.11. For a given machine M, there is a partition π_E on the set of states of M such that π_E has S.P. and an error $\pi_{s,t}$ is inessential if and only if

$$\pi_{s,t} \leqslant \pi_E.$$

Proof. It is clear from Definition 6.9 that if $\pi_{s,t}$ and $\pi_{t,r}$ are both inessential, then so is $\pi_{s,r}$. Thus

$$\pi_E = \sum \{\pi_{p,q} \,|\, \pi_{p,q} \text{ inessential}\}.$$

If

$$\pi_{s,t} \leqslant \pi_E$$

then $\pi_{p,q}$ is inessential for any input a in I, where

$$\delta(s, a) = p \qquad \text{and} \qquad \delta(t, a) = q.$$

Thus

$$\pi_{p,q} \leqslant \pi_E$$

and π_E has S.P. ∎

We now relate π_E to other partitions.

COROLLARY 6.11.1. For sequential machine M

$$\pi_E \geqslant \pi_e.$$

Proof. Obvious from the definitions of the errors. ∎

COROLLARY 6.11.2. If π_R is an output consistent partition with S.P. on M, then

$$\pi_E \geqslant \pi_R.$$

Proof. Errors in π_R cannot affect any outputs. ∎

This corollary implies the following.

COROLLARY 6.11.3. The machine M_{π_E} which computes the block of π_E is invariant under state reduction.

Thus the partition π_E is perhaps the most interesting partition discussed here. The reader may have noticed that we have failed to give an algebraic characterization of π_E as we did for π_e. The reason for this is in Theorem 6.12.

THEOREM 6.12. It is impossible to determine π_E using the *I-S*, *S-S*, *S-O*, and *I-O* partition pair algebras.

Proof. Machines J and K (Figs. 6.24 and 6.25) have the same Mm-lattice (hence the same partition pairs), the same *I-S* pairs, the same *S-O* pairs, and the same *I-O* pairs; yet

$$\pi_E = I$$

for machine J and

$$\pi_E = \pi_e = \{\overline{1,3};\overline{2}\}$$

for machine K. ∎

The next theorem summarizes the results and shows that the existence of different types of errors in a sequential machine guarantees that the machine can be nontrivially decomposed so that each component machine permits only one type of error.

THEOREM 6.13. Any sequential machine M can be decomposed into the serial connection of three machines

$$M_1 \ominus M_2 \ominus M_3$$

such that

(i) every error in M_1 is an essential error of M;

(ii) every error in M_2 is an inessential error of M;

(iii) every error in M_3 is a temporary error of M.

Proof. From Theorem 6.10 and 6.11 and Corollary 6.11.1, we know that the partitions π_E and π_e on the states S of M have S.P.,

$$\pi_E \geqslant \pi_e,$$

and an error $\pi_{p,q}$ is:

(i) temporary if and only if $\pi_e \geqslant \pi_{p,q}$;

(ii) inessential if and only if $\pi_E \geqslant \pi_{p,q}$.

But this shows (Theorem 4.3) that we can realize M from a serial connection of M_1, M_2, M_3 so that

$$M_1 \cong M_{\pi_E} \text{ and } M_1 \ominus M_2 \cong M_{\pi_e}$$

with the required error behavior. ∎

COROLLARY 6.13.1. If the state behavior of a machine M cannot be non-trivially realized by a serial or parallel connection of two smaller machines then either

(i) all errors in M are essential;

(ii) all errors in M are inessential but not temporary.

Proof. If two kinds of errors occur in M, then by Theorem 6.13, M can be decomposed into smaller machines. Thus we just have to show that no temporary errors can occur in M. If $\pi_{s,t}$ is a temporary error, then

$$\pi_{s,t} \leqslant \pi_e = M^n(0).$$

Since $M^k(0)$ has S.P. for $k = 0, 1, 2, \ldots$, we conclude that

$$I = M(0) > 0;$$

for otherwise M is nontrivially decomposable. But

$$M(0) = I$$

implies that for all pairs of states s, t of M

$$\delta(s, x) = \delta(t, x),$$

which implies that every partition π on S has S.P. Thus if M has more than two states, it can be nontrivially decomposed contradicting the assumption. Thus there are no temporary errors in M. ∎

EXAMPLE. Since

$$\pi_E \geqslant \pi_e$$

we know that a three-state machine cannot have simultaneously essential, inessential and temporary errors. Machine L of Fig. 6.26 shows that all three error types can exist simultaneously in a four-state machine. For this machine

$$\pi_E = \{\overline{1}; \overline{2,3,4}\} > \pi_e = \{\overline{1}; \overline{2}; \overline{3,4}\}.$$

EXAMPLE. Machine N of Fig. 6.27 is a two-input, five-state (Moore) machine that has three different error types. For this machine

$$\pi_E = \{\overline{0,1}; \overline{2,3,4}\} > \pi_e = \{\overline{0}; \overline{1}; \overline{2}; \overline{3,4}\}.$$

	a	b	c	a	b	c
1	1	4	1	0	0	0
2	3	1	3	0	0	0
3	2	1	4	0	0	0
4	2	1	4	1	1	0

Fig. 6.26.   Machine L.

	a	b	
0	0	3	0
1	1	4	0
2	3	0	0
3	2	1	0
4	2	1	1

Fig. 6.27.   Machine N.

Next we use the concept of temporary errors to characterize the relation between the two sequential machine models.

THEOREM 6.14. Let M be a reduced Moore machine and let M' be the corresponding reduced Mealy machine. Then the state behavior of M is isomorphic to the state behavior of M' if and only if there are no temporary errors in M.

Proof. From Theorem 1.3 we easily obtain that the S.P. partition π on S of M that maps the state behavior of M onto the state behavior of M' is given by

$$\pi = M(0).$$

The state behaviors are isomorphic if and only if

$$\pi = 0$$

and therefore

$$M(0) = 0.$$

This happens (Lemma 6.6) if and only if there are no temporary errors in M. ∎

Our next corollary shows how we can convert certain realizations of reduced Moore machines in the corresponding realization of the reduced Mealy machines.

COROLLARY 6.14.1. Let M be a reduced Moore machine whose state behavior is realized by a serial connection of the machines

$$M_k, M_{k-1}, \ldots, M_1, M_0$$

defined by the S.P. partitions

$$M^{k+1}(0) = M^k(0) > M^{k-1}(0) > M^{k-2}(0) > \ldots > M^1(0) > 0.$$

Then the connection of the machines

$$M_k, M_{k-1}, \ldots, M_1$$

realize the state behavior of the corresponding reduced Mealy machine M'.

Proof. Obvious from Theorem 6.14. ∎

6.6 INPUT ERRORS

We now discuss the state errors that can be caused by errors in the input sequence and derive several results about such errors. We limit ourselves to input errors that do not effect the length of the input sequence. This rather specialized application *may be omitted on first reading*.

DEFINITION 6.10. We say that a state error $\pi_{s,t}$ can be *input-induced* in M if and only if there exists a state u and two input sequences $\bar{x}$ and $\bar{x}'$ of equal length such that

$$\bar{\delta}(u, \bar{x}) = s, \bar{\delta}(u, \bar{x}') = t.$$

Let

$$\rho = \Sigma \{\pi_{s,t} \mid \pi_{s,t} \text{ is input-induced}\}.$$

LEMMA 6.7. For an n-state sequential machine M

$$\rho = \sum_{k=0}^{n} m^k(\pi),$$

where

$$\pi = m_{I-s}(I).$$

Proof. By definition

$\pi = m_{I-s}(I) = \Sigma \{\pi_{r,v} \mid$ there exist u in S and a, b in I such that $\delta(u, a) = r, \delta(u, b) = v\}$,

which is the sum over all state errors that can be induced by an input sequence of length one. Let $\pi = \rho_1$. The sum of the state errors that can be induced by input sequences of length one or two is given by

$$\rho_2 = m(\pi) + \pi.$$

Similarly, the sum of errors that are induced by input sequences of length three or shorter is given by

$$\rho_3 = m[m(\pi) + \pi] + \pi = m^2(\pi) + m(\pi) + \pi.$$

By induction we obtain that

$$\rho_1 \leqslant \rho_2 \leqslant \rho_3 \leqslant \ldots \leqslant \rho_n = \rho = \sum_{k=0}^{n} m^k(\pi). \blacksquare$$

THEOREM 6.15. Let M be an n-state sequential machine. Then all input induced errors are temporary if and only if

$$M^n(0) \geqslant \sum_{k=0}^{n} m^k(\pi),$$

where

$$\pi = m_{I-s}(I).$$

Proof. If $\pi_{s,t}$ is input-induced, then by Lemma 6.7

$$\pi_{s,t} \leqslant \sum m^k(\pi).$$

Thus

$$\pi_{s,t} \leqslant M^n(0)$$

and using Theorem 6.10 we conclude that $\pi_{s,t}$ is a temporary error in M. If all input-induced errors are temporary, then by Lemma 6.7 and Theorem 6.10

$$\sum_{k=0}^{n} m^k(\pi) \leqslant M^n(0). \ \blacksquare$$

We say that M is a *bounded-transient* machine if and only if all input-induced errors are temporary.

The previous theorem leads to a canonical form for bounded-transient machines. From Theorem 6.6 we know that the S.P. partition $M^n(0)$ defines the smallest machine M_1, that can be connected in series with a feedback-free machine, M_2, to realize M. On the other hand, the S.P. partition

$$\sum_{k=0}^{n} m^k(\pi)$$

defines the maximal input-free machine that can be used to realize M. If all input errors are temporary in M then

$$\sum_{k=0}^{n} m^k(\pi) \leqslant M^n(0).$$

This leads to our next result.

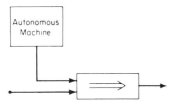

Fig. 6.28. Canonical form of a bounded transient machine.

COROLLARY 6.15.1. A sequential machine M has only temporary input errors if and only if it can be realized as a serial connection of an input-free machine to a feedback-free tail machine (as shown in Fig. 6.28).

The next corollary extends the previous theorem to inessential errors.

COROLLARY 6.15.2. Let M be an n-state sequential machine. Then all input-induced errors are inessential if and only if

$$\sum_{k=0}^{n} m^k[m_{I-s}(I)] \leqslant \pi_E.$$

Proof. Immediate from Lemma 6.7 and Theorem 6.11. ∎

EXAMPLE. Consider machine P shown in Fig. 6.29. For this machine

$$\pi = m_{I-s}(I) = \{\overline{1,2}; \overline{3,4}; \overline{5,6}; \overline{7,8}\},$$

$$\sum_{k=0}^{n} m^k(\pi) = \pi,$$

	0	1
1	3	4
2	4	3
3	5	6
4	6	5
5	7	8
6	8	7
7	1	2
8	1	2

Fig. 6.29. Machine P.

$$M(0) = \{\overline{1}; \overline{2}; \overline{3}; \overline{4}; \overline{5}; \overline{6}; \overline{7,8}\},$$

$$M^2(0) = \{\overline{1}; \overline{2}; \overline{3}; \overline{4}; \overline{5,6}; \overline{7,8}\},$$

$$M^3(0) = \{\overline{1}; \overline{2}; \overline{3,4}; \overline{5,6}; \overline{7,8}\},$$

$$M^4(0) = \{\overline{1,2}; \overline{3,4}; \overline{5,6}; \overline{7,8}\},$$

$$M^4(0) = M^5(0).$$

Thus

$$M^n(0) = \sum_{k=0}^{n} m^k(\pi)$$

and we conclude that this is a bounded-transient machine. Furthermore, we see that for this machine every input-induced error will be corrected in four operations of M since the minimal feedback-free tail that can be serially connected to an input-free machine to realize M has four stages.

NOTES

The study of feedback in sequential machines and its relation to errors was started by the authors [17]. The pair algebra approach to general feedback problems appeared in [18]. The use of the machine output for feedback and the effect of storing past inputs was studied by E. J. McCluskey in [23] where Theorems 6.8 and 6.9 were first derived. Bounded-transient machines were first studied by S. Winograd [29]. It has been shown recently by A.D. Friedman that every machine can be realized by a single binary feedback loop machine.

7 SEMIGROUPS AND MACHINES

7.1 THE SEMIGROUP OF A MACHINE

A sequential machine can be described as a set of mappings of the set of states into itself, where each mapping corresponds to an input. Input sequences therefore correspond to functional composition of these mappings. The mappings corresponding to the input sequences are finite in number and are closed under composition. Thus these mappings form a finite semigroup of transformations on the set of states of the machine. This semigroup uniquely determined by the machine reflects the computational capability of the machine and its structure is closely related to the machine structure.

In this chapter, we use these semigroups to solve basic capability problems about loop-free realizations:

(1) What set of machines is required to realize any sequential machine?

(2) Characterize those "computational capabilities" of a machine which have to be present in some component machine of any realization of the machine.

These results can be obtained from the partition-set system techniques of the previous chapters and some rudimentary group theory. Thus, we are led to the point of view that the semigroups study is more appropriate for expressing what happens in a machine decomposition rather than how decompositions may be constructed.

We consider the state machine first since here the definition is most natural.

DEFINITION 7.1. The *semigroup of a state machine*

178

$$M = (S, I, \delta)$$

is the semigroup generated by the inputs regarded as mappings of S into S where, for a in I,

$$a : S \longrightarrow S$$

is given by

$$(s)a = \delta(s, a).$$

By writing the input function as $(s)a$ instead of $a(s)$, we link up the function concatenation notation with the sequence notation. Thus we may write

$$[(s)a]b = (s)a \cdot b = (s)ab$$

and interpret $(s)ab$ as the result of applying input sequence ab to s or applying semigroup function ab to s. This is certainly desirable since the two concepts are really the same, but some caution must be used. An equation of the form

$$\bar{a} = \bar{b}$$

could mean that either

(1) $\bar{a} = a_1 \ldots a_n$ is the same element of $\mathscr{I}_0$ as
$\bar{b} = b_1 \ldots b_m$, that is
$m = n$ and $a_i = b_i$ for $1 \leqslant i \leqslant m$;

(2) the semigroup product $a_1 \ldots a_n$ is the same
as semigroup product $b_1 \ldots b_n$, that is
$\bar{\delta}(s, \bar{a}) = \bar{\delta}(s, \bar{b})$ for all s in S.

In this chapter, however, we interpret such an equation to mean that the semigroup products are the same (Interpretation 2).

EXAMPLE. We wish to find the semigroup of state machine A of Fig. 7.1. To do this, we start generating other semigroup elements from inputs 0 and 1. We begin by computing the result of strings of length two and augmenting the state table with these "sequence inputs" or "input words." The calculation for 01 looks like this:

$$(s_1)01 = [(s_1)0]1 = [s_3]1 = s_1$$
$$(s_2)01 = [(s_2)0]1 = [s_1]1 = s_2$$
$$(s_3)01 = [(s_3)0]1 = [s_3]1 = s_1.$$

After all length two input sequences are computed, the table looks like

	0	1
s_1	s_3	s_2
s_2	s_1	s_2
s_3	s_3	s_1

Fig. 7.1. Machine A.

	0	1	01	10	00	11
s_1	s_3	s_2	s_1	s_1	s_3	s_2
s_2	s_1	s_2	s_2	s_1	s_3	s_2
s_3	s_3	s_1	s_1	s_3	s_3	s_2

Fig. 7.2. Intermediate calculation of semigroup of A.

Fig. 7.2 and we are ready to generate strings of length three. Most of these result in state columns previously generated and we write these sequences above the first appearance of the column. For example, we discover that

$$010 = 0$$

and so we write 010 at the head of the 0 column. This results in Fig. 7.3. Finally, we try to extend the new three input column into four input columns but we discover that

$$(001)0 = 00$$

and

$$(001)1 = 11.$$

Thus, the possibility of finding new columns is exhausted. In order to write out the semigroup in table form, we give each column a name $(0, \ldots, 6)$ and calculate the products. This results in the table in Fig. 7.4.

	0	1	2	3	4	5	6
					100 000	011 111	110
	010 0	101 1	01	10	00	11	001
s_1	s_3	s_2	s_1	s_1	s_3	s_2	s_1
s_2	s_1	s_2	s_2	s_1	s_3	s_2	s_1
s_3	s_3	s_1	s_1	s_3	s_3	s_2	s_1

Fig. 7.3.   Full calculation of semigroup of A.

	0	1	2	3	4	5	6
0	4	2	6	0	4	5	6
1	3	5	1	6	4	5	6
2	0	5	2	6	4	5	6
3	4	1	6	3	4	5	6
4	4	6	6	4	4	5	6
5	6	5	5	6	4	5	6
6	4	5	6	6	4	5	6

Fig. 7.4.   Semigroup of machine A (accumulator A').

The relations we found in augmenting the input columns can be used to advantage in finding the semigroup table. For instances,

$$3 \cdot 6 = (10)(001)$$

by associative law

$$= 1(000)1$$

because $000 = 00$ (as noted in Fig. 7.3)

$$= 1(00)1 = (100)1$$

because $100 = 00$ (as noted in Fig. 7.3)

$$= 001 = 6.$$

Notice that the semigroup table itself can be regarded as the table of a state machine A'. State machine A' is an instance of what we call a "semigroup accumulator." The submachine of A' obtained by restricting the input set to $\{0, 1\}$ can be reduced to a machine isomorphic to A by using any of the S.P. partitions

$$\{\overline{2,3,6};\ \overline{1,5};\ \overline{0,4}\},$$
$$\{\overline{0,3,6};\ \overline{1,2,5};\ \overline{4}\},$$
$$\{\overline{1,2,6};\ \overline{5};\ \overline{0,3,4}\},$$
$$\{\overline{0,1,6};\ \overline{2,5};\ \overline{3,4}\}.$$

Thus, A' realizes A. A later theorem will guarantee the existence of such partitions for all machines satisfying a mild connectedness condition.

Also note that the submachine of A' determined by inputs $\{0, 1\}$ and states $\{4, 5, 6\}$ is isomorphic to A, and so A' realizes the state behavior of A. Thus, no extra S.P. decompositions have been created. The simple serial realization determined by S.P. set system

$$\phi = \{\overline{s_1,s_3};\ \overline{s_1,s_2}\}$$

is still undetectable by S.P. partitions, and so going from A to A' is seen to be limited as a state-splitting technique.

Next we extend our concept to Moore type machines. By appealing to the reduced machine realization, the definition becomes realization independent.

DEFINITION 7.2. If
$$M = (S, I, O, \delta, \lambda)$$
is a Moore type sequential machine, then we say that the semigroup of state machine
$$M' = (S_R, I, \delta_R)$$
is the *semigroup of machine* M where $M_R = (S_R, I, O, \delta_R, \lambda_R)$ is the reduced form of M.

In other words, to get the semigroup of M, we reduce it, take away the outputs, and compute the semigroup of the resulting state machine. Thus each semigroup element may be identified with a class of input sequences whose effect on the machine cannot be distinguished by subsequent machine experiments. To acheive this same effect in the Mealy case is trickier and we consider the Moore case for the sake of simplicity.

As pointed out in the example, a semigroup may be thought of as a special kind of machine. Thus we have a way of going from semigroup to machine which provides a kind of inverse to our previous construction.

DEFINITION 7.3. If H is a semigroup, then the machine
$$M_H = (H, H, H, \delta_H, \lambda_H)$$
where
$$\delta_H(s, a) = s \cdot a \qquad \text{and} \qquad \lambda_H(s) = s$$
is called the *semigroup accumulator* for H. If H is a group, we may call M_H a *group accumulator*.

An example of a group accumulator is provided by a 36-bit accumulator in a computer which accumulates the addition group modulo 2^{36}. This explains the choice of nomenclature.

The purpose of the remaining sections is to elucidate and exploit the relationships between machines and their associated semigroups and accumulators.

7.2 REALIZATION BY SEMIGROUPS

As mentioned in the example of the last section, a machine can often be realized by the semigroup accumulator for its associated semigroup. Other times, one must first add the identity transformation to the associated semigroup in order to realize the machine by the accumulator. The occurrence of these situations can be guranteed by the two connectedness conditions of the next definition. The effect of these conditions is to restrict our attention to machines which have no states that cannot be entered in normal use. Thus, these restrictions are really quite harmless.

DEFINITION 7.4. We say that machine

$$M = (S, I, O, \delta, \lambda)$$

has a starting state if and only if there is a state s in S such that for all t in S, there exists an $\bar{a}$ in $\mathscr{I}_0$ such that

$$t = \bar{\delta}(s, \bar{a}).$$

We say that M *has a strong starting state* if $\bar{a}$ can always be chosen in $\mathscr{I}$.

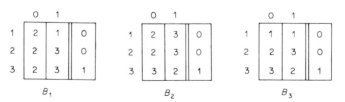

Fig. 7.5. Machines B_1, B_2, and B_3.

EXAMPLE. Figure 7.5 shows three machines. Machine B_1 has a strong starting state $s = 1$ because

$$\delta_1(1, 1) = 1$$
$$\delta_1(1, 0) = 2$$
$$\bar{\delta}_1(1, 01) = 3.$$

Machine B_2 has a starting state $s = 1$ because

$$\delta_2(1, \Lambda) = 1$$
$$\delta_2(1, 0) = 2$$
$$\delta_2(1, 1) = 3.$$

State 1 is not a strong starting state for B_2 because the only sequence which carries state 1 into state 1 is the null sequence Λ and Λ is not in $\mathscr{I}$. Machine B_3 has no starting state since state 1 cannot be reached from states 2 or 3 and states 2 and 3 cannot be reached from state 1.

In behavioral applications, it is often necessary to specify a starting state as part of the machine description. For structural applications, we require the existence of states from which every other state can be reached, but it is in no way important that the machine actually be "started" in such a state. Nevertheless, these concepts are very close, and this "starting state" terminology seems the most appropriate.

Observe that a state s is a strong starting state for M if and only if, for any t in S, there are an infinite number of $\bar{a}$ in $\mathscr{I}$ such that $t = \bar{\delta}(s, \bar{a})$. We can now contrast the following concepts:

1. Strongly connected: there are always transitions leading to any designated state.

2. Strong starting state: the possibility of transitions leading to any designated state can be preserved indefinitely.

3. Starting state: there is an initial possibility of transitions into any given state.

4. None of the above: some states of the machine cannot be reached. This shows that Definition 7.4 can accurately be considered as a connectedness condition.

We can now state the key result about the machine-semigroup relationship which will be exploited to relate machine and semigroup structures.

NOTATION. If H is a semigroup of functions of set S into S, then we write H_0 for the semigroup $H \cup \{e\}$ where e is the identity mapping of S into S.

THEOREM 7.1. If H is the semi-group of a machine

$$M = (S, I, O, \delta, \lambda)$$

and if M has a starting state, then semigroup accumulator M_{H_0} realizes M. If M has a strong starting state, then M_H realizes M.

Proof. Let s be a starting state of M. For t in S and a in H_0, define

$$a \in \alpha(t) \text{ if and only if } (s)a = t,$$

let $\quad \iota(a) = a \quad$ for a in I,

and let $\quad \zeta(a) = \lambda((s)a) \quad$ for a in H.

We first have to show that $\alpha(t)$ is nonempty. Let a in $\mathscr{I}_0$ be a sequence such that $\bar{\delta}(s, \bar{a}) = t$. If $\bar{a} = \Lambda$, then $(s)e = t$ and so e is in $\alpha(t)$. Otherwise, $\bar{a} = a_1 \ldots a_k$ and $\delta(s, b) = t$ where b is the product $a_1 \ldots a_k$. Thus we have b in $\alpha(t)$. Note that if s is a strong starting state, we do not need to use $\bar{a} = \Lambda$ and so there is no need to add e to H. This same assignment then works to establish the second statement of the theorem.

All that remains is to prove that (α, ι, ζ) is an assignment map. Suppose that a is in $\alpha(t)$ and b is in I. Then

$$(s)\delta_H(a, \iota(b))$$

by definition of ι and δ_H

$$= (s)ab$$

because $(s)a = t$ by definition of $\alpha(t)$

$$= (t)b$$

by notation

$$= \delta(t, b).$$

Therefore

$$\delta_H(a, \iota(b)) \text{ is in } \alpha(\delta(t, b))$$

and part (i) of Definition 1.14 is verified. To verify (ii), we assume a is in $\alpha(t)$ and a series of definitions yield

$$\zeta(\lambda_H(a)) = \zeta(a) = \lambda((s)a) = \lambda(t).$$

Thus we indeed have a realization. $\blacksquare$

EXERCISE. Verify this result for machines B_1 and B_2 of Fig. 7.5. Note that the identity *map* must be added to the semigroup of B_2 even though this semigroup has an identity *element* (namely, input 0). Machine B_3 shows that the theorem would be false if the connectedness condition were dropped.

We have now shown that any decomposition of a machine's semigroup is automatically a decomposition of the machine, since the semigroup realizes the machine. The question of which decompositions of M can be detected from the semigroup now arises. The answer is that only the loop-free decompositions can be so detected, but we require several lemmas to prove it.

The first lemma gives a more exact statement of how the semigroup realizes the machine.

NOTATION. If H is the semigroup of a machine M, then we write

$$M_H^* = (H, I, H, \delta_H, \lambda_H)$$

and

$$M_{H_0}^* = (H_0, I, H_0, \delta_{H_0}, \lambda_{H_0}).$$

In words, M_H^* is the submachine of semigroup accumulator M_H obtained by taking I (input alphabet of M) as the input set instead of H.

LEMMA 7.1 If H is the semigroup of machine M, then there is a homo-morphism of $M_{H_0}^*$ onto M whenever M has a starting state and there is a homomorphism of M_H^* onto M whenever M has a strong starting state.

Proof. Let s be a starting state or a strong starting state. In either case, the homomorphism is given by

$$h_1(a) = (s)a \qquad \text{for } a \text{ in } H \text{ or } H_0,$$
$$h_2(a) = a \qquad \text{for } a \text{ in } I,$$
$$h_3(a) = \lambda[(s)a] \qquad \text{for } a \text{ in } H \text{ or } H_0.$$

This is verified by the equations

$$h_1(\delta_H(b, a)) = (s)ba = \delta(h_1(b), h_2(a))$$
$$h_3(\lambda_H(b)) = \lambda[(s)b] = \lambda[h_1(b)].$$

Finally, to show that h_1 is onto, we have to find for each t in S a state a in H_0 (or H) which goes into t under a. This is equivalent to saying we need some a such that $(s)a = t$. Such an a can always be found because s is a (strong) starting state. Thus the lemma is proved. ∎

The next lemma says that restricting the inputs of the semigroup accumu-lator to I doesn't change the S.P. partitions.

LEMMA 7.2. If H is the semigroup of machine M, then

$$L_{M_H} = L_{M_H^*};$$
$$L_{M_{H_0}} = L_{M_{H_0}^*}.$$

Proof. All blocks of π in $L_{M_H^*}$ go into blocks of π under all a in I, and since H is just the closure of I under concatenation, the same must be true for a in H. The converse is obvious. The same statement can be made about π in $L_{M_{H_0}^*}$ since the identity map also sends blocks of π into blocks of π. ∎

THEOREM 7.2. All the state behavior loop-free decompositions of a machine M with semigroup H can be detected from the S.P. lattice of semigroup accumulator M_{H_0} (M_H) if M has a (strong) starting state.

Proof. The loop-free state behavior realizations of M are determined by its S.P. lattice L_M by Chapter 4. If M has a starting state, $M_{H_0}^*$ is a split version of M by Lemma 7.1 and the structure of L_M is embedded in $L_{M_{H_0}^*}$ by Theorem 5.2. But by Lemma 7.2, $L_{M_{H_0}^*} = L_{M_{H_0}}$ and so the structure of L_M is also embedded in $L_{M_{H_0}}$. If M has a strong starting state, the analogous remarks hold for M_H. ∎

In contrast to this, the transition from a machine M to its associated semigroup accumulator M_H or M_{H_0} destroys the partition pair structure of M, and the resulting partition pair structure is essentially the minimal structure imposed by the S.P. lattice. This is made precise by the next two exercises.

EXERCISE. Show that the partition pair operators on an accumulator M_H satisfy the inequalities

$$M(m(\pi)) \geqslant m(\pi) \quad \text{and} \quad m(M(\pi)) \leqslant M(\pi).$$

This means that all M partitions and m partitions have S.P.

EXERCISE. Show that the operators on an accumulator M_{H_0} satisfy the equations

$$M(m(\pi)) = m(\pi) \quad \text{and} \quad m(M(\pi)) = M(\pi).$$

This means that the M partitions, the m partitions, and the S.P. partitions are all the same.

One expects, therefore, that the important structural applications of semigroup theory to machines will be for the loop-free case. The purpose of the remaining sections is to obtain a more detailed understanding of this relationship. The reader is reminded, however, that the presentation here is not the only way that semigroups have been attached to machine theory. Several other interesting uses of semigroups appear in the machine literature, but these generally say little about structure, which is the main concern of this book.

7.3   THE STRUCTURE OF GROUP ACCUMULATORS

If a machine is such that every input of the machine permutes the states, than the semigroup of the machine is a group. This is because a sufficient repetition of an input leads back to the identity input. Thus, there is a broad, easily recognized class of machines whose associated semigroup is a group. The carryover of group structure to group accumulator structure is so direct that nearly all the results here are restatements of classic group theory.

First, we characterize S.P. partitions.

THEOREM 7.3. A partition π on the states of group accumulator $(G, G, G, \delta_G, \lambda_G)$ has the substitution property if and only if the blocks of π are right cosets of some subgroup H of G. For short, we call this partition π_H.

Proof. Since applying an input is the same as multiplying the state on the right and since right cosets go into right cosets under right multiplication, it is obvious that any such π_H has S.P.

Going the other way, let H be the block of π containing identity element e. $Ha \subseteq H$ for all a in H since π has S.P. and ea is in H. Therefore, H is a subgroup of G and the blocks of π must contain entire right cosets of H.

But if B is a block of π and b is an element of B, then $Bb^{-1} \subseteq H$ since e is in Bb^{-1} and hence B has no more elements than H. Therefore, B is a single right coset of H. ∎

COROLLARY 7.3.1. The S.P. lattice for a group accumulator M_G is isomorphic to the lattice of subgroups of G under inclusion. The correspondence is given by $\pi_H \longleftrightarrow H$.

Proof. Exercise. ∎

Thus the loop-free structure is reflected in the lattice of subgroups. The *Mm* structure has already been worked out in a previous exercise and the *I-S* structure can easily be seen as the left-right dual of the *S-S* structure. There is only one result about these other structures that is of much interest here and that is the following:

THEOREM 7.4. If $(G, G, G, \delta_G, \lambda_G)$ is a group accumulator and π_H is a partition with S.P. corresponding to subgroup H, then

$$M_{I-s}(\pi_H) = \pi_K$$

where K is the largest normal subgroup of G contained in H.

Proof. First we show that $\pi_K \leqslant M_{I-s}(\pi_H)$. To do this, we have to show that all the inputs in the same block of π_K carry each right coset of H into the same right coset, i.e., we have to prove that

$$Hxa = Hxb \quad \text{for } a \equiv b \quad (\pi_K) \text{ and } x \text{ in } G.$$

Assume that we have a, b, x satisfying

$$a \equiv b \quad (\pi_K) \text{ and } x \text{ in } G.$$

Because K is normal, we know from group theory that

$$xab^{-1}x^{-1} \text{ is in } K \subseteq H$$

Therefore,

$$Hx = H(xab^{-1}x^{-1})x = Hxab^{-1}$$

and multiplying by b, we get the desired equation

$$Hxb = Hxa.$$

Now we prove that $\pi_K \geqslant M_{I-s}(\pi_H)$. Suppose B is a block of $M_{I-s}(\pi_H)$ and a is an element of B. Each element of B must send coset Hx into a single coset and it must be the coset containing exa. Therefore,

$$HxB \subseteq Hxa \quad \text{or} \quad HxBa^{-1}x^{-1} \subseteq H.$$

Therefore, $xBa^{-1}x^{-1}$ is contained in H. From group theory, we know that the group generated by the set $xBa^{-1}x^{-1}$ is normal in G and is contained in H; and therefore contained in maximal normal group K.

In particular, for $x = e$, we have

$$eBa^{-1}e^{-1} = Ba^{-1} \subseteq K \quad \text{or} \quad B \subseteq Ka.$$

This means that B is contained in a block of π_K and the second part of the proof is complete. Combining the parts, we get our result. ■

COROLLARY 7.4.1. If M is a group accumulator for group G, H is a subgroup of G, and K is the largest normal subgroup of G contained in H, then G/K is the semigroup of machine M_{π_H}.

Proof. Those inputs identified by $M_{I-s}(\pi_H)$ are precisely those which have the identical effect on M_{π_H}. ■

When $H = K$, then M_{π_H} with like inputs identified is isomorphic to the group accumulator for G/K. When $K = \{e\}$, then M_{π_H} is a representation of G on a smaller set of states.

We now state and prove the main result about the decomposition of group accumulators.

THEOREM 7.5. Suppose that $(G, G, G, \delta_G, \lambda_G)$ is a group accumulator and H is a subgroup of G. Then there exists an $|H|$ block partition τ such that

$$\pi_H \cdot \tau = 0$$

and such that H is the semigroup of the tail machine of a simple serial decomposition based on π_H and τ. Furthermore, if identical inputs of the tail machine are merged, then the tail machine becomes isomorphic to $(H, H, H, \delta_H, \lambda_H)$.

Proof. To construct τ, choose a subset B of G such that the sets

$$B \cap Ha \quad \text{for } a \text{ in } G$$

have exactly one element. (B is a set of right coset representatives.) Then define

$$\tau = \{rB | r \text{ in } H\}.$$

To show that τ is a partition, let us suppose that

$$rB \cap sB \neq \phi \quad \text{for } r \text{ and } s \text{ in } H.$$

This means that

$$rb = sb' \quad \text{for some } b \text{ and } b' \text{ in } B.$$

But then

$$s^{-1}rb = b'$$

and so b and b' are both in Hb. Since B intersects this coset in a single element, $b = b'$. This implies that $r = s$ and so rB and sB are the same block. Therefore, the sets in τ are disjoint. Since τ contains $|H|$ sets of $|G|/|H|$ elements each, every element of G must be in some block of τ and so τ is a partition on G.

Given an element g of G, we define $B(g)$ to be the block of τ containing g. It is important to note that $rB(g) = B(rg)$ for r in H and g in G.

Next, we wish to show that for a and g in G,

$$Ha \cap B(g) \text{ contains a single element.}$$

This would prove that

$$\pi_H \cdot \tau = 0$$

and that the local tail machine would have no "d.c." conditions. (This justifies talking about *the* tail machine.) Now $B(g) = rB$ for some r in H and since $Ha \cap B$ is a single element by choice of B, so is

$$r(Ha \cap B) = rHa \cap rB = Ha \cap B(g),$$

which is what we wanted to show.

This last result easily extends to prove that

$$H \cap B([Ha \cap B(e)]g)$$

represents a single element of H which we designate by

$$f(Ha, g).$$

Letting δ_2 represent the transition function for the tail machine M_2, we wish to show that

$$\delta_2(B(r), (Ha, g)) = B(rf(Ha, g))$$

for all r in H and a and g in G. This says in effect that the operation of machine M_2 is effectively described by the group operation of H. The isomorphism guaranteed by the last statement of the theorem is given by

$$r \longleftrightarrow B(r) \qquad \text{for } r \text{ in } H$$

for the states and

$$f : (Ha, g) \longrightarrow H \qquad \text{for } a \text{ and } g \text{ in } G$$

for the inputs, $f^{-1}(a)$ being the class of merged inputs corresponding to a. Thus the whole theorem now depends on establishing the equation for δ_2. This means that we must verify that

$$[Ha \cap B(r)]g = Hag \cap B(rf(Ha, g))$$

as the left-hand side represents the next state of M_G and the right-hand side represents the next block of M_{π_H} intersected with what we claim is the next block of M_2 (block of τ). By definition, the right-hand expression is equal to

$$Hag \cap B(r[H \cap B([Ha \cap B(e)]g)]).$$

Distributing the r and moving it inside B, we get

$$Hag \cap B(rH \cap B(r[Ha \cap B(e)]g)).$$

Repeating this and using $rH = H$, we get

$$Hag \cap B(H \cap B([Ha \cap B(r)]g)).$$

Obviously, $B(H \cap B(x)) = B(x)$ and so this reduces to

$$Hag \cap B([Ha \cap B(r)]g).$$

But the single element given by this set must be the element

$$[Ha \cap B(r)]g$$

since this element obviously contained in both

$$Hag$$

and

$$B([Ha \cap B(r)]g).$$

This proves our equation and our theorem. ∎

	0	1	2	3	4	5
0	0	1	2	3	4	5
1	1	2	0	5	3	4
2	2	0	1	4	5	3
3	3	4	5	0	1	2
4	4	5	3	2	0	1
5	5	3	4	1	2	0

Fig. 7.6. Group S_3.

EXAMPLE. Consider the group S_3 of Fig. 7.6, the so-called symmetric or permutation group on three elements. Instead of the more usual decomposition based on normal subgroup $\{0, 1, 2\}$, we illustrate the theorem with non-normal subgroup $H = \{0, 3\}$. The right cosets of H are

$$H = \{0, 3\}, \quad H1 = \{1, 4\}, \quad H2 = \{2, 5\}$$

which means that

$$\pi_H = \{\overline{0,3}; \overline{1,4}; \overline{2,5}\};$$

and we choose

$$B = \{0, 4, 5\}$$

which means that

$$\tau = \{\overline{0,4,5}; \overline{1,2,3}\}.$$

The resulting decomposition is shown in Fig. 7.7.

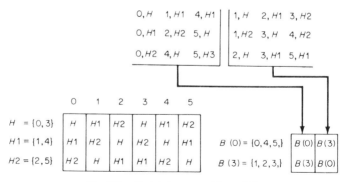

Fig. 7.7. Serial decomposition of S_3.

EXERCISE. Work out the decomposition with $H = \{0, 1, 2\}$ and $B = \{0, 3\}$ or the decomposition with $H = \{0, 3\}$ and $B = \{0, 1, 2\}$.

We now capitalize on the possibilities for repeated application of these results.

COROLLARY 7.5.1. If $M_G = (G, G, G, \delta_G, \lambda_G)$ is a group accumulator and $H_0, \ldots, H_n$ is a set of subgroups of G such that $H_0 = G$, $H_n = \{e\}$, and H_i is normal in H_{i-1} for $1 \leqslant i \leqslant n$, then M_G can be realized by a series connection of the accumulators M_{K_i} where

$$K_i = \frac{H_{i-1}}{H_i} \qquad \text{for } 1 \leqslant i \leqslant n.$$

Proof. Apply Theorem 7.5 with $G = H_0$ and $H = H_1$. By Theorem 7.4, $M_{\pi H_1}$ will be M_{K_1} after equivalent inputs are merged. We now repeat the application of Theorem 7.5 to tail machine M_{H_1} using $H = H_2$. We repeat this process until we get tail machine $M_{H_{n-1}}$ which is M_{K_n}. ∎

Recall that a simple group is a group which has no proper normal subgroups.

COROLLARY 7.5.2. Group accumulator M_G can be realized by a serial connection of simple group accumulators.

Proof. From group theory, we know that we can find a series of groups satisfying Corollary 7.5.1 such that each K_i is simple. This is done constructively by choosing each H_i to be a maximal normal proper subgroup of H_{i-1}. ∎

These last corollaries describe decompositions into group accumulators whereas we are primarily interested in decompositions into machines. Thus, *any* sequence of subgroups

$$G = H_0 \supseteq H_1 \cdots \supseteq H_n \supseteq \{e\}$$

gives a serial decomposition, even though H_i is not normal in H_{i+1}. This we already know from Corollary 7.3.1 and our knowledge of loop-free structure.

Theorem 7.5 is the only theorem of this section which does not have an exact analogy from group theory. When H is not normal, $M_{\pi H}$ is not a group and is not of much direct interest to a group theorist. Thus he has no reason to consider hooking on the Group H. However from the point of view of machine theory, $M_{\pi H}$ is just as interesting as M_G and therefore worthy of study. Thus, although group theory and machine theory overlap in some places, the motivation is different and the results take on a different flavor; and in the end, each follows its own course.

7.4 BEHAVIOR CONSIDERATIONS

The results of this book are chiefly concerned with machine structure rather than with the computational capabilities of machines. Two computer specifications may be radically different from a designers point of view and yet both computers may be capable of solving the same problems. Nevertheless, there are some similarities and overlap between the areas of structure and behavior and this section is intended to sketch this common ground.

Consider state machines C_1 and C_2 of Fig. 7.8. These two machines do not realize each other, yet either machine can be used to perform a given permutation on $S = \{1, 2, 3\}$, provided we allow the possible application of an input series to achieve this. For example, input c to machine C_2 performs the same permutation as input sequence ba to machine C_1. Similarly dc and a do the same permutation and so do b and d. Thus one might say that C_1 and C_2 "have the same capability."

This concept can be formalized as follows:

DEFINITION 7.5. State machine $M = (S, I, \delta)$ is said to *have the capability* of state machine $M' = (S', I', \delta')$ if and only if there exists functions α and ι where

  i) α maps S' into nonempty disjoint subsets of S;
  ii) ι maps I' into $\mathcal{I}$, the set of sequences over I;
  iii) $\delta(s, \iota(x)) \in \alpha(\delta'(s', x))$ for all $s \in S$, $s' \in \alpha(s)$, and $x \in I'$.

Machines M and M' are said to have the *same capability* if and only if they have the capability of each other.

Note the great similarity between the definitions of "M realizes M'" and "M has the capability of M'." The only difference is that in one case, ι maps I' into I (inputs into inputs) and in the other, ι maps I' into $\mathcal{I}$ (inputs into input words). Thus this is a generalization of the realization concept.

EXERCISE. Show that if M has the capability of M', then the semigroup of M' is a homomorphic image of a subsemigroup of the semigroup of M. If α is one-to-one, then the homomorphism is an isomorphism. The converse statements do not hold. Machines D_1 and D_2 in Fig. 7.9 have identical semi-

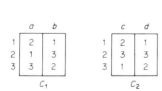

Fig. 7.8. Machines C_1 and C_2.

	0	1
1	2	4
2	3	2
3	1	3
4	4	5
5	5	1

D_1

	0	1
a	b	f
b	e	a
c	d	d
d	f	e
e	a	c
f	c	d

D_2

Fig. 7.9.   Two machines with the same semigroup.

groups (namely, the so-called alternating group on five elements) with identical input sequences corresponding; yet neither machine has the capability of the other.

EXERCISE. Show that "M has the capability of M'" is a transitive relationship.

Let $M = (S, I, \delta)$ be a machine such that:

$$S \text{ is an } n \text{ element set}$$
$$I = \{f \mid f : S \longrightarrow S\},$$
$$\delta(s, f) = f(s).$$

Machine M may be called a "universal" n-state machine because it realizes the state behavior of any n-state machine M'. To realize $M' = (S', I', \delta')$, choose α to be any one-to-one map and let

$$\iota(x) = \alpha^{-1}(\delta'[\alpha(s), x]) \qquad \text{for } x \text{ in } I'.$$

Note that $\iota(x)$ does map S into S and is therefore in I as it is supposed to be. [To make M into a universal n-state Mealy (Moore) machine, one of course adds $O = S \times I (O = S)$ and lets λ be the identity map.] Any machine M^* which has the capability of M has the capability of any n-state machine and may be considered a "universal n-state machine" in a behaviorial sense. Whereas M has n^n inputs, such an M^* may have a lot less. In fact, there is a universal M^* with n states and three inputs, and a universal M^* with $n + 1$ states and only two inputs. These are shown in Fig. 7.10. We leave the verification of these claims as an exercise. Note that sequence 10 on the $n + 1$ state machine has the same effect on the set $\{1, \ldots, n\}$ as input 1 to the n-state machine.

	0	1	2			0	1
1	2	2	1		1	2	$n-1$
2	3	1	2		2	3	1
3	4	3	3			⋮	⋮
⋮	⋮	⋮	⋮		k	$k+1$	$k-1$
k	$k+1$	k	k			⋮	⋮
⋮	⋮	⋮	⋮		$n-1$	n	$n-2$
$n-1$	n	$n-1$	$n-1$		n	1	s
n	1	n	1		s	1	1

Fig. 7.10. "Universal" n-state machines $(n \geqslant 3)$.

There is a certain persistence of capabilities that is described in the next two theorems. The proofs are not very enlightening from a structural point of view so we omit them for the sake of time and space.

THEOREM 7.6. If machine M is realized by a serial decomposition $M_1 \ominus M_2$ and if M has the capability of a machine whose semigroup is a simple group G; then either M_1 or M_2 has the capability of a machine with semigroup G.

Thus, in any loop-free realization of M, the capabilities for certain simple groups must be preserved. If M has the capability for machine D_1 of Fig. 7.9, this capability may be exchanged for that of its cousin D_2, but there always must be a capability for some member of the family.

In Chapter 5, we described an infinite class of realization for machine E of Fig. 5.8. Since the semigroup of this machine is a simple group, one component of each decomposition must have the capability of that group. Indeed, for each case this capability is contained in the tail machine. The "difference" in the tail machines may be attributed to the fact that the larger machines require longer input sequences to imitate the permutations of machine E.

	0	1	2
s	s	s	t
t	t	s	t

Fig. 7.11. Machine E.

NOTATION. Any two-state submachine of machine E of Fig. 7.11 will be called a *two-state reset machine*. The formal definition of a reset machine appears later.

We can now state the second theorem on preserving capabilities.

THEOREM 7.7. If machine M is realized by a serial decomposition $M_1 \ominus M_2$ and if M has the capability of a two-state reset machine, then either M_1 or M_2 has the capability of that same two-state reset machine.

It is shown in the next section that Theorems 7.6 and 7.7 describe the only capabilities that are preserved. They represent "prime" capabilities that cannot be "subdivided." This, of course, *does not mean that simple group accumulators cannot be decomposed*, as we have decomposed some previously. (Recall that even a nonnormal subgroup of H of G defines an S.P. partition π_H on the group accumulator M_G and thus yields a decomposition.)

Theorem 7.6 may be interpreted in terms of semigroups because of the following statement.

LEMMA 7.3. Machine M has the capability of some machine whose semigroup is a simple group G if and only if G is a factor group of some subgroup of the semigroup of M.

Proof. The involved proof is uninformative and so we leave it as an advanced exercise. ▋

Theorem 7.6 can now be restated as follows: If machine M is realized by a serial decomposition $M_1 \ominus M_2$ and if the semigroup of M has a subgroup with simple factor group G; then either the semigroup of M_1 or the semigroup of M_2 must contain a subgroup with factor group G.

Thus, we are dealing with results which can be and have been stated almost exclusively in semigroup terminology, but we prefer the machine concepts for the treatment here.

The fundamental limitation in introducing these semigroups to machine theory is this: when considering a sequence of inputs to be just as good as a single input, what does one do about the corresponding output strings? It does not seem sufficient to arrive at the right state when the output sequences are different. One approach is to generalize and say that certain nonidentical output sequences may be considered the "same." This is certainly reasonable if some outputs are "blank" or "don't print." Models for such situations are provided by the "quasi-machines" and "abstract machines" of Ginsburg, but these tend to lead away from machine structure and fall outside the scope of the material here.

The chief interest here in these behavioral considerations is the fact that they lead to certain invariants of decomposition. Although we do not anticipate much application to design, it does give some insight into what a decomposition does.

7.5 DECOMPOSITION INTO SIMPLE COMPONENTS

The purpose of this and the subsequent section is to provide techniques for decomposing any machine into a loop-free connection of simple machines, i.e., machines whose semigroups are simple groups and machines which are two-state reset machines. (These are sometimes called "irreducible" machines.) This will provide a converse for Theorems 7.6 and 7.7. These techniques generally increase the memory requirements considerably, so that design applications seem at best to be very remote. Nevertheless, it is interesting that such realizations exist in theory; and so we proceed for those readers interested in these proofs for their own sake.

There are really two problems here. The first is to decompose a machine into simple components and the second is to decompose a machine into simple components such that the original machine has the capability of each component. Restated, the second problem is to ensure that only those simple components predicted by Theorem 7.6 and 7.7 are used. The second problem will be deferred to the next section where a more complex alternative to the present construction will be described.

The construction is accomplished by three kinds of decomposition. The first is a set system decomposition into "permutation-reset" machines. The second is a decomposition of permutation-reset machines into permutation machines and reset machines. The third is a decomposition of permutation machines and reset machines by using previously discussed partition techniques. As a first step toward making these precise, we now define the permutation-reset machines.

DEFINITION 7.6. Machine $M = (S, I, \delta)$ is called a *permutation* machine if and only if each input permutes the set S. Machine M is called a *reset* machine if and only if each input is an identity or a constant mapping. Machine M is called a *permutation-reset* (P-R) machine if an only if each input is a permutation or a constant mapping.

These concepts are illustrated in Fig. 7.12

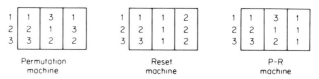

Fig. 7.12. Concepts of Definition 7.6.

We begin with the easy part of the construction, that of decomposing a P-R machine.

LEMMA 7.4. If $M = (S, I, \delta)$ is a P-R machine, then M can be realized by a serial decomposition $M_1 \ominus M_2$ where M_1 is a permutation machine and M_2 is a reset machine. Furthermore, M_1 may be taken as a group accumulator whose group is a subgroup of the semigroup of M.

Proof. Conceptually, the construction here is very simple. Machine M_1 is the accumulator for the group generated by the permutations of M and M_2 is a reset machine with the same states as M. To interpret a state of $M_1 \ominus M_2$, one applies the state of M_1 (which is the permutation generated by the permutation inputs to M) to the state of M_2(considered as a state of M). Permutation inputs are implemented by applying the input to M_1 (leaving state of M_2 unchanged) and constant inputs are accomplished by an appropriate reset of M_2 (leaving the state of M_1 unchanged). We use the notation c_s to indicate a constant input to M which maps all states onto state s.

Proceeding formally, let S_1 be the set of permutations on S generated by the permutation inputs in I. Assuming that δ is extended over the whole input semigroup of M and letting "$\cdot$" represent this semigroup multiplication, we may define

$$M_1 = (S_1, I_1, \delta_1) \qquad \text{and} \qquad M_2 = (S_2, I_2, \delta_2)$$

as follows:

S_1 defined as above;

$I_1 = I$;
$\delta_1(a, b) = a \cdot b$ for a in S_1 and permutation inputs b in I;
$\delta_1(a, c_s) = a$ for a in S, and constant inputs c_s in I.

We use an input symbol to represent a state in S_1 because a is generated by elements of I. In effect, M_1 is the semigroup accumulator for group S_1. Continuing with our definition:

$S_2 = S$;
$I_2 = S_1 \times I$;
$\delta_2(s, (a, b)) = s$ for s in S, a in S_1, and permutation input b in I;
$\delta_2(s, (a, c_t)) = \delta(t, a^{-1})$ for s in S, a in S_1, and constant input c_t in I.

Note that M_2 is indeed a reset machine (in the first case the input is an identity mapping and in the second case a constant mapping).

Our assignment map into $M_1 \ominus M_2 = (S_1 \times S_2, I, \delta')$ is

$$\alpha(s) = \{(a, t)|\delta(t, a) = s\},$$

$$\iota = \text{identity}.$$

To verify that this is an assignment map, let b be a permutation in I and (a, t) be in $\alpha(s)$ (i.e., $\delta(t, a) = s$). Then

$$\delta'((a, t), \iota(b)) = (a \cdot b, t)$$

is by definition of α in

$$\alpha[\delta(t, a \cdot b)]$$

$$= \alpha[\delta(\delta(t, a), b)]$$

$$= \alpha[\delta(s, b)]$$

which verifies equation (i) of Definition 1.14.

Now assume that c_r is a constant input and (a, t) is again in $\alpha(s)$. Then

$$\delta((a, t), c_r) = (a, \delta(r, a^{-1}))$$

is by definition of α in

$$\alpha[\delta(\delta(r, a^{-1})), a]$$

$$= \alpha[\delta(r, a^{-1} \cdot a)]$$

$$= \alpha[r]$$

$$= \alpha[\delta(s, c_r)]$$

and again equation (i) is verified and so we have a realization. This established the result. ∎

EXAMPLE. We now apply the construction to machine F of Fig. 7.13. The permutations on F are generated by input 0 and so we have $S_1 = \{e, 0, 00, 000\}$ which we choose to represent by $\{s_1, s_2, s_3, s_4\}$. The front machine which results from our construction is machine F_1 shown in Fig. 7.13. The states of F_2 are to be the same as F and the connection table is given by δ. The resulting tail machine is also shown in Fig. 7.13, its transitions being defined by the formulas in the proof, although in actual practice these can be obtained directly from the front machine and the connection table as in Chapter 5. The inputs to the tail machine of the form $(s_i, 0)$ lead to identity inputs and those of the form $(s_i, 1)$ lead to constant inputs.

The decomposition of M into $M_1 \ominus M_2$ given in the proof of Lemma 7.4 has the following nice properties:

1. Because of Corollary 7.5.2, accumulator M_1 is easily decomposed into machines whose semigroups are simple groups. Because of Lemma 7.4 and elementary group theory, the component machine of such a prime factori-

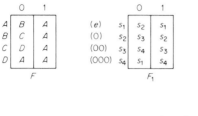

	0	1
A	B	A
B	C	A
C	D	A
D	A	A

F

		0	1
(e)	s_1	s_2	s_1
(0)	s_2	s_3	s_2
(00)	s_3	s_4	s_3
(000)	s_4	s_1	s_4

F_1

	s_1	s_2	s_3	s_4
A	A	B	C	D
B	B	C	D	A
C	C	D	A	B
D	D	A	B	C

Connection table

	$s_1,0$	$s_2,0$	$s_3,0$	$s_4,0$	$s_1,1$	$s_2,1$	$s_3,1$	$s_4,1$
A	A	A	A	A	A	D	C	B
B	B	B	B	B	A	D	C	B
C	C	C	C	C	A	D	C	B
D	D	D	D	D	A	D	C	B

F_2

Fig. 7.13. Decomposition of P-R machine F.

zation are precisely those predicted by Theorem 7.6. These component machines can all be group accumulators.

2. Because all partitions on the states of a reset machine have S.P., tail machine M_2 can be realized by a parallel combination of two-state reset machines.

The status of our construction is now evident. If we can show that every machine can be decomposed into P-R machines, then we know that any machine can be built out of "prime" machines. Furthermore, if we can find a decomposition into P-R machines such that no new simple factor group can be obtained from the resulting component semigroups, then we have the full converse of Theorems 7.6 and 7.7.

	0
1	2
2	3
3	1
4	5
5	4

Fig. 7.14. Machine G.

Observe also that the construction of Lemma 7.4 works even when M is not connected. For example, if one applies the construction to machine G of Fig. 7.14, one gets the group accumulator for the cyclic group of order six (from which only one input is needed) followed by a five-state reset machine (from which only two states are needed). Machine G does not have the capability of the order six accumulator but it does have the capability of each prime factor of the accumulator, as predicted by the theory. The effect of the tail machine is to designate a starting state for G.

EXERCISE. Decompose machine G according to Lemma 7.4 and verify the statements of the previous paragraph.

The decomposition of any machine into P-R machines is assured by the next result.

LEMMA 7.5. If $M = (S, I, \delta)$ is an n-state sequential machine, then there exists an S.P. set system ϕ on S such that the corresponding machine M_ϕ is a P-R machine (when transitions are properly chosen) and such that M can be realized by a serial connection of M_ϕ and some tail machine with at most $n - 1$ states.

Proof. Choose ϕ to be the collection of all $(n - 1)$ elements subsets of S,

$$\phi = \{B \subset S|\ |B| = n - 1\}.$$

We know ϕ has S.P., since for B in ϕ,

$$|\delta(B, x)| \leqslant n - 1$$

and thus all the states B are mapped by x into a common block of ϕ. If x in I is a permutation input, then δ_ϕ for M_ϕ must have

$$\delta_\phi(B, x) = \delta(B, x) \qquad \text{for } B \text{ in } \phi.$$

Obviously, δ_ϕ under x carries distinct blocks of ϕ into distinct blocks of ϕ and so x must be a permutation input. In fact, x for M_ϕ performs the same permutation as x for M under the correspondence

$$s \longleftrightarrow S - s.$$

Now suppose that x in I is not a permutation. Then for some block B_ϕ,

$$\delta(S, x) \subseteq B_\phi$$

and we define

$$\delta_\phi(B, x) = B_\phi \qquad \text{for all } B \text{ in } \phi$$

which of course makes x a constant (reset) input. Therefore, M_ϕ is a P-R machine. Since all the blocks of ϕ contain $n - 1$ elements, an $(n - 1)$-state tail machine can be constructed for M_ϕ to realize M. ∎

EXAMPLE. In Fig. 7.15, we show a machine H and a decomposition by

	0	1
1	2	2
2	3	1
3	4	3
4	1	2

Machine H

	0	1
A (1,2,3)	B	A
B (2,3,4)	C	A
C (1,3,4)	D	A
D (1,2,4)	A	A

Machine H_ϕ

	A	B	C	D
a	1	2	3	4
b	2	3	4	1
c	3	4	1	2

Connection table

	$A0$	$B0$	$C0$	$D0$	$A1$	$B1$	$C1$	$D1$
a	a	a	a	a	b	a	c	b
b	b	b	b	b	a	c	b	b
c	c	c	c	c	c	b	b	a

Tail machine

Fig. 7.15. Decomposition of machine H.

the construction in the proof. The connection table was carefully chosen to avoid introducing unpredicted elements into the semigroup of the tail machine. Some other choices would impose a three-cycle input on the tail machine. Unfortunately, we know of no proof that such a nice connection table can always be found, and so we are forced to abandon this elegant construction in the next section in favor of a more complicated construction for which we can guarrantee a nice connection table.

We have now reached our objective for this section.

THEOREM 7.8. Any machine M has a loop-free decomposition in which each component is either a simple group accumulator or a two-state reset machine.

Proof. By repeated application of Lemma 7.5, n-state machine M can be realized by a series of $n - 1$ P-R machines where the kth machine in the series is a $(n + 1 - k)$-state P-R machine. By our previous discussion, these P-R machines can be further decomposed into prime machines. ∎

7.6 THE COMPLETE CONSTRUCTION

The object of this section is to show how a machine may be decomposed into prime machines without introducing "unnecessary" prime machines. This is accomplished by exhibiting a suitable decomposition into P-R machines to which the decomposition of the previous section can be applied. The more immediate goal of the construction is to achieve a decomposition to which the following lemma may be applied.

LEMMA 7.6. If $M = (S, I, \delta)$ is a state machine, Ω is a collection of distinct subsets of S, and $\mathscr{I}'$ is a subset of $\mathscr{I}$ such that input sequences $\bar{a}$ in $\mathscr{I}'$ maps distinct sets in Ω onto distinct sets in Ω, then the semigroup generated by $\mathscr{I}'$ when considered as transformations of Ω into Ω is a factor group of a subgroup of the semigroup of M.

Proof. We omit a proof because it has little insight for structure theory. Paraphrased, the theorem states that groups generated by permutations on overlapping subsets are the same as groups generated by permutations on disjoint subsets. ∎

We now introduce a generalization of the notation M_π of Chapter 2.

NOTATION. Given a machine $M = (S, I, \delta)$ and an S.P. set system ϕ on S, we use the notation

$$M_\phi = (S', I, \delta')$$

to represent any machine whose states are associated with the blocks of

ϕ under a mapping $\lambda': S' \longrightarrow \phi$ (perhaps in a many-to-one manner) in such a way that

$$(*) \quad \lambda'(\delta'(s', a)) \supseteq \delta(\lambda'(s'), a)$$

for all s' in S' and a in I. The function λ' can be thought of as an output function for M_ϕ which interprets each state of M_ϕ as a block of ϕ. In other words, the states of M_ϕ can be thought of as blocks of ϕ (perhaps with repetitions) whose input maps are consistent with the input maps of M.

The basic constructions are given in the proof of the next lemma.

LEMMA 7.7. If machines $M = (S, I, \delta)$ and M_ϕ are given where $\phi > 0$ is a set system with S.P. on S, then a S.P. set system ψ on S, a machine M_ψ satisfying (*), and a machine $M_{\phi/\psi}$ can be found such that

  (i) $\psi < \phi$;
  (ii) $M_\psi = M_\phi \ominus M_{\phi/\psi}$;
  (iii) $M_{\phi/\psi}$ is a P-R machine;
  (iv) the group part of the semigroup of $M_{\phi/\psi}$ is a factor group of a subgroup of the semigroup of M.

Proof. We first construct ψ and $M_{\phi/\psi}$ according to the methods of H.P. Zeiger:

Construction of ψ. Speaking informally, we plan to pick a subset ϕ^* of ϕ such that the blocks of ϕ^* can be mapped onto one another by input maps in $\mathscr{I}_0$ and such that other blocks of ϕ cannot be mapped onto blocks in ϕ^*. We then choose ψ to be a special S.P. set system larger than the "set system" ϕ-ϕ^*. The machine $M_{\phi/\psi}$ need only refine those blocks of ϕ that are in ϕ^*, as the other blocks of ϕ are automatically in ψ; and the special properties of these input maps which permute blocks of ϕ^* enable one to do this without introducing unnecessary semigroups.

Proceeding formally, we define a binary relation R on the blocks of ϕ as follows: for B_1 and B_2 in ϕ, we write

$$B_1 \, R \, B_2$$

if and only if

$$\delta(B_1, \bar{a}) = B_2 \qquad \text{for some } \bar{a} \text{ in } \mathscr{I}_0.$$

In English, R is the relation "B_1 can be mapped onto B_2 by some input sequence." Clearly, R is a reflexive transitive relation and we can find a nonempty subset ϕ^* of ϕ such that

  (i) B_1 and B_2 in ϕ^* implies $B_1 \, R \, B_2$;
  (ii) $B_1 \, R \, B_2$ for B_2 in ϕ^* implies B_1 in ϕ^*;
  (iii) B_1 in ϕ^* implies $|B_1| > 1$.

Because R is a reflexive and transitive relation, there is at least one subset which satisfies condition (i) and at least one which also satisfies condition (ii). Since $\phi > 0$, one can also find one which satisfies condition (iii) as well. Next we define

$$\psi^* = \{\delta(B, \bar{a})|B \text{ in } \phi \text{ and } \bar{a} \text{ in } \mathscr{I}_0\}.$$

Note that $\psi^* \supseteq \phi$ since $\delta(B, \Lambda) = B$. Now we can define the desired ψ.

$$\psi = \max [(\psi^* - \phi^*)\cup 0].$$

In effect, ψ was obtained by removing ϕ^* from ϕ, adding (maximal) proper subsets of blocks of ϕ onto which blocks of ϕ can be mapped by input sequences, and adding those one element blocks necessary to make ψ a set system. To verify that ψ has S.P., observe that ψ^* is constructed to carry blocks into blocks and removing ϕ^* preserves this property since the only blocks of ϕ to be mapped onto blocks of ϕ^* are blocks of ϕ^* [by condition (ii)]. Taking the max also preserves S.P. so ψ has S.P. Part (i) of the lemma is now easily verified since obviously $\psi \leqslant \phi$ and ψ does not contain those blocks of ϕ that are in ϕ^*.

Construction of $M_{\phi/\psi}$ *and* M_ψ. For the purpose of this construction and the remainder of this proof, we use the symbols A, B, and C for blocks according to the following conventions:

A is used for blocks of ϕ^*;
B is used for blocks of $\phi - \phi^*$;
C is used for blocks of $\psi - \phi$

We now single out any block of ϕ^* and call it A_0. For any A_i in ϕ^*, we choose an input sequence $\bar{x}_i$ from $\mathscr{I}_0$ such that $A_i = \delta(A_0, \bar{x}_i)$. Such an $\bar{x}_i$ must exist by definition of ϕ^*. For each $\bar{x}_i$, we choose an $\bar{x}_i^*$ in $\mathscr{I}_0$ such that

$$\delta(s, \bar{x}_i^* \bar{x}_i) = s \quad \text{for all } s \text{ in } A_i.$$

Such an $\bar{x}_i^*$ must exist. (*Proof*: we know there is an $\bar{x}$ in $\mathscr{I}_0$ mapping A_i onto A_0. Therefore $\bar{x}_i \bar{x}$ maps A_0 onto itself and $(\bar{x}_i \bar{x})^{k+1}$ is the identity map on A_0 for some $k \geqslant 0$. Choose $\bar{x}_i^* = \bar{x}(\bar{x}_i \bar{x})^k$).

Our construction hinges on the following observation: If $C \subset A_i$ (for some C in $\psi - \phi$), then

$$\delta(C, \bar{x}_i^*) \text{ is equal to some } C_0 \text{ in } \psi - \phi \text{ such that } C_0 \subset A_0.$$

(*Proof*: Sequences $\bar{x}_i$ and $\bar{x}_i^*$ must transform A_0 and A_i respectively in a one-to-one way in order to satisfy $\delta(s, \bar{x}_i^* \bar{x}_i) = s$. Now $\delta(C, \bar{x}_i^*)$ must be contained in some block C' of ψ and C' must be contained in $\delta(A_i, \bar{x}_i^*) = A_0$ because ϕ has S.P. But C' cannot contain more elements than $\delta(C, \bar{x}_i^*)$ because then $\delta(C', \bar{x}_i)$ would properly contain C ($\bar{x}_i$ being one-to-one) and C would be excluded from ψ by construction, a contradiction.) This ability to find blocks of $\psi - \phi$ in terms of δ and $\mathscr{I}_0$ is really the key to the construction.

So far, we are given

$$M = (S, I, \delta),$$

$$M_\phi = (S', I', \delta'),$$

and
$$\lambda': S' \to \phi$$

which satisfy the equation (*). Furthermore, we have chosen A_0 and, for each A_i, input sequences $\bar{x}_i$ and $\bar{x}_i^*$. We are ready to define

$$M_{\phi/\psi} = (S^*, S' \times I, \delta^*).$$

We define
$$S^* = \{C \text{ in } \psi - \phi | C \subset A_0\}.$$

The function δ is defined by three cases. In actual practice, the function λ^* given below defines our connection table and we are making choices consistent with equation (*) for λ^* (i.e., equation (**) below) in order that the serial composition realize some M_ψ. Don't cares are filled to produce constant inputs.

Case I. If $\lambda'(\delta'(s', a)) = B$, choose any C_0 in S^*, and let

$$\delta^*(C, (s', a)) = C_0 \qquad \text{for all } C \text{ in } S^*.$$

This is a constant input. We are really just filling a column of d.c. conditions since the front machine keeps track of the blocks of ϕ.

Case II. If $\lambda'(\delta'(s', a)) = A_i$ and $\delta(\lambda'(s'), a)$ is properly contained in A_i, then $\delta(\lambda'(s'), a)$ is contained in some $C_0 \subseteq A_i$ by construction of ψ and let

$$\delta^*(C, (s', a)) = \delta(C_0, \bar{x}_i^*) \qquad \text{for all } C \text{ in } S^*.$$

The set $\delta(C_0, \bar{x}_i^*)$ is contained in S^* by definition of $\bar{x}_i^*$ and is a block of $\psi - \phi$ because of our previous observation. This is a constant input.

Case III. If $\lambda'(\delta'(s', a)) = A_i$ and $\delta(\lambda'(s'), a) = A_i$, then $\lambda'(s') = A_j$ for some A_j in ϕ^* by definition of ϕ^* (i.e. $\lambda'(s') \ R \ A_i$) and let

$$\delta^*(C, (s', a)) = \delta(C, \bar{x}_j a \bar{x}_i^*) \quad \text{for } C \text{ in } S^*.$$

By definition of j, $\bar{x}_j$, i, and $\bar{x}_i^*$, and because of the preliminary observation, $\delta(C, \bar{x}_j a \bar{x}_i^*)$ is indeed an element S^*. Since $\bar{x}_j a \bar{x}_i^*$ is a one-to-one map of A_0 onto A_0, (s', a) is a permutation input to $M_{\phi/\psi}$.

Since the three cases exhaust the input set $S' \times I$, part (iii) of the lemma is proved. Letting $\mathscr{I}'$ be all the inputs sequences of the form $\bar{x}_j a \bar{x}_i^*$ that are used in case III and letting $\Omega = S^*$, we see that Lemma 7.6 applies and part (iv) is proven. All that remains is to establish (ii). By choice of the input set $S' \times I$ for $M_{\phi/\psi}$,

$$M_\psi = M_\phi \ominus M_{\phi/\psi}$$

is a machine, but we must find a map λ^* of $S' \times S^*$ (the states of M_ψ) onto the set ψ such that equation (*) is satisfied. Symbolically, if

$$M_\phi \ominus M_{\phi/\psi} = (S' \times S^*, I, \delta_\psi)$$

we must choose λ^* to satisfy

$$\lambda^*(\delta_\psi((s', C), a)) \supseteq \delta(\lambda^*(s', C), a).$$

Expanding $\delta_\psi((s', C), a)$, this equation may be written

$$(**) \quad \lambda^*(\delta'(s', a), \delta^*(C, (s', a)) \supseteq \delta(\lambda^*(s', C), a).$$

For the function λ^*, we choose

$$\lambda^*(s', C) = B \text{ if } \lambda'(s') = B \text{ in } \phi - \phi^*,$$
$$\lambda^*(s', C) = \delta(C, \bar{x}_i) \text{ if } \lambda'(s') = A_i \text{ in } \phi^*.$$

Obviously, λ^* is an onto map because $C \subset A_i$ is the image of $(s', \delta(C, \bar{x}_i^*))$ where $\lambda'(s') = A_i$ and B is the image of (s', C) for all C whenever $\lambda'(s') = B$.

To verify (**), we must consider five cases.

Case I. If $\lambda'(\delta'(s', a)) = B$ and $\lambda'(s') = B_2$, then equation (**) is equivalent (regardless of δ^*) to

$$\lambda'(\delta'(s', a)) \supseteq \delta(\lambda'(s'), a)$$

which is just (*) for M_ϕ.

Case II. If $\lambda'(\delta'(s', a)) = B_1$ and $\lambda'(s') = A_1$, then equation (**) reduces to

$$\lambda'(\delta'(s', a)) \supseteq \delta(\delta(C, \bar{x}_1), a)$$

which is true because

$$\lambda'(s') = A_i \supseteq \delta(C, \bar{x}_1)$$

and so

$$\lambda'(\delta'(s', a)) \supseteq \delta(\lambda'(s'), a) \supseteq \delta(\delta(C, \bar{x}_1), a).$$

Case III. If $\lambda'(\delta'(s', a)) = A_1$ and $\lambda'(s') = B_1$, it follows (definition of ϕ^*) that $\delta(\lambda'(s'), a)$ is properly contained in A_1, Case II in the definition of δ^* applies, and

$$\lambda^*(\delta'(s', a), \delta^*(C, (s', a)) = \lambda^*(\delta'(s', a), \delta(C_0, \bar{x}_1^*))$$
$$= \delta(\delta(C_0, \bar{x}_1^*), \bar{x}_1) = \delta(C_0, \bar{x}_1^* \bar{x}_1) = C_0$$
$$\supseteq \delta(\lambda'(s'), a) = \delta(\lambda^*(s', C), a).$$

Case IV. If $\lambda'(\delta'(s', a)) = A_1$ and $\lambda'(s') = A_2$ and $\delta(\lambda'(s'), a)$ is properly contained in A_1, then the equations are identical with Case III.

Case V. If $\lambda'(\delta'(s', a)) = A_1$, $\lambda'(s') = A_2$, and $\delta(\lambda'(s'), a) = A_1$, Case III in the definition of δ^* applies and

$$\lambda^*(\delta'(s', a), \delta^*(C, (s', a)))$$
$$= \lambda^*(\delta'(s', a), \delta(C, \bar{x}_2 a \bar{x}_1^*))$$
$$= \delta(\delta(C, \bar{x}_2 a \bar{x}_1^*), \bar{x}_1)$$
$$= \delta(C, \bar{x}_2 a \bar{x}_1^* \bar{x}_1) = \delta(C, \bar{x}_2 a)$$
$$= \delta(\delta(C, \bar{x}_2), a) = \delta(\lambda^*(s', C), a).$$

These five cases exhaust all the possibilities for $S' \times S^*$ and I, equation (**) is therefore verified, part (ii) of the lemma is proven, and this proof is complete. ∎

The pieces of our construction are complete and all that remains is to put them together.

THEOREM 7.9. A machine $M = (S, I, \delta)$ with semigroup H can be realized by a loop-free realization of two-state reset machines and simple group accumulators for those simple groups which are factor groups of subgroups of H.

Proof. We observe that one-state machine M_I automatically satisfies equation (*). Lemma 7.7, therefore, guarantees a sequence of set systems (for some k)

$$I = \phi_0 > \phi_1 \cdots > \phi_k = 0$$

and a set of machines

$$M_{\phi_i/\phi_{i+1}} \qquad i = 0, \ldots, k-1$$

satisfying the conditions of the lemma and such that

$$M_0 = M_{I/\phi_1} \ominus M_{\phi_1/\phi_2} \ominus \cdots \ominus M_{\phi_{k-1}/0}.$$

But M_0 realizes M since equation (*) confirms equation (i) of Definition 1.14 under the map $\alpha(s) = \{s' | \lambda'(s') = s\}$ and $\iota =$ identity. Because of Lemma 7.7 (iii) and (iv), Lemma 7.4, and Corollary 7.5.2, the $M_{\phi_i/\phi_{i+1}}$ can be further decomposed to give the desired realization. ∎

The need for two-state reset machines cannot be detected from the semigroup, because a machine may have a semigroup which is a group and still require a reset machine in its prime decomposition. Examples of such machines are provided by machine B_2 of Fig. 7.5 and machine G of Fig. 7.14. A more exact characterization can be stated in terms of capabilities.

THEOREM 7.10. A machine $M = (S, I, \delta)$ can be realized by a loop-free connection of component machines M_i such that each M_i satisfies one of the following two conditions:

    (i) the semigroup of M_i is a simple group and M has the capability of M_i;
    (ii) M_i is a two-state reset machine and M has the capability of M_i.

Proof. Lemma 7.3 applied to Theorem 7.9 gives the whole theorem, except for showing that M has the capability of the reset component machines. We omit the involved argument which shows that M does actually have the capability of the reset machines which come up in our construction. ∎

Theorem 7.10 is the converse of Theorems 7.6 and 7.7 and so the capabilities which must appear in any loop-free decomposition are characterized.

NOTES

The main results relating the semigroup of a machine to its decompositions were obtained by K. B. Krohn and J. L. Rhodes [22]. The proof of these results by using set systems and permutation-rest machines is due to H.P. Zeiger [33], and the exposition in this chapter follows his approach.

REFERENCES

1. D. B. Armstrong, "A Programmed Algorithm for Assigning Internal Codes to Sequential Machines," *IRE Transactions on Electronic Computers*, Vol. EC-11, No. 4 (August 1962), 466–72.

2. D. B. Armstrong, "On the Efficient Assignment of Internal Codes to Sequential Machines," *IRE Transactions on Electronic Computers*, Vol. EC-11, No. 5 (October 1962), 611–22.

3. G. Birkhoff, "Lattice Theory," *American Mathematical Soc. Colloquium Publication*, Vol. XXV (1948).

4. G. Birkhoff and S. MacLane, *A Survey of Modern Algebra*. New York: The Macmillan Company, 1948.

5. H. A. Curtis, "Multiple Reduction of Variable Dependency of Sequential Machines," *Journal of the Association for Computing Machinery*, Vol. 9, No. 3 (July 1962), 324–44.

6. H. A. Curtis, "Use of Decomposition Theory in the Solution of the State Assignment Problem for Sequential Machines," *Journal of the Association for Computing Machinery*, Vol. 10, No. 3 (July 1963), 386–412.

7. T. A. Dolotta and E. J. McCluskey, "The Coding of Internal States of Sequential Machines," *IEEE Transactions on Electronic Computers*, Vol. EC-13, No. 5 (October 1964), 549–62.

8. A. Gill, *Introduction to the Theory of Finite-State Machines*. New York: McGraw-Hill Book Company, 1962.

9. S. Ginsburg, *An Introduction to Mathematical Machine Theory*. Reading, Mass.: Addison-Wesley, 1962.

10. D. R. Haring, "Some Aspects of the State Assignment Problem for Sequential

Circuits," Report ESL-R-147, Electronics Systems Laboratory, Massachusetts Institute of Technology (September 1962).

11. J. Hartmanis, "Symbolic Analyses of a Decomposition of Information Processing Machines," *Information and Control*, Vol. 3, No. 2 (June 1960), 154–78.

12. J. Hartmanis, "On the State Assignment Problem for Sequential Machines I," *IRE Transactions on Electronic Computers*," Vol. EC-10, No. 2 (June 1961), 157–65.

13. J. Hartmanis, "Maximal Autonomous Clocks of Sequential Machines," *IRE Transactions on Electronic Computers*, Vol. EC-11, No. 1 (February 1962), 83–86.

14. J. Hartmanis, "Loop-Free Structure of Sequential Machines," *Information and Control*, Vol. 5, No. 1 (March 1962), 25–43.

15. J. Hartmanis, "Further Results on the Structure of Sequential Machines," *Journal of the Association for Computing Machinery*, Vol. 10, No. 1 (January 1963), 78–88.

16. J. Hartmanis and R. E. Stearns, "Some Dangers in State Reduction of Sequential Machines," *Information and Control*, Vol. 5, No. 3 (September 1962), 252–60.

17. J. Hartmanis and R. E. Stearns, "A Study of Feedback and Errors in Sequential Machines," *IEEE Transactions on Electronic Computers*, Vol. EC-12, No. 3 (June 1963), 223–32.

18. J. Hartmanis and R. E. Stearns, "Pair Algebras and Their Application to Automata Theory," *Information and Control*, Vol. 7, No. 4 (December 1964), 485–507.

19. D. A. Huffman, "The Syntheses of Sequential Switching Circuits," *Journal of the Franklin Institute*, Vol. 257, No. 3 (March 1954), 161–190, and No. 4 (April 1954), 275–303.

20. R. M. Karp, "Some Techniques of State Assignment for Synchronous Sequential Machines," *IEEE Transactions on Electronic Computers*, Vol. EC-13, No. 5 (October 1964), 507–18.

21. Z. Kohavi, "Secondary State Assignment for Sequential Machines," *IEEE Transactions on Electronic Computers*, Vol. EC-13, No. 3 (June 1964), 193–203.

22. K. B. Krohn and J. L. Rhodes, "Algebraic Theory of Machines," *Proceedings of the Symposium on Mathematical Theory of Automata, New York, April 25–26, 1962, Microwave Research Institute Symposium Series* Vol. XII. Brooklyn, N.Y.: Polytechnic Press, 1963.

23. E. J. McCluskey, "Reduction of Feedback Loops in Sequential Circuits and Carry Leads in Iterative Networks," *Information and Control*, Vol. 6, No. 2 (June 1963), 99–118.

24. G. H. Mealy, "A Method for Synthesizing Sequential Circuits," *Bell Systems Technical Journal*, Vol. 34, No. 5 (September 1955), 1045–79.

25. E. F. Moore, "Gedanken-Experiments on Sequential Machines," *Automata Studies*. Princeton, N.J.: Princeton University Press, 1956.

26. E. F. Moore, editor, *Sequential Machines: Selected Papers*. Reading, Mass.: Addison-Wesley, 1964.

27. M. C. Paull and S. H. Unger, "Minimizing the Number of States in Incompletely Specified Sequential Switching Functions," *IRE Transactions on Electronic Computers*, Vol. EC-8, No. 3 (September 1959), 356–67.

28. R. E. Stearns and J. Hartmanis, "On the State Assignment Problem for Sequential Machines II," *IRE Transactions on Electronic Computers*, Vol. EC-10, No. 4 (December 1961), 593–603.

29. S. Winograd, "Input-Error-Limiting Automata," *Journal for the Association for Computing Machinery*, Vol. 11, No. 3 (July 1964), 338–51.

30. M. Yoeli, "The Cascade Decomposition of Sequential Machines," *IRE Transactions on Electronic Computers*, Vol. EC-10, No. 4 (December 1961), 587–92.

31. M. Yoeli, "Decomposition of Finite Automata," Technion, Israel Inst. of Technology, Technical Report No. 10. (March 1963.)

32. M. Yoeli, "Cascade-Parallel Decompositions of Sequential Machines," *IRE Transactions on Electronic Computers*, Vol. EC-12, No. 3 (June 1963), 322–24.

33. H.P. Zeiger, "Loop-Free Syntheses of Finite State Machines," M.I.T. Ph. D. Thesis, Electrical Engineering Department (September 1964).

INDEX

Abstract network, 82, 85–88, 97–99, 101, 149, 151
Armstrong, D. B., 36
Assignment, 28
Associated partitions, 86–88, 102, 110, 143, 150, 151
Authors (*see* Hartmanis, J.)

Block, 4

Capability, 192–194, 205
Clock, 113, 114
Closed set of machines, 98
Closure operator for machine network, 98, 99
Combinational logic, 19, 28, 85
Congruence relation, 12
Connection table, 138–140, 144, 198, 199
Cosets, 11, 12, 14, 186, 188
Curtis, C. H., 36

D.c. conditions (*see* "Don't care" conditions)
Defining a machine by equations, 31, 33
Defining a machine by network, 85
Distributivity, 9, 128, 133
Dolotta, T. A., 36
"Don't care" conditions, 33, 34–36, 88–93, 94, 95, 110, 111, 146–147, 169

Equivalence, 3
Equivalent machines, 23
Equivalent states, 23, 55
Error:
    inessential, 171, 173
    input-induced, 175
    permanent, 167
    state, 167
    temporary, 167, 168, 170, 173, 174
Error graphs, 170
Extended machine functions, 22
Extended partition pairs, 92
Extension, 3, 78

f as feedback, 157, 158
Factor group (*see* Quotient group)
Feedback-free, 160, 162, 164
Feedback partition, 149, 151, 156
Flow table, 17
Friedman, A. D., 177
Function, 2, 16, 28, 76–79, 82, 91, 138, 201

Gill, A., 36
Ginsburg, S., 36, 195
"Goes into," 18
Greatest lower bound, 6, 7, 65
Group, 11, 186–191, 193, 194, 197, 200, 205
Group accumulator, 181, 184

Haring, D. R., 36
Hartmanis, J., and R. E. Stearns, 36, 57, 96, 118, 147, 177
Homomorphism:
  group, 12
  lattice, 9
  machine, 20
  state machine, 21
Huffman, D. A., 36

Identity element, 11, 184
Identity map, 24, 28, 39, 183, 184
Identity partition, 8, 41
Incidental d.c. conditions, 35
Information flow inequalities, 77, 78, 79, 87, 90–91
Inverse element, 11
I-O pair, 71, 72, 75
I-S pair, 71, 72, 75
Isomorphism:
  group, 12
  lattice, 8, 123, 126
  machine, 19, 24

Karp, R. M., 36
Kohavi, Z, 36, 147
Krohn, K. B., 205

Lattice, 7, 41, 65, 68, 133
Least upper bound, 6, 7, 65
Logic delay form, 82–84, 88, 149
Loop-free network, 98, 101, 172, 185, 200, 205
Loop-free realization, 99, 101, 172, 185

McCluskey, E. J., 36, 177
Machine:
  component, 82, 93
  local, 94
  Mealy, 16, 26, 174
  Moore, 16, 26, 174
  permutation, 195
  permutation-reset, 194–195
  π-image, 38
  reset, 195
  state, 18
  tail, 109–113
  universal, 193

Mapping (*see* Function)
Mealy, G. H., 36
M operator:
  pair algebra, 64
  partition pairs, 61, 72, 160, 186
m operator:
  pair algebra, 64
  partition pairs, 61, 72, 186
Mm lattice:
  pair algebra, 64, 65
  partitions, 72–76, 172
  system pairs, 137
Mm pair, 64
Moore, E. F., 36

Network (*see* Abstract network)
Nonredundant set of partitions, 100, 101
Normal subgroup, 12, 187, 191, 194, 200, 201, 205
Null sequence, 22, 183

"One-to-one," 2, 8, 12, 19, 29, 30
"Onto," 2, 8, 12, 19, 138
Operations:
  lattice, 7
  partition, 4, 135
  set system, 133, 135
Operators (see *M* operator *and m* operator)
Output consistency, 56, 57, 120, 121, 123, 125–127

Pair algebra, 63, 72, 92, 136, 147, 157, 166
Parallel decomposition, 48–51, 128
Partial ordering, 6
Partition, 4
Partition pair, 58, 60, 72, 91
Paull, M. C., 147
Predecessor, 97
Prime parallel realization, 109

Quotient group, 12, 191, 194, 200
Quotient partition, 5, 6, 94–96, 110, 121–128

Realization:
  accumulator, 183

Realization (*cont.*):
  definition, 28
  feedback-free, 160
  loop-free, 99
  network, 85
  reduced, 120
  state behavior, 30
  with d.c. conditions, 90
Reduced machine, 23, 24, 26, 29, 55–57,
    147, 158, 164–167, 170, 174, 181
Reduced realization, 120, 127
Relation, 3, 12, 13, 201
Restriction, 2, 78
Rhodes, J. L., 205

Serial connection:
  machines, 42
  state machines, 43
Serial decomposition, 45, 97, 114, 131,
    138, 143, 145, 162–164, 172, 188,
    193, 194, 196, 199, 201
Semigroup:
  definition, 10
  Moore machine, 181
  state machine, 179
Semigroup accumulator, 181, 183–185
Set systems, 133, 138, 143, 145, 146, 157,
    158, 164–166, 181, 199, 201
Similar machines, 25
Simple group, 191, 193, 194, 197, 200,
    205
S-O pair, 71, 72, 75
S. P. (*see* Substitution property)

S-S pair, 71, 72, 75
Standard form, 82, 88, 149
Starting state, 182, 183
State behavior realization, 30, 45, 48, 78,
    87, 90–92, 94, 99, 101, 109, 114,
    115, 151, 160, 162, 173, 181
State graph, 17, 25
State-splitting, 119, 130
Stearns, R. E. (*see* Hartmanis, J.)
Strongly connected, 19, 183
Strong starting state, 182, 183
Subgroup, 11, 12, 187, 191, 194, 201
Sublattice, 8, 56, 68, 123, 126, 146
Submachine, 19, 29, 120, 180, 181
Substitution property:
  pair algebra, 68
  partitions, 38, 40, 41, 51–55
  set systems, 137, 138
System pair, 135–137

Unger, S. H., 147

Weak pair algebra, 89, 90
Weak partition pairs, 89–91, 92, 147
Weak system pair, 146
Winograd, S., 177

Yoeli, M., 57, 147

Zeiger, H. P., 147, 201, 205
Zero partition, 8, 41